ANTICIPATING THE FUTURE

ANTICIPATING THE FUTURE

BARRY BUZAN
GERALD SEGAL

SIMON & SCHUSTER
A VIACOM COMPANY

First published by Simon & Schuster, 1998
An imprint of Simon & Schuster Ltd
A Viacom Company

Simon & Schuster
West Garden Place
Kendal Street
London W2 2AQ

Simon & Schuster of Australia
Sydney

A CIP catalogue record for this book is available
from the British Library.

0-684-81773-X

1 3 5 7 9 10 8 6 4 2

Typeset by Hewer Text Composition Services, Edinburgh
Printed and bound by The Bath Press, Bath

For Rachel and Serena,
who are just beginning to live the future.
May there be gold at the end of their rainbow.

Contents

FOREWORD   *ix*

INTRODUCTION   *xiii*

PART I
LOOKING BACKWARD   *1*

1 GLOBALISATION AND WORLD WARS   *7*

2 EUROPEAN EXPANSION   *21*

3 CIVILISATIONS, EMPIRES AND   *43*
    BARBARIANS

4 FROM PRE-HISTORY TO CIVILISATION   *63*

5 LOOKING BACKWARD, LOOKING   *73*
    FORWARD

PART II
THE HERE AND NOW   87

6 THE PLANETARY ENVIRONMENT   91

7 POPULATION   105

8 IDENTITY   117

9 KNOWLEDGE   129

10 CAPITAL   143

11 SOVEREIGNTY   155

12 MILITARY POWER   165

13 WHERE ARE WE NOW?   175

PART III
MEMORIES FROM THE FUTURE   189

14 ON PROGRESS   191

15 THE VIEW FROM 2050   211

16 THE VIEW FROM 2500   251

17 THE VIEW FROM 7000   267

FURTHER READING   275

INDEX   289

Foreword

Why would two academics want to write a book like this? The judgements are sweeping (although we hope not glib), the language is deliberately un-academic (although we hope not simplistic), and there are no footnotes (although there is a list of suggested reading). When we began this project four years ago we had three motives in mind.

Our obvious starting point, and it has been one for various other authors, was to assess where humankind stands today on the verge of a new millennium. Unlike most of the millennial literature, we felt it important to stress the extent of human progress. While we recognise the often close run contest between triumph and tribulation, we find that in the long view the human story is fundamentally upbeat.

We also wanted to do something different. Much of the late twentieth-century literature about the state of the world tends to deal only with changes over the past century or so. We thought it important to stand back much further, reflecting on twenty millennia of the human experience.

Our third objective was to show that academic specialists need not shy away from phrases like 'reflecting on twenty millennia of human experience'. The authors' collective curriculum vitae includes over three dozen books, many of which were written for a specialist audience. Some of our usual readers will be appalled that we even thought of writing on such a huge and speculative subject. But we felt that social science theory and detailed knowledge of specific areas of the world (the academic expertise of the authors) are worth much more if they can be used to say something meaningful about bigger pictures for wider audiences. It was those spirits that led the authors to write earlier books on 'mind mapping' and a layman's guide to world affairs.

When we began talking about millennial issues, it became clear that we had a major argument to make. An important part of the stimulus to write this new book was the feeling that uncritical judgements were being made about such things as 'A Pacific Century', 'The Clash of Civilisations' and 'The Decline of the West'. We felt too many millennial authors ignored evidence from the broader sweep of human history. In our age of micro-specialists, we felt there was a virtue in taking a longer look back, a more anticipatory look forward – and all so that we could understand better where we are today.

Even a book half as ambitious as this one would owe an enormous debt to a number of experiences and people. All the more so for a book with a millennial sweep. The authors, both with strong North American connections but now long-time UK residents, have lived in various parts of the globe and spend their professional lives dealing with regional and global issues. The genesis, gestation and synthesis of this book owe a great deal to discussions with friends, colleagues and strangers around the world.

More specific votes of thanks are also offered with deep gratitude to Deborah Buzan, Phil Gordon, John Keane, Jean-Pierre Lehmann, Michael Leifer, Barbara Liebgott, Richard Little, Edwina Moreton, H.O. Nazareth, David Percy, Nick Rengger, Michael Segal, Ole Wæver and Jaap de Wilde. Important research assistance was provided by the ever-efficient and swift research staff at the International Institute for Strategic Studies. Barry Buzan would also like to thank the ESRC (Economic and Social Research Council) which funded research on another project that was also useful for this one.

Finally, a word on the art and practice of joint authorship. We approached this work on the basis of a series of agreed outlines. Segal wrote the first drafts of the introduction and 6–14 while Buzan did the same for chapters 1–5 and 15–17. Yet there is no place in the published text where we feel there is only one author. Each of us has written into the drafts of the other over many revisions, and any ideas that either of us could not live with were dropped. One of us was (and still is) more instinctively optimistic. That may have something to do with the fact that as a parent, he needs to believe that the world his daughter will grow up in has the capacity to manage its problems. But the foundation of the book is our shared belief in the capacity of human beings, both individually and collectively, to learn. Both of us still adhere to the currently somewhat unfashionable view that the unfolding of natural science has been and will continue to be a good thing. We marvel at both the accomplishments and the prospects of the hard sciences, and believe that they solve more problems than they create. Both of us also have faith in social learning. Coming from the social 'sciences' this might seem to be an even more difficult position to sustain. But while we might wish that learning in the social world moved more swiftly, more systematically, and with less pain and suffering, we both feel that human history has been basically progressive and see little reason to think that this line of advance has somehow come to an end. It is these twin faiths that are the essence of this book.

Barry Buzan
Gerald Segal
London 1997

INTRODUCTION

This is not another book about the new millennium – it is something far more audacious. It is a book about where humankind now stands in its own history. It is based on an understanding of where we have come from in the past several millennia, and where we are placed for the next few. The central idea is that we can best understand where we are now, with reference to where we have been and where we might be going. Unlike much conventional cynicism, we think that there are firm grounds for optimism about the human condition, and that the new millennium marks an important turning point in many vital aspects of human history. Our two core themes are thus *progress*, and *transformation*.

Much millennial pessimism arises from taking a too short-term view. There are plenty of Cassandras about, ranging from the milder sort who find it hard to escape a gloomy projection of the status quo, to the wilder sort who believe that we stand on the brink of some sort of ecological or social disaster. But a longer perspective suggests that human beings have made remarkable progress, albeit unevenly, and sometimes with major setbacks. We find no compelling evidence that this trend is about to stop. We are impressed by the steady long-term geographical spread and civilisational deepening of the human enterprise, by the relentless expansion of knowledge, by the huge material gains that have enabled ever more people to realise their human potential, and by the learning curve that despite all the setbacks seems to generate ever larger, more sophisticated, more capable, and in many ways more just economic, social and political orders. Our vision of human progress is not just material, but also political and moral. We recognise the perils of the future, but the longer view of history suggests that awareness of such risks is part of what helps humans stay on the path of progress. That such awareness is now sharper and better organised than it has ever been before is in itself grounds for optimism. Our full stall on progress is set out in chapter 13.

Our second core theme is transformation. The late twentieth century seems to be a time in which many large-scale historical patterns reach their turning points. Everyday conversation and media discussion offer some limited insight into this phenomenon with catch-phrases such as 'the End of the Cold War Era', and 'the rise of East Asia'. These do indeed capture important turning points. The ending of the forty-year Cold War, and even more so of the seventy-five-year twentieth century, seemed to bring to an end an era of violent ideological struggles about how best to organise the economic and political life of modern societies. The rise of East Asia is supposed to point towards restoration of an older pattern in which the East Asian civilisations dominated the world economy and Europe was a relative backwater. Asia accounted for at least a third of world GDP at the beginning of the nineteenth century, and that is roughly where they will be again two hundred years later. There is no doubt that some East Asian states have made remarkable progress in recent decades in lifting themselves out of poverty, and that they are virtually the only parts of the developing world to have put themselves successfully on the road to modernisation.

But in the long view of history these are merely local events. Our perspective focuses on three much broader developments which set the context for all of these shorter-term movements. The first of these is the shift from a world directly dominated by the West, to what we call *the Westernistic era*. This era is defined by the interplay between the spread of Western ideas around the globe on the one hand, and the reassertion of non-Western cultures on the other. Our age is Westernistic because most of the economic and political ideas around which it is organised come from the West. The East Asians succeeded because they adopted and adapted capitalism and political pluralism, much like countries in the Atlantic world did in the previous two centuries. The rise of the Asian phoenix was made possible by acceptance of Western ideas. Any abandonment of their key Western features will undermine Asia's ability to continue meeting the challenges of the future. As East Asians and others join the prosperity of the Atlantic world, they enrich the ever-adaptable notions of the West. The Westernistic era will see a more multicultural world, but one bound together by a shared legacy of widely accepted Western ideas. The important question is not about Western decline. It is about the change in the nature of the relationship between a still potent West and the other cultures of human civilisation some of which are recovering their voice and their economic and political power.

The second broad turning point rests on a much longer time line. It is about what we call the culmination of the making of a single human space on the planet, a process that has been underway ever since the first modern humans began to migrate to the distant corners of the world. In this perspective we stand on the edge of a new phase of human existence. It is only within living memory that humans have effectively discovered and mapped all parts of the earth's surface, and only some thirty years ago that we first saw our planet as a whole from outer space. It will not be too long before the size of the world's population stabilises for the first time in history. This filling up and knowing of the planet mark a sharp departure from the fundamental conditions that have shaped human history over all the past millennia. They bring us into a new relationship not only with ourselves, but also with the earth as an ecosystem and even the earth in the cosmos. They may even redefine our notions of progress.

A third, and potentially more far-reaching turning point is our new-found ability to change the very components of ourselves. This process – for example manifest in our ability to control conception and therefore free women to take greater control of their lives – has had a far-reaching impact. And there is more to come. Although human history is replete with scattered efforts to understand who we are and how our bodies work, it is only in our era that we have become able to alter our bodies and perhaps even our minds. This is not just a matter of new drugs or the uncertain virtues of psychoanalysis, but much more a matter of our new ability to fix our broken or worn out body parts and change our genetic makeup. We may also be on the verge of learning how to slow ageing and/or make a direct interface between humans and machines. But we certainly have learned to take control of when we give birth, how to implant new organs and how major parts of our genetic code work. We have only just begun a fundamental debate about how much we want to do with our new powers over our bodies. When do we wish to define the start or end of life? How much more tinkering with human form and function should we tolerate? These are new and awesome questions and these issues are also aspects of the central discussion about the meaning of progress that forms a central theme of this book.

In order to capture the twin themes of progress and transformation we need to take an unusually long view of the human condition. But we did not want to follow the tradition of wrist-breaking millennium books and world histories. We wanted an essayish, accessible book for those interested in how to think about where we are and where we are going. This means we have to move fast over a very large and varied terrain. To make this strategy work, we have adopted an unusual approach, part history, part current affairs analysis, and part science fiction.

Part I of the book deals with history. The human story is a relatively certain subject matter, though one that can be endlessly reinterpreted. We begin with the present and work backward through the main eras: the twentieth century, the rise of Europe, the era of classical and ancient civilisation, and prehistory back to the end of the last ice age. This is not history in fine detail. It paints only in broad brush-strokes, and concentrates only on grand themes. The purpose of this account is to tell us where we are now in relation to where we have come from, and to identify what if any historical momentum propels us into the future.

The Price of (Mis) Reading History

Every time history repeats itself the price goes up.

Anonymous.

Part II focuses on the present. Here the relative certainty of the past dissolves into a series of questions, debates and puzzles, reflecting the pervasive uncertainty of our own time about itself. We examine the current condition of humankind in terms of seven themes: environment, population, identity, knowledge, capital, sovereignty and military power. Their purpose is to reflect current preoccupations, and to relate these to where we have come from and where we seem to be heading.

But one of the insights from history is that the human experience has so far always been marked by deep patterns of uneven development. At any point in history since the beginning of civilisation, and still today, we find peoples in radically different stages or types of development. It makes as much sense to lump together an understanding of the fate of a refugee in Rwanda and a bond trader in Frankfurt, as it does to believe that life for a resident of London in the late twentieth century is much the same as it was in the fifteenth century. The differences in modern space are akin to differences in vast swathes of time. The existence of these different worlds makes it difficult to form single generalisations about humankind in the past, now, or for the future. Human history has to be told as a set of overlapping stories.

Orwell on Past, Present and Future

Who controls the past controls the future: who controls the present controls the past.

George Orwell, *Nineteen Eighty-Four*, pt. 1, ch. 3 (1949).

Part III takes its inspiration partly from science fiction, partly from history, and partly from Peter Schwartz's *Art of the Long View*. Unlike most scenario writers we do not try to creep forward into a prediction of the future, for even the clearest picture of a fuzzy object must itself be fuzzy. Instead, we try out a new method of linking the present to the future. Taking our cue from Part I, we *start* from the future, and look back at the late twentieth century as it might be seen by historians located fifty, five hundred and five thousand years in the future The future perspective uses distance in time to gain insight into the present, for it is only by understanding the present that we gain leverage on the future. We are interested in the feasible project of anticipating the future, not in the impossible one of predicting it.

ON PREDICTION AND PRESCRIPTION

Only those who have not read any good science fiction would argue that you cannot anticipate the future. The notion of foreseeing does not mean that the future can be understood as well as the present or the past. But it is important to recall that the meaning of the present and even the past are sharply contested. It is not until much time has passed that we understand the past, and even then our sense of the truth is always being adjusted. To an important extent our sense of the future is similarly adjusted as it comes closer to today. Whether it is a matter of looking forward or back, we cannot help but judge on the basis of where we are today. Hence the central importance of understanding where we are now.

Most people are loath to predict. When asked to do so, say in the context of scenario-planning for business, the preference of most people is to stay close to the present. In earlier times, when change was much less rapid, there was perhaps less risk in trying to foresee the future. But in our modern world, many aspects of life are changing increasingly rapidly, thereby making prediction less predictable. The current vogue in business schools has moved away from long-term planning and now puts more emphasis on quick thinking and adaptable structures and people. Business cycles are usually less than five years and are shrinking. Military specialists are happier to stray out a bit further, if only because it takes at least a decade for new weapons systems to be devised and deployed. Demographers are often happy to operate up to twenty or thirty years hence, for they can tell you now how many people will be in the workforce in twenty years' time and roughly how many people will be where on the planet. Astronomers, of course, are only happy dealing in the vast numbers of years that it takes light to reach our planet. That may help explain why there is a sign at the American Jet Propulsion Laboratory that says 'we do precise guesswork'.

Kelly on Past and Future

To see into the future one must see into the past . . . Adaptation – at its core – requires a sense of the future. In a changing environment, either opaque or clear, systems that anticipate the future are more likely to persist.

From Kevin Kelly, *Out of Control*, p. 566.

Prediction, as Ernest Gellner pointed out, 'does not exclude the possibility of comprehension'. There is value in expressing a vision '. . . in the hope that its clear and forceful statement will make possible its critical examination'. But all those who anticipate the future need to remember, as the old Arab proverb has it, 'he who predicts the future lies even if he tells the truth'. Prophecy is a leftover from more primitive and superstitious times, and is much despised in our scientific era. The business guru Peter Schwartz, whose *The Art of the Long View* is a modern classic about scenario-building and the art of prediction, nevertheless argues that in order to act with confidence and live a full life, one must be willing to look ahead and consider uncertainties by using mental radar. Those who react to uncertainty with denial will never break new ground and find the deep satisfaction of having risen to and met a challenge. These are challenges that every good parent should well understand, for they implicitly make such assessments when thinking about their children's future. At a minimum, a willingness to contemplate scenarios is a vehicle for learning. The illusion of certainty is not preferable to an understanding of risks and realities. Herman Kahn's *On Thermonuclear War: Thinking About the Unthinkable* was not a prediction of nuclear war, but it was a useful effort to overcome the disease of denial. By thinking the unthinkable, he helped ensure that it never happened. Thus while there can be no accurate picture of tomorrow, there can be better decisions about the future and understanding of the present. What we need is that old adage about good theatre, 'the willing suspension of disbelief'.

Schwartz on Forecasting

The single most frequent failure in the history of forecasting has been grossly underestimating the impact of technologies.

From Peter Schwartz, *The Art of the Long View*, p. 173.

Of course we suspend disbelief with great caution. Early twentieth-century futurists, although good at foreseeing our venture into space, failed to believe that the motor car would be such a huge success and problem. It was only ten years ago that much gazing into the future assumed that we faced a real risk of destroying life on our planet through the use of nuclear weapons. That risk was real, and might still return, but for the time being is much reduced. Our current apocalyptic vogue is concerned with environmental catastrophe. This too is more a sign of the times than an accurate anticipation of the future. It is based on a delusion that life is somehow in a delicate balance, when the reality has always been a more random world of competition where species die and mutate. It is all too easy to quote the by-now laughable predictions of others, but it is worth recalling that Lord Kelvin, the President of the Royal Society in 1895 said that 'heavier-than-air flying machines are impossible', that Harry Warner of Warner Brothers said in 1927 'who the hell wants to hear actors talk?' and that in 1943 Thomas Watson, the Chairman of IBM, said 'I think there is a world market for maybe five computers'.

Our look at the present in Part II does allow us to ask certain questions about the future. Will states survive, and if so, where and why? Similarly, how will cultures change? Anticipations of the future are more often based on extrapolations from the current state of scientific research. Thus it is worth asking if humans will live longer and whether genetic engineering will affect basic features of life forms. Some have even suggested that in the long-term, men of the species will become redundant. Science might also be able to make possible a therapy for global warming or travel at Star Trek-like warp speed. Science might make it possible to fend off a comet strike, or minimise its effects. Might we make terraforming a reality and make possible human existence on other planets? And then there is the possibility of discovering life on distant planets. Obviously we are in no position to predict the reality of such hopes or fears, but in our look back from the future, we will have views on the subject.

It is not our main purpose in this book either to predict or to prescribe, though we will unavoidably do some of both. In Part III, the process of anticipation commits us to some prediction. Especially in the look back from 2050 we have allowed ourselves the entertainment of a fairly detailed scenario for the next thirty years based on how we see the themes identified in Parts I and II unfolding. But except implicitly, the art of anticipation does not lend itself to prescription. Prescription is about the realm of choice in human affairs, whereas anticipation puts the emphasis on the momentum of events. One of our anticipations is that choice plays a big role in humanity's future.

ON THE MILLENNIUM

Lest our enthusiasm for the historic significance of the late twentieth century be dismissed as mere pandering to millennial enthusiasm, it is worth reflecting for a moment on the wholly arbitrary character of the date itself. According to the US Naval Observatory, the Greenwich Observatory and the Encyclopaedia Britannica, the millennium begins on 1 January 2001. The logic, however counter-intuitive, is that our calendar started with the year one, and therefore every decade and century must start with a one. This quirk is owed to Dionysius Exiguus, the sixth-century abbot of a Roman monastery, who settled the dispute on the proper day for Easter. He arbitrarily named Anno Domini, 'the birth year of Our Lord', as 1 AD. Remember that the classical civilisations of the Mediterranean did not have the concept of zero until the Arabs brought it from India. There was no zero in Roman numerals. But such clinging on to the errors of history is not the best way to understand the start of the millennium. Celebrations on 31 December 1999 will be held at the Vatican, Times Square, The Great Wall of China, the Taj Mahal, the Acropolis, the Eiffel Tower and more than a dozen other locations in a global satellite link.

If you must choose a date for the start of the millennium, then 1 January 2000 is the most common sense choice. On 6 April 1997 there were one thousand days (1,440,000 hours) until the year 2000. There is even a site on the World Wide Web to help you count down by the second. But there is nothing very precise about the first second of a new millennium. The world has many time zones and therefore many different times when the millennium starts.

And then there is the matter of our Gregorian calendar being only one of several ways of measuring time. According to Islam, what we call 2000 will be 1420. Even if we stick with the Christian calendar, nit pickers can easily argue for a different starting date for the millennium. Until AD 800, New Years Day in France used to be 1 March. For nearly two centuries afterwards it was 25 March and from 996 to 1051 it coincided with Easter. From the seventh century to 1338 the English considered Christmas Day to be the first day of the year, and then it was moved to 25 March for civil purposes and to Easter for religious ones.

A large part of our confusion about dates is due to inadequate scientific knowledge and the difficulty of grasping the implications of the fact that our planet rotates on its axis once every 23.9345 hours, or 23 hours and 56 minutes and four seconds. It is less than the twenty-four hours we know as a day. The earth travels once around the sun every 365.25636 days, and therefore calendars have to make compromises. In 46 BC Julius Caesar reformed the previously erratic Roman calendar. He took the length of the year to be 365.25 days, beginning on 1 January. As a result of a tremendous mistake by Roman priests, the calendar had to be reformed again in 10 BC. Even so, because the Julian year exceeds the true year by 0.00781 days, by 1582 the spring equinox had slipped back from 21 March to 11 March. To prevent further slippage, Pope Gregory XIII reformed the calendar. As part of the reforms, ten days of 1582 were removed, with 5 October becoming 15 October.

Catholic countries adopted the Gregorian calendar quite quickly but the Protestants lagged. England put it into practice in 1752 and Finland not until 1918. As European power spread around the world, every country eventually settled on the Gregorian calendar as the way of marking the change of year. Individual countries often still retain their traditional calendar, but they will all recognise some importance in what will be the year 2000 in the Gregorian calendar. Chinese New Year in the year 2000 will not be until 4 February, but that will be 4698 in the Chinese calendar. Jews will have their New Year in 2000 on 30 September, but then according to their calendar it will be the year 5760.

Gregory XIII was a Catholic Pope, and of course his calendar is supposed to have begun with the birth of Christ. Leaving aside whether Christ was a real character in history, it is certainly far from clear when he was born (not to mention how he was conceived). Most students of the subject say the latest Christ could have been born was 4 BC. Perhaps we should have celebrated the second millennium in 1996.

Given this close connection to the birth of Christianity, it is not surprising that the previous thinking about the meaning of millennia is closely connected to Christian religions and dark-age Europe. The tradition of revolutionary millenarianism and mystical anarchism was prevalent before and after the first millennium change in Western Europe. Christian eschatology worried about 'the end of days' or 'the final state of the world' at the coming of the millennium. The Book of Revelations (xx, 4–6) noted that after the Second Coming, Christ would establish a messianic kingdom on earth and would reign over it for a thousand years before the Last Judgement and the resurrection of the dead. The period before the first millennium was to be one of danger and settling of scores, but the aftermath was to be a time of joy, serenity, prosperity and justice. In the event, the year 1000 passed off quite uneventfully. Millenarianism remained a potent set of ideas, especially for the poor in Europe, for centuries to come, but legends about the panics of 999 were, to an important extent, essentially a creation of eighteenth-century writers anxious to portray the medieval society as superstitious.

For much of the subsequent millennium little attention was paid to the year 2000. Before the nineteenth century, years were most often counted in years of reign for various monarchs. Michel de Notredame's (Nostradamus 1503–1566) rhyming predictions for life 500 years hence was of a different tradition, but was symbolic of the sporadic fascination with the next millennium. Of course, by the time we arrived within sight of the second Christian millennium, we had lost our belief in magic and clerical power. Some 30 million people are expected to visit the Vatican in the year 2000 for what will almost be a secular jamboree for the millennium. Our trust in science has made it easier for us to see the year 2000 as an excuse for major celebrations, and very little of the old belief in the importance of the date is left.

Nevertheless, as it turns out, the beginning of a third millennium is important, albeit for very different reasons than the ticking of a clock. We are not expecting either the Last Judgement or the rising of the dead. But we are at a very special time in human history. In order to understand how and why that is, read on . . .

PART I
LOOKING BACKWARD

History is very long and its seemingly infinite train of facts quickly becomes overwhelming. Few people have the time or the inclination to master it all, and for these few the task is a life's work. In this short look a long way back we are not going to tell the story from beginning to end as a detailed sequence of events. Instead, we will start from where we now stand in the present, and work backwards. Doing it this way means that we can begin on the familiar ground of our own time and go from there into the less familiar past.

Wilde on History

The one duty we owe to history is to rewrite it.

Oscar Wilde, Gilbert, in *The Critic as Artist*, pt. 1 (published in *Intentions*, 1891).

We want to answer two questions: (1) how did we get to the situation in which we now find ourselves? (which we will take up in Part II); and (2) are there patterns and momentums in the historical story that point to where we might be going? (which we will take up in Part III). To do this does not require understanding the detailed lives of the 200 generations of humans that have existed since the first rise of civilisation. Instead, we can look at broad patterns in the development of human social, political and economic organisation. How is it that in the mere 15,000 years since the end of the last ice age, we have evolved from a sparse population of a few million people scattered around the planet in small hunter-gatherer bands, to a global population of 6 billion organised into 5,000 nationalities, 180 states, and a more-or-less globally integrated economy? What organisational and technological inventions made this astonishing transformation possible? What lessons, if any, can be learned from the fate of the many great civilisations and empires that created human history before the modern age?

(Differing) Views on Reading History

History not used is nothing, for all intellectual life is action, like practical life, and if you don't use the stuff – well, it might as well be dead.

A.J. Toynbee, Television broadcast, 17 April 1955, NBC-TV.

Science and Technology revolutionize our lives, but memory, tradition and myth frame our response. Expelled from individual consciousness by the rush of change, history finds its revenge by stamping the collective unconscious with habits, values, expectations, dreams. The dialectic between past and future will continue to form our lives.

Arthur M. Schlesinger, Jr., 'The Challenge of Change,' in *New York Times Magazine* (27 July 1986).

There is a sort of myth of History that philosophers have. . . . History for philosophers is some sort of great, vast continuity in which the freedom of individuals and economic or social determinations come and get entangled. When someone lays a finger on one of those great themes – continuity, the effective exercise of human liberty, how individual liberty is articulated with social determinations – when someone touches one of these three myths, these good people start crying out that History is being raped or murdered.

Michel Foucault, interview in *La Quinzaine Littéraire* (15 March 1968; repr. in Didier Eribon, *Michel Foucault*, 1989; tr. 1991).

Men make their own history, but they do not make it just as they please; they do not make it under circumstances chosen by themselves, but under circumstances directly found, given and transmitted from the past. The tradition of all the dead generations weighs like a nightmare on the brain of the living.

Karl Marx, *The Eighteenth Brumaire of Louis Bonaparte*, sct. 1 (1852; repr. in *Selected Works*, vol. 2, 1942).

Only strong personalities can endure history, the weak ones are extinguished by it.

Friedrich Nietzsche, *Thoughts out of Season*, pt. 2, sct. 5 (1874).

We have need of history in its entirety, not to fall back into it, but to see if we can escape from it.

José Ortega y Gasset, *The Revolt of the Masses*, ch. 10 (1930).

GLOBALISATION
AND WORLD WARS

1

The twentieth century is short (just over seven decades), and yet full of devastating wars and sparkling economic prosperity. Future historians will probably appoint 1989 as its terminal year. In that year the Berlin wall fell, and the central front of the Cold War dissolved. The division of Germany that had been one of the primary foundations of the post-1945 world order came to an end. The Soviet Union accelerated the internal unravelling that two years later was to break it into fifteen new states. The military and ideological confrontation between the superpowers that had dominated world politics for over forty years simply evaporated. More than that, the fall of communism seemed to mark the end of a century-long struggle, in which several ideologies (monarchism, liberal democracy, communism and fascism) battled amongst themselves to see which would shape the future of industrial society. By the end of the twentieth century liberal democracy had won this struggle decisively, leading some commentators to declare 'the end of history', or more modestly, the triumph of the West.

Alongside this titanic political struggle, and in many ways part of it, was a massive increase in globalisation. The twentieth century will be remembered not only for its world wars, but also for the growth of a global economy and communication system,

7

the creation of world-spanning international and transnational organisations, the transformation of many Western ideas into global ones, and the rise of consciousness about the planetary environment and its fragility. This has been a century of conflict and collaboration, and progress and disaster, on an unprecedented scale and with unprecedented intensity.

LANDMARKS

At first glance, the historical landscape of the twentieth century is dominated by three massive features. Immediately behind us is the Cold War, in the turbulence of whose collapse we still live. Half a century before that sits the Second World War, now beginning to pass out of living memory, but whose shadow still noticeably affects present day events. At the beginning of the century sits the First World War, whose causes, consequences and awful carnage are now beginning to feel almost as distant as the wars of the nineteenth century. One can almost see the First and Second World Wars together with the inter-war period as a single event, a kind of European Civil War in which the European powers conducted their last great conflict over whether one of them, this time Germany, would exercise imperial control over the continent.

The outcome of the Second World War set the stage for the confrontation between the United States and the Soviet Union, and between communism and liberal democracy, that became labelled the Cold War. With only a few adjustments the cease-fire lines of 1945 in Europe and Asia become the ideological and military front lines of the Cold War. Crucially, most of Germany and all of Japan fell within the Western sphere. This meant that the industrial heartlands of the ex-fascist powers were politically purged by the Western powers and forcibly converted to liberal democracy. The addition of these powers to the West, especially once their economic recovery was complete, helped tip the balance against the Soviet Union and communism in the forty-year struggle to determine the political shape of industrial society.

The Main Events of the Cold War

- 1947   US initiates a world-wide policy of containment against Soviet power and communist influence: Marshall Plan and the Truman Doctrine in 1947
- 1948–9   Berlin Crisis
- 1949   founding of NATO, and the victory of Mao's communists in the long-running Chinese Civil War
- 1950   Sino-Soviet alliance
- 1951   Japanese-American Security Treaty
- 1950–3   Korean War
- 1955   founding of the European Economic Community (EC)
- 1960   Sino-Soviet split
- 1962   Cuba missiles crisis
- 1961–75 Vietnam War, and the first period of East-West détente
- 1979–89 Afghan War, and the second period of détente
- 1986   onset of domestic reform in the Soviet Union
- 1989   fall of the Berlin Wall
- 1991   collapse of the Soviet Union

If we look a little deeper, in between and underneath the high political events of the global clash between the superpowers, four other things were going on that were of at least equal long-term historical importance. One of these was the rapid opening up and expansion of the global economy in terms of trade, production, and from the late 1970s onwards, finance.

The growth of world trade, 1913—90

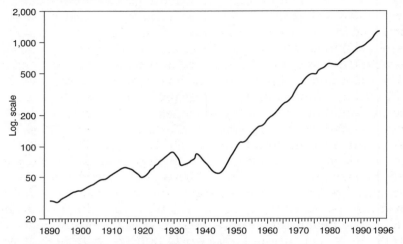

Long Term Development of World Merchandise Trade, 1890–96
Volume Indices, 1950 = 100

Note: Data for the periods 1914–1920 and 1939–1947 are not available.
Source: WTO, UN, OECD and IMF.

This was accompanied by an extraordinary growth in the number of translational corporations from a handful to over 40,000 by the early 1990s. By 1993 the sales of foreign subsidiaries and factories had reached one fifth of the entire world economy and comfortably more than total world exports. These developments increasingly made national economies not only more interdependent with each other, but also dependent on the smooth functioning of an ever more complex and powerful global market.

The second was decolonisation and the rise of the Third World in global politics as dozens of newly independent states more than quadrupled the membership of the international community. In 1914 there were 44 states; in 1930, and still in 1945, 64; in 1960, 107; in 1978, 148; and by the late 1990s more than 180. It was the Second World War that triggered a general withdrawal from the whole business of overseas empires. Before 1945, the world was organised as a system of unequal political relations, in which the European powers (and a few others) treated each other as equals, while treating the rest as inferiors (protectorates, dominions, colonies). Inferiors at best had unequal treaties imposed on them (extraterritoriality); often they were militarily occupied and directly controlled (colonies), and in the worst cases their populations were enslaved, massacred or displaced. With decolonisation, virtually all states and peoples agreed to treat each other as legal equals. Huge differences of power and development of course remained, and many of the new states had in practice not much more economic leeway than they possessed under colonial rule. But this political transformation was nevertheless one of the great events of the twentieth century.

The third underlying feature of the century was the growth of international (and transnational) organisations. Before 1914, international organisations were few in number, modest in function, and recent in origin: the Universal Postal Union (1874), the International Telegraph Union (1865), and suchlike. World politics functioned as it always had, on the basis of diplomacy and war conducted between states. There were no permanent forums or organisations for the general conduct of world affairs. After the First World War, this changed dramatically. The League of Nations was the first great experiment in permanently institutionalising world politics. Although it was, in the context of the inter-war years, a disastrous failure, the League represented an idea whose time had come. Despite the fiasco of collective security during the 1930s, the victorious powers in 1945 had no hesitation in setting up the United Nations (UN) as a permanent world political forum. From these beginnings have proliferated the hundreds of intergovernmental organisations that are now seen as essential to the management of humankind's political and economic affairs. These organisations are a very long way from constituting a world government, and it is a mistake to see that as their purpose. But they are a distinctive mark of the twentieth century.

The fourth underlying feature of the twentieth century was the dramatic, though often painful evolution of liberal political and social systems. This was largely a Western phenomenon, and was tied in to the processes of industrialisation, mass politics and world wars that were reshaping Western society. The creation of political and social systems that were more genuinely representative and responsive to popular will was crucially linked to the ability to sustain economic prosperity. Virtually no society that had sustained political and social pluralism seemed to surrender its liberal system. By the end of the century, there were virtually no advanced industrial countries that did not have such liberalism.

The rise of international governmental and non-governmental organisations, 1909–90

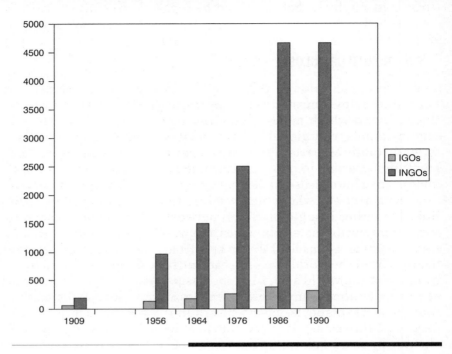

One of the main features of this system, and one with a deep impact on social order, was the emancipation of women. This not only marked a decisive break with the West's own traditions, but also constructed a major difference, and often a source of tension, between the West and most other cultures. Liberating half the population initiated a process that fundamentally changed economic, social, sexual and family relations throughout Western and Westernised society. Wider family structures were narrowed to the 'nuclear family', and then as divorce rates increased, even the nuclear family became less durable. Although there was much concern in the developed West about the ensuing social crisis, in fact the late twentieth-century levels of crime were lower than in the nineteenth century. The worrying in the late twentieth century had a great deal to do with the fact that comparisons were being drawn to the unusual period of the 1950s and early 1960s when there was astounding economic growth, but the consequences of social change had not yet begun in earnest. By the late twentieth century the developed world was experimenting with new forms of family and social structures that might be better suited to a post-industrial society.

THE GROWTH OF A GLOBAL SYSTEM

Perhaps the single most striking feature of the twentieth century is the extent to which much of the human species has been drawn together into a truly global international system. In purely physical terms virtually all parts of the planet are now connected to all other parts. It is possible to phone, fax or telex from almost anywhere to almost anywhere else, which means that communication is instantaneous across the whole planet. More than 30 million people are linked together in a global e-mail network which enables them to swap information as easily as if they were all in the same room. Radio and television mean that events from wars to weather reports in any part of the world can be heard and seen virtually in real time by much of the world's population. It is possible to fly from almost anywhere to almost anywhere else in less than a day, which means that the whole planet is open to travellers (unless they are debarred for political reasons). It is possible to ship bulk goods quickly and cheaply by sea, road, rail and air from almost anywhere to almost anywhere else, and to move money almost instantaneously, which means that production, finance and trade operate on a global scale. In terms of transport and communications, and therefore in terms of goods and information, for all but the poorest people, the planet is now a single space.

This fundamental development was, as we shall see in the next chapter, underway before the twentieth century, but it is in this time that it has become pervasive in the daily life of most people in the world. The effects are both benign and malign. In economic terms, most of the world lives in a single global market. Think about what you do when you wake up in the morning. The radio alarm, even the bed you are lying on, are likely to be made abroad. The milk and toast may be local, but the cereal, juice and jam are more likely to be foreign. Of course the newspaper you read is a global product. All this is because the prices of most commodities and most currencies are set by patterns of supply, demand and speculation that operate planet-wide. Finance and insurance operate through global markets, and the world's major stockmarkets are all tied together into a continuously operating system. Much industrial production and trade is organised in far-reaching multinational networks. Automobiles and civil airliners, for example, are almost all constructed from materials and manufactured components originating in many different countries. Tens of thousands of companies are organised as transnationals, and the internal exchange of goods and services amongst their constituent parts now accounts for over a third of all world trade and about 50% of trade among the most developed countries. Individuals with money commonly take holidays and do business in countries other than their own, and find it easy to arrange travel to almost all parts of the planet.

It is possible, and indeed necessary, for both political and economic actors to think of the global economy as a single structure if they are to operate within it successfully. Curiously, however, most economic statistics are still collected and organised on a state by state basis. This makes globalisation more difficult to see than it should be, and encourages out-of-date and politically distorted thinking in terms of balance of trade and competition between states. It is also alarmingly obvious that the development of this global economy is highly uneven: wealth, organisation, communication, knowledge and productivity, although found everywhere, are much more concentrated in some parts of the global system than in others. Consequently, the better-organised and more powerful parts of this system shape the whole pattern of relations regardless of whether this serves the interests of the weaker parts or not.

Because of the increase in human numbers, and the success of industrialisation, the idea that the world has become a single physical space also applies to the human impact on the planetary ecosystem. Humankind has now become so numerous, and with the aid of countless machines so active, that the scale of its day-to-day activities threatens to alter the composition of Earth's order of life and its atmosphere. Many species are being pushed out of existence annually as the human tide uproots, alters or poisons the habitats on which they depend. Gases produced by agricultural, industrial and energy production are changing the composition of the atmosphere, and altering its quality both as a generator of weather and as a screen against solar radiation. The ecosphere has always been changeable, but in this century the activities of humans have begun to impose their own, 'unnatural' changes. Our economic activities are now beginning visibly, and potentially drastically, to affect our own conditions of life.

The relative world decline of the core west's (Europe + North America) population

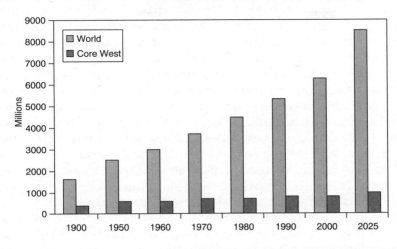

The spread of industrialisation, and the impact of technologies of transportation and communication that bind the planet together, have created a genuinely global system of diplomatic and military relations amongst the world's states. It is possible to make alliances, to conduct day-to-day diplomacy, and to fight wars on a planetary scale. Several major centres of industrial, financial, organisational and military power exist not just in Europe and North America, but also in Asia, and to a lesser extent Latin America. More than half a dozen countries have substantial arsenals of nuclear weapons, and double that number possess the technological means to build them if they wish. In this century humankind has for the first time acquired the means to commit species suicide, removing itself and much else from the planet in a great orgy of destruction. Throughout the four decades of the Cold War (1947–89) we lived with the daily fear that a war between the United States and the Soviet Union would have that result. This capability for self-destruction now exists as a permanent feature of the human condition.

Running in parallel with the physical linking up of the planet into a single space is the globalisation of many of the main ideas by which human beings organise their communities, their communications, and their activities. Most obvious is the global spread of the natural sciences, mathematics and medicine. The empirical, experimental scientific method developed in the West has become universal, and when added to global communication means that scientific research has almost become a single enterprise conducted on a planetary scale, albeit still restrained in some areas by the imperatives of military and commercial secrecy. Less well developed, but growing fast, is the use of English as a *lingua franca* for everything from international business and diplomacy to air traffic control and scientific conferences. Where this fails, legions of multilingual people (and increasingly, machines) are available to facilitate communication across language barriers by providing interpreting and translation services.

There is also an historically unprecedented globalisation of two major ideas about political organisation and legitimacy: the state and nationalism. As a result of decolonisation, it is a singular feature of contemporary world politics that humankind is almost entirely organised politically into units apparently all of the same type. The global political space is divided into some 180 states all of which claim exclusive right of self-government over a specified territory (sovereignty). Although there are territorial disputes and uncertainties among them, nearly all accord each other diplomatic recognition. This means that they accept each other's right to exist, and acknowledge each other as legally equal entities. On this basis, nearly all of them adhere to a complex set of diplomatic rules and procedures which enables them to communicate and negotiate with each other, to be permanently represented in each other's countries, to participate in international law as equal subjects, and to be members of the numerous international treaties and organisations that are a part of the contemporary global system. There is even some development of international law and norms on matters ranging from piracy and navigation rights to human rights and war. These are often supported more in principle than in practice, but their very existence indicates a significant globalisation of the organising ideas that frame political life.

Nationalism [the idea that shared ethnicity, culture, history, and particularly language, should provide the legitimate basis for claims to self-government] has also become a world-wide idea. It has transcended its European origins to become a potent political force all over the planet, surmounting a host of cultural and civilisational boundaries on its way. The idea that ethno-national groups should have political standing is quite recent, becoming powerful only with the French revolution at the end of the eighteenth century. Ideally, it harmonises with the idea of the sovereign state, producing a nation-state, in which a distinct people embody their culture and territory in the sovereign exercise of self-government. Some more or less pure nation-states do exist: among them Japan, Denmark, Poland, Korea. But the global reality is one in which several thousand nations exist, often uncomfortably, inside a framework of fewer than two hundred states.

In addition to nationalism and the territorial state, it is also clear that the debate about ideology – the sets of ideas around which states and peoples (try to) organise their political, economic and societal life – has become global. In the recently concluded Cold War a world-wide contest between communism and liberal capitalism dominated the politics of the planet for over four decades. These two ideologies, although both universalist in aspiration, represented strongly opposed views about how to organise the political economy of modern industrial societies: state power, command economy and totalitarian government on one side, and individualism, market economy and pluralist government on the other. The essential character of each made it intrinsically opposed to the other, and each being backed by a superpower, their contest penetrated into the political life of the whole of humankind. By 1989–92 liberal capitalism had won this war decisively, itself then taking on the character of a global standard against which any new contender had to measure itself in terms of productive efficiency, technological innovation, and cultural attractiveness.

The ideological contest of the Cold War can be seen as an extension, or a second round, of an earlier three-way contest amongst liberal capitalism, and two totalitarian ideologies, communism and fascism. Although fascism learned much of its totalitarian technique from communism, it opposed the universalism of liberal and Marxist doctrine with exclusivist claims of national and racial superiority. The ideas and organisations for this first round contest had been developing all through the nineteenth century. But it was the sustained national mobilizations of the First World War that demonstrated the real potential for mass politics and totalitarian state control over economy and society. The subsequent revolutions in Russia, Italy, Germany and elsewhere, elevated them to the realm of great power global politics. The rise of totalitarianism to state power dominated the 1920s and 30s, and shaped the central alignments of the Second World War. Eventually, three liberal capitalist great powers (Britain, France, the United States) opposed three fascist ones (Germany, Italy, Japan). The one communist great power (the Soviet Union) first seemed to align with the fascists but was then forced into alliance with the liberal capitalists after being attacked by Germany in June 1941. In what was for over three years a very finely balanced contest, the fascist powers eventually overreached themselves. Losing the war pushed fascism to the political margins, effectively eliminating it from the second round of the ideological struggle, the Cold War, which was in full swing within two years of the allied victory over Germany.

The violent history of the twentieth century's power rivalries demonstrates the globalisation of ideas and struggles not only about the organising framework and the legitimising principles of political life, but also about the way in which the political economy of human societies should be constructed. All three ideologies spread widely beyond their countries, cultures and political economies of origin, and all still retain roots in the political life of almost every nation. Communism remains in political power almost exclusively in Asia, despite being an idea of European origin.

The historic characteristic of the twentieth century is thus the construction of a single global space encompassing a wide range of human activities: communication, transportation, economy, politics, war, science, environment; and up to a point, law, culture and language. This does not mean that humankind is unified on a planetary scale in any more than a very limited sense. To be interconnected is not necessarily to be either integrated or harmonious. As illustrated even by the microcosm of the disintegration of Yugoslavia, there is a great deal in terms of culture, politics, economics and history that still divides individual from individual, class from class, nation from nation, state from state, and civilisation from civilisation.

What this single global space does mean is that humans, classes, nations, states and civilisations are much more closely, quickly and deeply in contact with each other than ever before, whether for mutual benefit or harm, whether intentionally or unintentionally, and whether contact is wanted or not. Their sustained and often intense impact on each other is a daily fact of existence. One result is that people share more ideas, rules, and principles of political and economic organisation than ever before. They are not anywhere near being united in the sense of possessing a single culture or an overarching political authority. But they are unified in the sense that all are components in an array of international systems – military, political, economic, societal and environmental – where the action and circumstances of each are substantially and regularly affected by what others do, even on the other side of the planet. Although humankind is durably and deeply fragmented along many lines, most of its parts are interconnected, and often interdependent in a host of important ways, and to a degree that has no historical precedent.

From where we stand now, the politics of intense, multi-level, planetary interdependence is not more than half a century old. What were the antecedents of these amazing and turbulent developments that constitute our own time? What was it that set up the circumstances which propelled our global system into being with such speed and violence?

EUROPEAN EXPANSION

2

A TALE OF TWO EUROPES: LATE NINETEENTH VERSUS LATE FIFTEENTH CENTURY

In order to see how the twentieth century's global systems of trade, war, diplomacy, communication and transport came into being, we have to switch our focus to the peculiar history of Europe. Europe's history during this half millennium is both the main driver behind the process of globalisation and the precursor to today's 'triumph of the West'. One way of understanding this story is to see it as an unprecedented accumulation of power concentrated in one small part of the world. This surplus of power enabled Europeans to fight continuously amongst themselves, in the process honing their war-making skills, technologies and organisations to take over and transform almost the whole of the planet. In 1500, Europeans comprised 14% of the world's population and controlled 7% of the world's land area. By 1800 they were 18% of the population and controlled 35%. By 1914 they were over 30% of the world population, had substantially re-peopled three continents (the Americas and Australia), and controlled 84% of the world's land. In the process of this expansion, Europeans laid the foundations not only of a wider West, but also of the global system in which we now live.

European power is often understood in terms of superior firepower or wealth. While these two elements of power did eventually emerge, the real basis of European power lay in its

21

ideas. As Albert Einstein noted, Western success was a feature of 'Western science' which was based on the invention of the formal logical system (in Euclidian geometry) and the discovery of the possibility of causal relationships by systematic experiment (in the Renaissance). The full story of the West is too complex to tell here (see chapter 14) but the belief in progress, and eventually the rights of individuals and the competitive markets were also to become key ingredients in its success.

Because the Europeans were the first to put together this mix of inventions and ideas, they had the unique privilege of finding their own path to modernity at a time when their dominance meant that they suffered little interference from the rest of the world – however much they interfered with each other. Developments that took place in Western Europe between 1500 and 1914, and the effects of those developments on the rest of the world, shaped much (though not all) of what is familiar in the twentieth century across the whole planet: the modern state, the industrial economy, the global trading system, the scientific method, and the world-wide system of transportation and communication. In their retreat from empire Europeans left behind a world remade politically and economically, sometimes badly, in their own image. Their excess power eventually enabled them to embark on the orgies of self-destruction in 1914 and 1939 that destroyed their global dominion.

If we take 1914 as our vantage point, what we see is a picture of extraordinary European – and particularly northern and western European – dominance (map 1). In Western Europe, we see a system of recognizably modern states. All are territorially coherent, have clear boundaries, and claim sovereignty [the exclusive right to self-government]. All have standing armed forces and well-developed administrative bureaucracies. Some of them are heavily industrialised (Britain, Germany, France, and the European offshoot in the United States), and most of the rest are at various stages along the road to industrialisation. A network of railways and telegraphs has been laid in most countries and connected up between them. Most of the rest of the world consists either of countries made by Western Europeans (as in the Americas), colonised by Western Europeans (most of Africa and Asia), or penetrated and dominated by Western Europeans (China, the Ottoman Empire, Siam, Persia). Some of the more powerful European states even had colonies within Europe, most notably Britain in Ireland. Except for Japan, which had successfully

Map 1

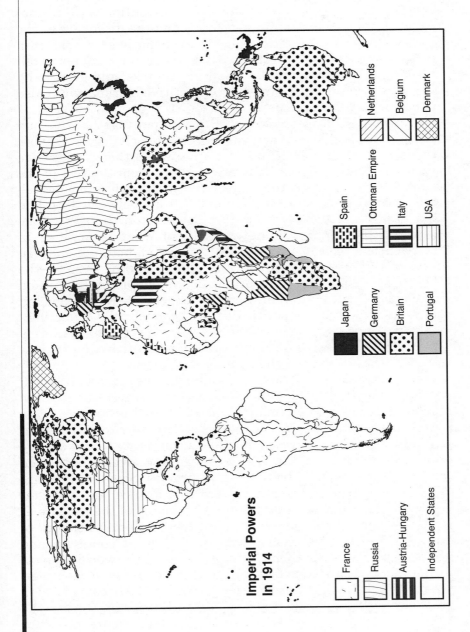

Imperial Powers
In 1914

	France
	Russia
	Austria-Hungary
	Independent States

	Japan
	Germany
	Britain
	Portugal

	Spain
	Ottoman Empire
	Italy
	USA

	Netherlands
	Belgium
	Denmark

Map 2

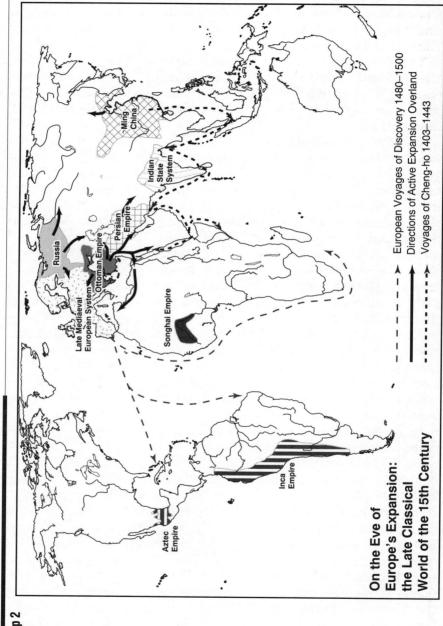

On the Eve of
Europe's Expansion:
the Late Classical
World of the 15th Century

- - - - ▶ European Voyages of Discovery 1480–1500

━━━━▶ Directions of Active Expansion Overland

••••••▶ Voyages of Cheng-ho 1403–1443

Ming China

Indian State System

Persian Empire

Russia

Ottoman Empire

Late Mediaeval European System

Songhai Empire

Aztec Empire

Inca Empire

created a European-style industrial state and a local empire, and Russia, which had extended its empire across Northern and Central Asia, there were no other significant centres of power, and few meaningfully independent countries outside Western Europe and the Americas.

Yet if we look back a little more than four hundred years, to the fifteenth century, we get an entirely different picture (map 2). Before 1500, Europe looks less like the familiar map of modern states, and more like the incoherent patchwork of medieval times.

The Papacy and the Holy Roman Empire still held significant authority over the state system, and there were other strong remnants of the feudal arrangements in which sovereignty was fragmented amongst a variety of actors (church, king, local aristocracy, cities, guilds). To be sure, one can see the outlines of modern states emerging in England, France, Spain and Scandinavia, and also interstate power rivalries, such as that between England and France (the Hundred Years' War, 1337–1453). But like many of today's Third World countries, these states were still weakly formed. They were prone to civil wars, depopulating plagues, and large boundary changes, and the dynastic interests of ruling aristocracies often prevailed over what we might think of as state interests. Europe itself was not yet closely bound together by networks of transportation and communication: a typical journey from London to Venice would take nearly a month. Consequently wars and conflicts in one area within it remained quite separate from those elsewhere.

In global terms, Europe was a largely self-contained backwater. Medieval Europe had briefly projected power into the eastern Mediterranean during the Crusades of the twelfth century, and in the fifteenth century Christian Europeans were completing the expulsion of Islamic, Moorish power from Spain. European seamen and traders were beginning to find their way around Africa and across the Atlantic. But in the south-east, Constantinople had fallen to the Ottoman Empire in 1453, and Islamic Turkish power was destroying the remnants of the Byzantine Empire, beating back the power of Venice, and occupying most of the Balkans. In Asia, the Chinese admiral Cheng-Ho undertook a series of voyages between 1405 and 1443 with a powerful trading fleet, establishing Chinese influence all around the northern perimeter of the

Indian Ocean. He reached as far as the Red Sea and the Somali coast, taking in India, Burma, Malaya, Sumatra, Java and Vietnam, all this before the Portuguese had managed to get as far south as Senegal in their slow creep down the West African coastline. Arab traders plied the sea routes connecting China to the Red Sea, and had already imported Islam into Indonesia and China.

In the fifteenth century, then, Europe was neither significantly more powerful nor significantly more advanced (many would say less), than other centres of civilisation. It had no empire to rival that of Ming China or the Incas, its emerging states were preoccupied with fighting each other, and it was under major assault from expanding Ottoman power. Four things happened during the intervening centuries to transform this unpromising-looking fifteenth-century picture into the global domination of the nineteenth century. First was the emergence of a new type of political construction in Europe: the national state. Second was the development of industrial society: the aptly named 'industrial revolution'. Third was the persistence of conflict within Europe. And fourth was the expansion of European power and population overseas.

THE NATIONAL STATE

It is easy to take the modern state for granted, and to assume that something like it (classical Athens or Rome for example) has existed since the dawn of civilisation. But this apparent continuity is an illusion. From the fifteenth to the seventeenth centuries a type of political form developed in Europe that was significantly different from the city-states, kingdoms and empires that preceded it. This development produced the modern national (and eventually democratic) state, and it is not without significance that the emergence of this political form corresponded closely to Europe's rise to world power.

The National State

The national state is distinguished by a number of features. Most obvious is its strong sense of territory, expressed in clearly demarcated borders, and the claim of its government to centralised sovereignty: the absolute right of self-rule within that territory. This contrasts with the traditional form of empires, in which the claim to government was often partial, and shared with local rulers, and in which the territorial domain was often vague, tending to fade out rather than being given a sharp boundary. In addition, the national state was marked by a ruling stratum wider than that in traditional empires, comprising both nobility and mercantile classes. The historical sociologist Charles Tilly nicely describes this as a synthesis of the forces of coercion and the forces of capital and argues that it made such states more effective in war than other political forms. As it developed, the national state brought more of the population into the governing process, transforming subjects into citizens, and shifting sovereignty from the monarchy (absolutism) to the whole population (popular sovereignty).

If we look backwards from 1914, we can identify some of the main developments in this rise. At the end of the nineteenth century the European states ranged politically from semi-democracies (Britain, France, Netherlands) through mixed systems of parliamentary and autocratic government (Germany) to absolutist autocracies (Russia). All of them were influenced by the newly emerging idea of nationalism [the principle that the right of self-rule resides in ethno-linguistic groups]. The coherence of these groups was often far from clear, and traditions had to be 'invented' in order to make nationalism work. Nevertheless, in the more democratic states, nationalism was part of the complex of ideas and forces that led to the acceptance of popular sovereignty as the foundation of government. This new way of organising people had first burst onto the scene at the end of the eighteenth century, when it unleashed the hitherto untapped power of mass armies in revolutionary France. Nationalism was a strength for most of the western

European countries, where long centuries of war and internal consolidation meant that ethno-cultural boundaries and political ones had been more or less made to coincide. Where this was so, political and cultural identities reinforced each other and enhanced a sense of community within the state. One cost of this was that building unity at home made rivalry with those beyond the frontiers sharper.

Such ethno-nationalism was a particular problem for the multinational empires (Russian, Austro-Hungarian and Ottoman), and those states with colonies in Europe (Britain over Ireland). For them, nationalism was corrosive of internal cohesion. Yet a different and more positive experience of nationalism was becoming apparent in some of the white settler states (United States, Canada, Australia) albeit at the expense of the native populations. The settlers too felt they were creating nations, but of a civic rather than ethnic form. Such multi-cultural nationalism was to prove to be one of the United States' great contributions to Western ideas about governance. Their multi-ethnic society was built on the basis of democracy and federalism (although not a federalism linking ethnically separate states). Canada and Australia were eventually to find a similar formula that would lay the basis for the belief that stable and prosperous government could be based on complex identity.

The nineteenth-century European state system had a well-developed international society. The norm was that all states recognised each other's claims to sovereignty, and that they established permanent diplomatic representation in each other's capitals. A body of international law existed which enabled states to regulate some aspects of their relations. The preservation of the balance of power – in other words, agreement that no single state should be allowed to become predominant in Europe – had considerable standing as a European norm.

Looking back earlier, into the eighteenth and seventeenth centuries before the French Revolution, the picture was different in several important respects. During this period nationalism was only barely discernible as a political force. Almost everywhere except Britain and the Netherlands, absolutist monarchs claiming all the powers of government held sway, locating sovereignty in themselves (Louis XIV's remark, 'L'État c'est moi') rather than, as later, in the people. Monarchical rule meant that the principle of dynastic succession loomed large in European international relations. Wars were frequent, often involving either disputes over rights of succession as the rival royal houses (Bourbons, Habsburgs) manoeuvred to increase their sway, or disputes over religious affiliations (mostly consequent on the splits in Western Christianity that spread after Luther's posting of his ninety-five theses in 1517). There was little desire to restrain the resort to war, and not until the eighteenth century did distinctive state interests begin to displace dynastic concerns. Diplomacy for war avoidance only became common in the nineteenth century.

As we move backwards in time towards 1500 and earlier, dynastic concerns become stronger, political authority and military power within states become less centralised and more feudal. Before 1500, the practice of diplomacy and the claim of state sovereignty on which it rested could only be found amongst the Italian city-states, where they had been invented during the Renaissance of the fifteenth century (and from where they spread to the rest of Europe during the sixteenth century).

Looked at from the perspective of the states themselves, these four centuries thus represent a dramatic transformation in the whole nature of political organisation in Europe. The agrarian-based semi-feudal arrangements still prevailing in the fifteenth and sixteenth centuries gave way to the still agrarian-based, but sovereign and absolutist state system of the seventeenth and eighteenth centuries. These in turn gave way to the industrial-based national states, the rise of nationalism, and the beginnings of democratic government and mass society that grew during the nineteenth century. This series of political and economic developments not only changed the internal character of European states, but also transformed the way that they related to each other. It had also made them exceptionally powerful in relation to the rest of the world, which remained stuck in the less effective and slower moving political forms of the ancient and classical era.

THE INDUSTRIAL REVOLUTION

The industrial revolution is conventionally understood as centring on the application to manufacturing of both new methods of organisation (factories, mass production), and new technologies (iron, steam, electricity, chemicals, telecommunications etc.). Its most obvious consequence was to increase not only the amount of goods produced, but also the variety and type of goods. Expanded production reduced the cost of goods and opened the possibility for mass consumption of basics such as cloth, ironware and pottery. Innovation meant that new and different products were continuously being pumped into society on a large scale: railways, steamships, aircraft, radios and so on. Two things underlay this increase and diversification of production: first, a systematic and continuous accumulation of scientific and technical knowledge, and second, the large-scale application of non-human and non-animal sources of energy to the production process. The earliest energy sources were water and wind mills, but the great symbol of the industrial revolution was the steam engine, which allowed an energy source to be set up almost anywhere, independent of natural conditions (but dependent on a supply of fuel, usually coal). The large-scale application of mechanical and chemical energy to the process of production marked a decisive break with earlier history in which production was limited by the availability of human and animal labour. With industrial means, the amount and diversity of production became potentially unlimited.

Percentage shares of world manufacturing output, 1750–1980

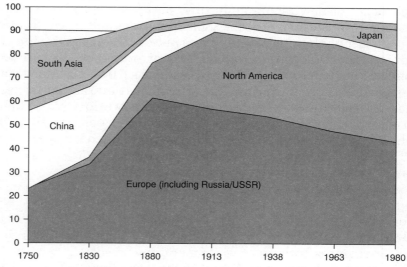

Source: Paul Bairoch, 'international industrialization levels from 1750 to 1980', Journal of European Economic History, 11:2, (1982), pp. 296, 304.

The industrial revolution was not just about production. It was made possible by ideas about the rights of individuals and their interrelationship through markets, and in turn revolutionised the material condition of humankind and society itself. These threads are inseparable. Perhaps the major difference between pre-industrial (i.e. agrarian) societies and industrial ones was their attitude towards change. Agrarian societies tend to be socially and politically conservative. They see time and history as more cyclical and repetitive than linear and progressive, and often go out of their way to suppress inputs that might disturb their social order. The Romans, for example, knew of the water mill, but their slave-based economy gave them little incentive to make use of it. In the middle of the fifteenth century, the Chinese Empire decided to cease overseas trading. It forbade the construction of ocean-going ships, and limited the power of the merchant classes. Agrarian societies were not immune to innovation, and they did evolve both socially and technologically. But innovation was subordinate to other values, and society was not geared to the expectation of change.

The shift to industrial production makes it impossible to sustain such conservative social and political arrangements. Industrial societies make innovation a priority over other values, and feed on the resulting change. They open themselves to the impact of new technologies and new knowledge, and allow the impact of these to reshape their societies and their states. So long as technology remains an open-ended source of change, industrial societies are in a condition of permanent revolution. Their class structures, their sources of political authority and legitimacy, and their relationships among the individual, society and state, are all exposed to continuous adaptation and restructuring to meet new conditions. Industrial society has even helped reshape the relationship between the sexes.

The early stages of the industrial revolution not only shifted masses of peasants off the land and into the cities, but empowered the commercial classes in relation to the aristocratic ones, and created new classes of workers and professionals. As the production revolution continued, it empowered the individual in relation to both society and state. More advanced industrial society requires both its producers and its consumers to be more sophisticated. It requires flexibility in the deployment of individuals, allowing people to be mobile both in terms of where they live and what kind of work and status they can aspire to.

Industrial societies have to educate their citizens, and in doing so they give them power. In doing so they increase their own power as states and cultures. Industrial societies make far more effective use of their human potential than any other social form yet invented. Because of this, it was not just superior weapons that enabled the first generation of industrial societies in Europe to dominate the world. Their undoubted greed and unrestrained aggressiveness were supported by an across-the-board superiority in organisation, knowledge and flexibility.

The logic of this development runs in parallel with that of the development of the national state in western Europe discussed above. The industrial revolution did not begin until the middle of the eighteenth century, and then mostly in Britain. During the seventeenth and eighteenth centuries, the European economy was still overwhelmingly dominated by agricultural and mineral production and trade. Not until the middle of the nineteenth century was industry moving decisively into its coal, iron and

Production of world manufacturing industries, 1830–1980 (1900 = 100)		
	Total Production	Annual Growth Rate
1830	34.1	(0.8)
1860	41.8	0.7
1880	59.4	1.8
1900	100.0	2.6
1913	172.4	4.3
1928	250.8	2.5
1938	311.4	2.2
1953	567.7	4.1
1963	950.1	5.3
1973	1730.6	6.2
1980	3041.6	2.4

Source: Paul Bairoch, 'International industrialization levels from 1750 to 1980', Journal of European Economic History, 11: 2 (1982).

steam phase, becoming the dominant sector of the economy, and spreading to other European countries and the United States. Only around 1850 did Britain, then the premier industrial power, actually overtake China as the leading world centre of industrial production.

The industrial revolution is thus a later development than the formation of the national state, which had already been underway for more than three centuries by the time the industrial revolution was beginning. It is in the late eighteenth and more especially the nineteenth century that the confluence between the two becomes significant. During the eighteenth century, absolutist monarchical power was at its height. But the American, and then the French, revolutions signalled the beginning of the end for absolutism, and the beginning of a rapid and comprehensive movement towards popular sovereignty [the location of the right to self-government in the people rather than in the rulers] and ever wider participation of the citizenry in the process of government. People shifted from being subjects to being citizens. Their participation could be democratic, but it could also be expressed in mass movements of a distinctly authoritarian hue such as those that emerged during the twentieth century. Starting from these revolutions nationalism was often in effect invented as a binding force and thus took hold as a major new element in the making of the modern state. Before the French Revolution it was not controversial for states to contain many different peoples, and for rulers to speak a different language from their subjects. In the new age, appeals to nationalism were used to blur internal differences. Nationalism was not only a way of vesting sovereignty in the people. It was also a way of creating strong overarching communal identities to set against the divisive and potentially conflictual new class structures of industrial society identified by Marx.

EUROPEAN POWER STRUGGLES

The third trend in European history during this period, a continuous struggle for power, is the most familiar one, and we can deal with it briefly. The essential story here is the tension between on the one hand a collective desire of European international society to prevent any one power from becoming predominant, and on the other, the episodic attempts by particular European states to seek mastery of the continent. The fear was that one state or dynasty would become so powerful as to threaten the power and independence of the others. Until just a few decades ago, the European states lived in a world in which war was frequent, the seizure of territory by force was often considered legitimate, and territorial expansion was a widely pursued goal. From this perspective, the Cold War was merely the latest (and perhaps last) episode in a long history of alarms that one power would dominate Europe, and countervailing attempts by other powers to prevent that from happening. This balance of power pattern, summarised in table 1, has recurred frequently in European history.

The struggle against hegemonic control in Europe		
PERIOD	ASPIRANT HEGEMON	MAIN OPPOSITION
1947–1989	Soviet Union	NATO
1870–1945	Germany	France, Russia, Britain
1667–1715, 1789–1815	France	Austria, Prussia, Sweden, Britain, Russia
1519–1648	Habsburgs (Spain, Austria, Italy, Holland)	France, Ottomans, Britain

Before the Cold War, the European Civil War centred on fears that Germany would make its empire within Europe. The so-called 'German problem' arose from the consolidation of a powerful industrialised German state during the middle of the nineteenth century. Prior to the rise of Germany, from the early decades of the nineteenth century right back to the 1670s, the state that most inspired fears of hegemonic intent in Europe was France. Further back, from 1519 to 1648 Europe's fear of hege-mony was focused on the Habsburg dynasty, which by a combi-nation of successful dynastic marriages and military campaigns, had accumulated a huge European empire. During the fifteenth century the fear of the Habsburgs was so great that France was even willing to make alliances with the hated Ottoman Muslims against fellow Christians in Austria.

The century and a half of struggle against Habsburg hege-mony that culminated in 1648 was also the time of the religious upheavals of the Reformation and Counter-Reformation, and these two lines of action were closely intertwined. Dissatisfac-tion with the Roman church had been building since the four-teenth century, but became common during the sixteenth century with the spread of Lutheran and Calvinist heresies across much of northern Europe and southern France. The Catholic church's counterattack against these challenges to its religious monopoly dominated the first half of the seventeenth century. These religious divisions were critical to the power politics of the day. The Treaties of Westphalia in 1648 successfully took religious issues out of power politics, but did nothing to stem the rivalries and wars amongst the European powers.

The processes of industrial and political modernisation going on in Europe clearly did not mute the cycles of hegemonic challenge and response, which continued right up to the Cold War. But modernisation did affect the means with which those rivalries were conducted. The First and especially the Second World War demonstrated that industrialisation and popular sovereignty had made the European states too powerful to fight amongst themselves without danger of creating damage on such a huge scale as to risk the stability, and even the existence, of both winners and losers. It was also becoming clear by then that nationalism and popular sovereignty were beginning to foreclose the option of territorial seizures that had for long been standard practice. When nations became fusions of people, culture and territory it was neither legitimate, nor in the long run practical, to transfer arbitrarily chunks of territory between winners and losers. Unfortunately, the power-enhancing effects of modernisation manifested themselves earlier than the power restraining ones. The result was that Europe allowed its long tradition of internal conflict to culminate in the ruinous wars of the twentieth century that destroyed its world power.

EUROPEAN EXPANSION

The impact of modernisation had a much earlier and more dramatic effect on the relationship of the Europeans with the rest of the world than on their relationships with each other. It propelled Europe from being an obscure backwater in the fifteenth century, to being the centre of the world during the nineteenth century. As shown on map 1, at the end of the nineteenth century the European powers plus the United States and Japan controlled, either directly or indirectly, most of the world. This control represented the culmination of a period of expansion that began in the fifteenth century and continued for five hundred years.

European expansion		
Period	Source	Area of Expansion
19th Century	– United States	– Alaska, Western and Southern states, Philippines, Caribbean
	– various European	– Africa, Southeast Asia
	– European migrants	– Americas, Siberia, Australia, Africa
	– South Asian migrants	– East Africa, Caribbean
	– Chinese migrants	– North America
18th Century	– Russia	– Central Asia, Eastern Siberia, Alaska and Pacific coast
	– Spain	– Mexico, Pacific coast, northern South America
	– Britain	– North America, India
	– African slaves	– Americas
17th Century	– Russia	– Siberia
	– Britain, France	– North America, India
	– Britain, France, Holland	– East Asian and South American trade
	– Holland	– coastal Africa
16th Century	– Russia	– Urals, Western Siberia
	– Spain	– Central America, Caribbean, Peru, Philippines
	– Portugal	– African coasts, India, Indonesia

Much of this European expansion, although resting on the ideas and systems of human organisation derived from the Enlightenment, in practical terms rode on the back of superior sea power. From the fifteenth century onward, Western Europeans began to produce sturdy and well-armed seagoing vessels which enabled them to penetrate and then dominate the trade of Asia. When the Europeans applied industrial technology to shipbuilding, their steam-powered armoured warships were able to break the military resistance of Japan and China. The sharp tip of European expansion is thus the shift from land to sea power, both commercially and militarily.

During the nineteenth century, expansion was combined with mass migrations of Europeans. The United States, together with Canada, received more than 30 million immigrants from Europe. It also extended colonial control across the Pacific to the

Philippines, and into Central America and the Caribbean. Russia occupied Central Asia and the Vladivostok region, sending more than half-a-million settlers eastward into Siberia. Nearly four million Europeans emigrated to South America, whose countries had established their independence from Spain and Portugal in the early part of the century. Another two million went to Australia and New Zealand, and nearly one million to Africa, mostly to South Africa and Algeria. During this century the Europeans penetrated and then colonised nearly all of Africa, eroded and penetrated the Ottoman Empire and Persia, extended colonial control over most of Southeast Asia, and, along with the United States, forced China and Japan to open themselves to Western trade, culture and political influence. Although the slave trade from Africa to the Americas ended in 1870, Europe, and to a lesser extent the United States, also played a key role in the migrations of Indians into East Africa, and of Chinese to North America and Southeast Asia. At the height of their power, Europeans not only controlled much of the planet, they also changed its ethnic composition, eating habits and even people's sense of their place in the world. (The pattern of European expansion before the nineteenth century is set out in map 3 below.)

THE REST OF THE WORLD

A Eurocentric view of world history is fully justified for the first half of the twentieth century, and also for much of the nineteenth. But the further back one looks, the less significant Europe becomes, and the more the rest of the world comes into view as a set of players in their own right. In the nineteenth century, Islam continued to expand in Africa. Up until its defeat in the Opium War (1842), China was still a major centre of manufacturing, and was able to restrict European access. Japan similarly managed to sustain its self-enforced isolation until the mid-1850s. In the eighteenth century, China was expanding vigorously into Central and Southeast Asia. Persia managed to conquer much of north-west India (1739), and the Ottomans, though in retreat, fought regular and not always unsuccessful wars with Austria, Russia, and Persia. In the seventeenth century, the Mogul Empire was strong in South Asia, and the

Map 3(a)

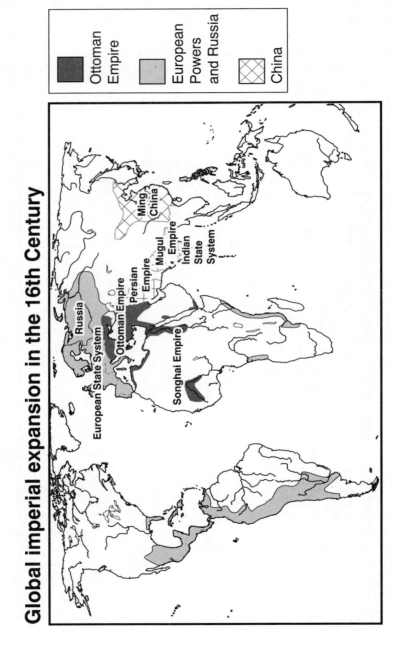

Global imperial expansion in the 16th Century

Map 3(b)

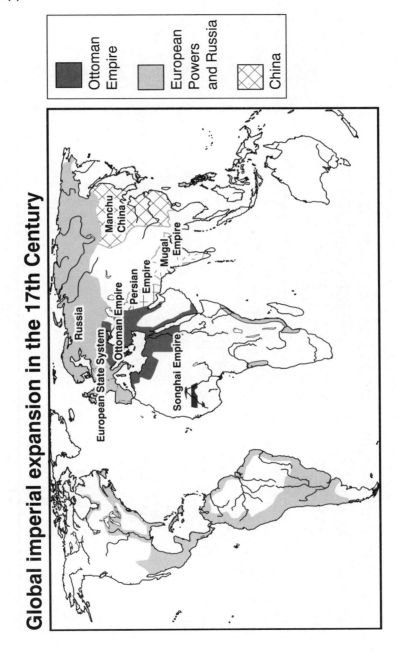

Global imperial expansion in the 17th Century

Ottoman Empire

European Powers and Russia

China

Russia

Manchu China

Mugal Empire

Persian Empire

Ottoman Empire

European State System

Songhai Empire

Map 3(c)

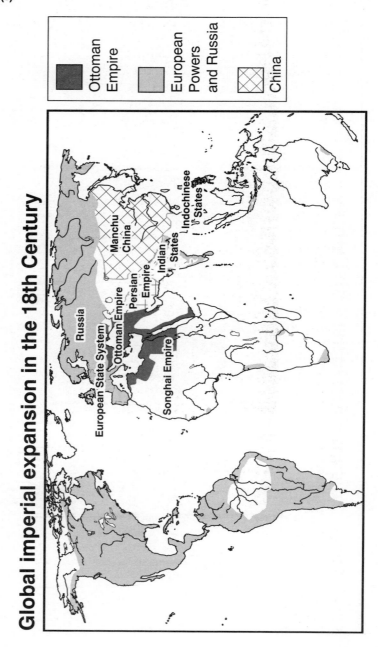

Global imperial expansion in the 18th Century

Ottoman Empire

European Powers and Russia

China

Ottoman Empire was able to mount its last offensive against Vienna (1683). China ousted the Dutch from Taiwan (1662) and took control of Korea (1627), while Japan instituted its policy of closure against foreigners.

During the sixteenth century, while Spain was conquering Central and South America, and Portugal was taking Brazil and opening the trade routes to India and China, the Ottoman Empire was still in its expansionist phase. Right on Europe's doorstep, it was taking Egypt, much of the Middle East, and Hungary, and laying siege to Vienna. It was in alliance with France against the Habsburgs, while at the same time fighting a long series of wars with Persia. In India the Mogul Empire was expanding its power, while the Ming Empire in China was beating off attacks by barbarians in the north, and attempted Japanese invasions of Korea.

What these events suggest is that the rise of Europe took place against the background of an earlier, quite different, and in its own way vigorous system of international relations. Europe eventually became almost totally dominant, leaving a legacy that shaped much of the political, economic and even cultural life of humankind in the twentieth century. But there was no magical point of transformation in 1500. For at least the first three centuries of Europe's rise, the older international system was still potent, and in much of Asia dominant. The next chapter will explore this older history which the meteoric rise of Europe did so much both to obscure and to destroy.

CIVILISATIONS, EMPIRES AND BARBARIANS

3

The world that existed before the rise of Europe consisted of two main components: (1) a set of populous core areas of agrarian civilisation, and (2) surrounding these cores, large areas dominated by a much smaller population of nomadic barbarians. An extensive periphery thinly occupied by hunter-gatherers makes for a possible third element, but this played a very marginal role in the story we have to tell here. There was a sustained and overall quite evenly balanced struggle between the military power of the barbarians and the military and cultural power of the civilisations. In terms of its impact on the shape of history, this struggle was often of greater importance than the battles that went on within and between the centres of civilisation themselves.

The story of this ancient and classical world stretches back for nearly five thousand years from AD 1500 to around 3250 BC. It covers the great bulk of recorded human history, and is therefore a vital element in any attempt to discern larger patterns in the progress of our species. As we saw in the previous chapter, a few of its last empires (Chinese, Ottoman, Mogul) overlapped with the rise of Europe before finally being overwhelmed in the eighteenth and nineteenth centuries by the newly industrialised might of the European powers. Some important legacies from this era fed into the rise of Europe and the West, most notably Judaism and Christianity; Greek art, science and philosophy; Roman law; mathematics and commerce from the Islamic world; and Chinese technology. All of the major (and most of the minor) religions and ethical systems stem from this time (Buddhism, Christianity, Confucianism, Hinduism, Islam, Judaism, etc.) as do the makings of the great linguistic, cultural and ethnic formations that we think of as civilisations (European/Western, Arab, Turkic, Persian, Indian, Confucian). So too do the barbarians, still to be found living in isolated pockets such as Afghanistan and Somalia, but now mostly perceived as archaic romantic figures found in fantasy films and comic books.

This history is too vast and too diverse to tell in detail here. We cannot chart the rise and fall of its numerous empires or trace the development of its many civilisations and their endless struggles with successive waves of barbarian invaders. What we can do is look at five basic patterns that define its essential qualities. These are: (1) the expansion of the areas controlled or influenced by agrarian civilisation, (2) the repeated rise and fall of empires, (3) the regular clashes between nomadic barbarians and settled civilisations, (4) the growth of long-distance trade, and (5) the relative stagnation of technology.

THE EXPANSION OF CIVILISATION

When the European expansion began around AD 1500 there were six main centres of high civilisation all of which had existed for at least two millennia: Southern Mexico, the Andean highlands and coastal strip, Europe, the Middle East, South Asia and East Asia. There seemed also to be the beginnings of a possible seventh in the central lands of West Africa, along the upper Niger river. Fifteen hundred years earlier there were five such centres: the Mediterranean, the Middle East, South Asia, China, and Central America. In 1500 BC there were three: the Middle East, the Indus valley and China. In 3000 BC there were two: Sumer and Egypt. Before 4000 BC we are in a world without cities, empires, high cultures, writing and wheels.

Map 4(a)

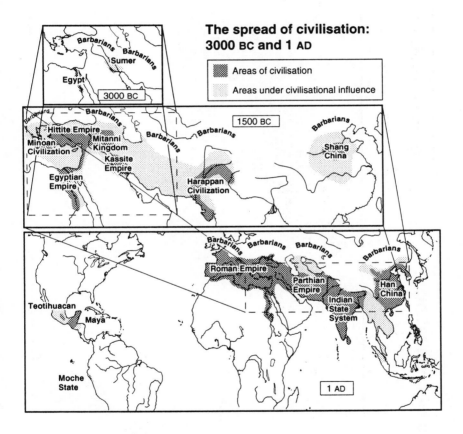

The spread of civilisation: 3000 BC and 1 AD

Areas of civilisation

Areas under civilisational influence

Map 4(b)

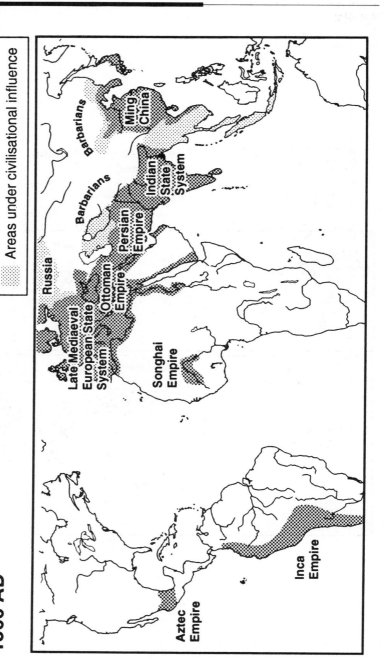

The spread of civilisation:
1500 AD

Areas of civilisation

Areas under civilisational influence

Barbarians

Ming China

Barbarians

Indian State System

Persian Empire

Russia

Ottoman Empire

Late Mediaeval European State System

Songhai Empire

Aztec Empire

Inca Empire

One main thread in this story – and also in the larger story of the progress of humankind – is thus the development of civilisation from one centre to many, and the subsequent expansion of each of these centres (albeit with many setbacks) at the expense of peoples with less centralised political relations and less stratified and specialised social and economic ones. Some centres of civilisation were probably spurred into existence by the influence of others, but several seem to have been self-starting creations responding to similar combinations of environment, population, trade and technology.

From its earliest beginnings, civilisation was defined by settled agricultural societies that developed cities. Civilisations almost always arose in areas, particularly river valleys, where agricultural conditions were good enough to support quite dense populations, and where there were easy trade contacts between different environmental zones. Cities are the key. Before them, there was no civilisation, and before civilisation there were no cities. Cities accumulated wealth and knowledge; developed elaborate social hierarchies and specialised divisions of labour (soldiers, artisans, administrators, priests, astronomers, kings); generated sophisticated cultures and religions; served as focal points for trade; developed accounting and writing; and mobilised military power in the form of armies and political power in the form of kings, emperors and bureaucracies. The basis of their political economy was the creation, storage, distribution and defence of food surpluses (grain: usually maize, rice or wheat). Cities became capable of controlling and co-ordinating surrounding agricultural populations, in the process becoming city-states. Some of them became good enough at this to bring other towns and cities into their orbit, and sometimes to serve as the centres of vast empires.

Once established, civilisations tended to expand their area of cultural, economic and political influence. Empires came and went, but only rarely did civilisations collapse. The Indus valley civilisation that flourished between 2700 and 1700 BC had by 1500 BC disappeared completely, even its cities having died. Something similar occurred to the lowland Mayan civilisation in Central America around AD 900. But the general rule was that over time, civilisations grew, albeit with many setbacks along the way. Around 3000 BC only a few small areas were civilised. By AD 1500, civilisation stretched in a more or less continuous swathe from East Asia, through Southeast and South Asia, and the Middle East, to North Africa and Europe. In addition, there were two substantial islands of civilisation in Central and South America. It was this process of slow expansion from many centres that was terminated by the unprecedented global expansion of European power after AD 1500.

Most of these ancient and classical civilisations functioned fairly autonomously, especially the outliers. The centres of civilisation in Mexico and Peru had little if any sustained contact with each other, and until they were obliterated by the Spaniards, virtually none with the civilisations of Eurasia. China had some regular cultural and trade contact with the civilisations to its west, but distance and difficult geography conspired to keep trade small, cultural contact limited and slow moving, and military contact almost non-existent until long after the first arrival of the Portuguese. The situation was somewhat different in central and western Eurasia, where centres of civilisation shared boundaries, and were within relatively easy military and commercial reach of each other. From AD 1500 to the fifth century BC, the civilisation in the Middle East was in direct economic and political contact with, and often at war with, those in the Mediterranean/Europe and South Asia. Despite this more intense contact, however, each of these civilisations retained its distinctive cultural character. Each generated and maintained its own languages and religions. Even the thousand-year Greek (and Roman) occupation of the Middle East stretching from Alexander's conquests (334–23 BC) through the Hellenistic and Roman empires, to the expulsion of Byzantine power from the region by the Arabs during the seventh century AD, did not eliminate the indigenous languages and cultures of the region, or its status as a distinct centre of civilisation. Indeed, the Græco-Roman occupation preceded the spectacular expansion of Middle Eastern civilisation inspired by Islam. Not until the rise of Europe was any one civilisation so successful in extending its range of control and influence.

THE RISE AND FALL OF EMPIRES

Within each civilisational area, the normal pattern was the rise and fall of city-state empires. Some of these empires were huge, lasted many centuries, and dominated their whole civilisational area, while others were ephemeral. At times rival empires contended for power within a single civilisational area, and at yet other times periods of fragmentation occurred, in which no empire dominated, and civilisation retreated to small city-states and minor kingdoms.

The rhythms and proportions of the waxing and waning of empires varied greatly from place to place. Some civilisational areas were more exposed to barbarian invasions than others, some suffered environmental disasters, some were devastated by disease, some had unstable succession mechanisms, and some developed social forms (the Hindu caste system, the Greek city-state, the Islamic umma) that made empires less necessary or more difficult. In China, empires tended to be strong and long lasting, and to follow closely one from another. Only occasionally did long periods of fragmentation into 'warring states' occur. This pattern was reversed in South Asia, where empires tended to be infrequent and short lived, and fluctuating patterns of warring states the general rule. In the Middle East, the tendency was firmly in favour of empires, some of them (especially Egypt) long lived. But more so than was the case in either East or South Asia, this civilisation frequently generated rival empires within its area. Some civilisations, most notably the ancient Greeks and the Maya, firmly resisted empire, finding their main expression as systems of (often warring) city-states. As we have seen, modern (i.e. post-Roman) European civilisation was also notable for its 'warring states' and its resistance to universal empire.

The waxing and waning of imperial power reflected the general character of the ancient and classical empires as political forms. The key to understanding this process is the city-state, which was the fundamental building block of the era. Empires tended to grow around powerful cities such as Athens, Babylon, Carthage, Ch'ang-an, Constantinople, Cuzco, Delhi, Nineveh, Patna, Rome, Tenochtitlan, or Ur. When empires disintegrated, they collapsed back to the city-state level. So when imperial control collapsed it did not normally endanger civilisation. Power simply fragmented back down to city-states and small kingdoms. The Islamic world, for example, flourished as a vast zone of trade and common culture even when it was politically fragmented into weak and often short-lived political units. Only when the cities themselves died, and social organisation reverted to village level, was civilisation threatened.

The main incentive for building empires was the desire to control and tax trade routes. Imperial control was usually good for trade in that it provided protection and stimulated demand for, and production of, goods. In turn, the tax revenues from trade (and also the loot from successful conquests) funded the monumental display and the military might of the empire. These empires were extractive, but offered important services in return: security of trade routes and food supply; protection against barbarian raiders; provision of public goods (roads, temples, coinage, property rights, promotion of lingua francas, standards for weights, measures and values); and military demand for goods and services.

The empires of the ancient and classical era were in some ways remarkably flexible units. They had neither fixed geographical limits nor a uniform degree of political control. The rise of great military captains – Alexander the Great, Chandragupta Maurya, Charlemagne, Genghis Khan, Hammurabi, Julian, Sargon, Timur – often made empires, while weak rulers, or fragmenting rules of royal succession, often dismantled them. Random events such as plagues or barbarian assaults could weaken or destroy empires. So too could more structural problems, such as reaching the limits of expansion, and so losing the input of new resources of land (Ottomans) or slaves (Rome) which had previously been used to buy off internal problems or to sustain the economy. Secessionism was a constant problem, borders were always in question, and the balance between central and local power was continually in flux.

But there was a learning process, and as history unfolded, the techniques of imperial control improved, enabling larger and more durable constructions to be built. In such a turbulent environment military power and skilful, energetic, and ruthless leadership were the keys to successful empire. But even possession of these did not guarantee more than short-term success. Creating a broader and more deeply rooted ruling elite better able to survive variations in the talent of leaders was one key. Another was the attraction of the imperial idea itself. This took root especially strongly in China and the Middle East, so that even during periods of fragmentation, the warring states were often motivated by the desire to re-establish a wider imperial domain. Over the five millennia of this era, there is a pattern of progressive development from Sumer to Rome in which the techniques of imperial construction and control became more effective. Ruling elites became broader, which enabled empires to become larger and/or better integrated. Rome even extended citizenship to its peoples, and in Western Europe, nostalgia for Rome lasted for more than a thousand years after its fall.

For the most part, this process of the rise and fall of empires occurred within civilisational areas rather than being the result of interaction between them. Long-distance trade and cultural exchange were possible during the ancient and classical era, but military and political interaction required states to bring significant armed force to bear on each other, and logistical constraints made this difficult. Until the Europeans broke the pattern, only occasionally was a whole civilisational area overrun by its neighbour, as in the case of Alexander's conquest of the Persian Empire. Han China and Imperial Rome, for example, knew of each other's existence, but never made strategic contact.

THE CLASHES BETWEEN BARBARIANS AND CIVILISATIONS

The term 'barbarians' has been used by many civilised peoples (Greek, Chinese, European) to label others who are outside their own culture. For the period of ancient and classical civilisations, the term has a more specific meaning. It refers to tribes of nomadic herdsmen and hunters who occupied the steppe lands (especially, but not only, the steppe lands of central Eurasia). These peoples were not primitive hunter-gatherers, but neither were they settled agriculturists. Their way of life depended on some of the same technologies that underpinned the urban, agricultural civilisations (domesticated animals, wheeled wagons, metal tools). But they were nomadic and tribal, and did not develop cities. Their economy was based on animal herding rather than agriculture, and they lacked the sophisticated class structure and division of labour that typified urban agrarian civilisation. Their way of life gave them some distinctive military advantages, especially when horses began to be used as a means of transportation some time after 2000 BC. They were skilled horsemen, and tough, mobile and willing fighters.

From the very beginning of this period, barbarians were in sustained contact with civilisation as traders, neighbours, raiders, and not infrequently conquerors. Great leaders such as Timur, Attila, Muhammad and Genghis Khan occasionally arose amongst them capable of welding the normally divided and fractious tribes into huge hordes that were the most formidable military machines of their day. At various times throughout the four thousand years from 2500 BC to AD 1500 barbarian power conquered every major centre of civilisation in Eurasia. Barbarian raiders and conquerors frequently did great damage to both city life and agricultural production. But although they often destroyed or usurped empires, they rarely threatened civilisation itself, often being absorbed by the seductive cultures and larger populations of the settled world.

The final collapse of barbarian power is almost as important in defining the end of the classical and ancient era as is the rise of the national state in Europe. The advent of firearms from the fourteenth century AD onward spelled the permanent doom of the long-standing nomadic military superiority based on light cavalry. Equipped with guns, peasant infantry could stand off barbarian raiders, and so push the area of civilised control into the steppe. The Russian expansion across Siberia, beginning in the sixteenth century, and the assertion of durable Chinese control over the eastern reaches of Central Asia during the Manchu expansion of the eighteenth century, marked the final extinction of classical barbarian control in the steppe.

Throughout this era all of the Eurasian civilisations experienced periodic waves of barbarian assaults. Because the barbarians' lifestyle and herd-based economy made them mobile, they could suddenly turn up anywhere with little or no warning. They had the strategic advantage of occupying the interior steppe lands of Eurasia, which gave them access to all of the centres of civilisation. Trading, raiding, and missionary activity generated sustained contact between barbarians and civilisation, and the transfer of technology and culture made some of the barbarians semi-civilised. But for the barbarians, the great cities, storehouses and trade routes of civilisation constituted an irresistible temptation to plunder, whether in raids, or in more sustained periods of extractive imperial rule.

Seven main waves of barbarian outsurge

Wave/Time	Barbarians	Target
Seventh: 13th century AD	Mongols	China, Russia, Central and Western Asia
Sixth: 10th–15th centuries AD	Turks	Central and South Asia, Middle East, Southeast Europe
Fifth: 7th–8th centuries AD	Arabs	Middle East, Central Asia, North Africa, Spain
Fourth: 3rd–7th centuries AD	Indo-Europeans and Turks	Northern China, Roman Empire, South Asia
Third: 8th century BC	Indo-Europeans	Middle East, Northern China
Second: 13th century BC	Indo-Europeans	Greece, Middle East
First: 19th–15th centuries BC	Indo-Europeans	Northern China, Middle East, South Asia

It is possible to see these movements in terms of concentric circles of peoples, being pushed westward by pressures emanating from an Asian core located north of China. The first wave was of Indo-European (Aryan) race, and it was these peoples that challenged civilisations in Europe, South Asia and the Middle East during the first two millennia BC. The Aryans (who provided much of the ancestral population of present day Europe, India and Persia) were pushed from behind by a second wave of Turkic peoples, mostly responsible for the assaults on civilisation during the first millennium AD. These, in turn, were pushed by the Mongol peoples, who staged their own direct assault on civilisation in the twelfth and thirteenth centuries AD. The sources of this process are rather obscure, and not important to the general picture. Among the factors operating were relative success and failure in warfare amongst the barbarians, innovations in military technology, climate changes in the steppe lands, and periodic Chinese successes in pushing back the barbarian frontiers. When defeated or oppressed, nomadic peoples could and did move *en masse* to seek greener pastures.

THE GROWTH OF LONG-DISTANCE TRADE

The development of a truly world-wide economy is a hallmark of European expansion and Western domination. But long-distance trade existed well before the Europeans first circled the planet with sea routes around Africa and across the Atlantic and Pacific Oceans. Indeed, the main motive of the European explorers was to reopen patterns of trade from classical times that had broken down because of the fall of Rome and the rise of Islamic power. The general pattern of this story is set out in table 4.

Key events in the development of world trade	
Time	**Development**
2nd millennium BC	Development of long-distance trade between Middle East, and Europe and Indus Valley.
6th century BC	Persian Empire connects Mediterranean and Asian trade.
5th century BC to 5th century AD	Silk roads link the empires and civilisations of Asia and the Mediterranean by land through Central Asia and the Middle East, and by sea through South Asia and the Middle East.
6th and 7th centuries AD	Breakdown of the Mediterranean economy and decay of silk roads trade to Europe. Hostility between Islam and Christendom disrupts trade links.
8th century AD	Revival of trade in Asia. Europe isolated and stagnant.
12th–14th centuries AD	Crusades and Mongol empire temporarily revive Eurasian trade.
14th and 15th centuries AD	Revival of European trade.
16th century AD	Europeans re-establish direct sea links to Asia, bypassing the Middle East, and for the first time bring the Americas into the world economy.

For some two thousands years before the voyages of da Gama and Columbus, a trading network existed that embraced all of Eurasia and northern and eastern Africa. That network itself

Map 5 – The fourth century AD: trade, empire and barbarians in classical Eurasia

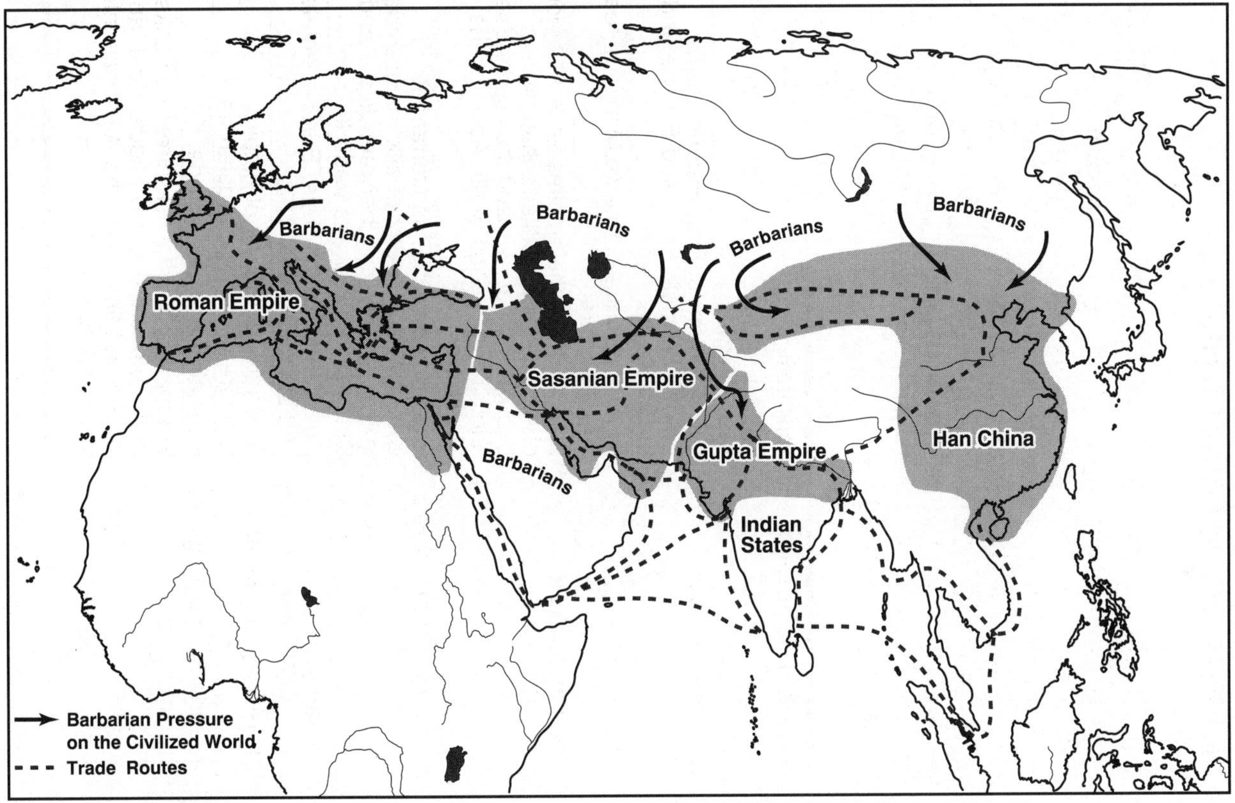

Barbarians

Han China

Barbarians

Barbarians

Gupta Empire

Indian States

Barbarians

Sasanian Empire

Barbarians

Barbarians

Roman Empire

Barbarians

→ Barbarian Pressure on the Civilized World

--- Trade Routes

grew out of the extensive patterns of regional trade that sur-
rounded and supported all of the emerging centres of civilisation
(see map 5).

Before the industrial age, trade was largely driven by the
differences among regions in terms of what they could produce.
For example, river valley civilisations such as those in Egypt
and Mesopotamia could produce surpluses of food grains, but
were often without local supplies of metals, wood, stone and
jewels which had to be brought in from afar. Coastal and river
navigation even with primitive craft enabled bulk goods to be
traded over long distances. The earliest civilisations in Sumer
and Egypt grew up around navigable rivers, which became the
spines of subsequent empires after 3000 BC. From 2000–1500 BC
trade links spread from the centres of civilisation in the eastern
Mediterranean (i.e. Crete, Egypt, Babylon) throughout Europe.
By 1700 BC, there were trade links between the civilisations in
Egypt, Mesopotamia and Indus valley.

The Scale of Trade

The archaeologist Brian Fagan reveals the scale
and sophistication of early trade with an account
of a famous shipwreck dating from the fourteenth
century BC off southern Turkey. It contained an
amazing array of goods from as far apart as the
Baltic and Africa, including more than five metric
tons of copper ingots (enough metal to equip a
small army), a ton of resin, numerous blue glass
ingots, hardwood, amber, tortoise shells, elephant
tusks, pottery, olives and ostrich eggs.

Although Mediterranean civilisation was uniquely favoured
by the availability of extensive inland seas, similar processes
were at work around the other emerging cores of civilisation,
with overland and river-carried trade and cultural contact
reaching much further afield than the military and political
control of the ancient empires. Ancient and classical empires
typically lived symbiotically with major trading networks.
Trade provided taxes to support the empire, and the empire
provided security, markets and infrastructure to support trade.
The Roman Empire was a largely self-contained trading system,
providing roads, ports, currency and security, and creating a

demand for goods to supply major cities and the frontier armies. China likewise developed extensive internal trade in bulk and luxury goods, though not having the advantage of inland seas, it depended more on the development of canals to connect up its navigable river systems.

As a rule, trade developed earlier and more extensively within civilisational areas than between them, and trading networks were always more extensive than zones of imperial control. Not until around 500 BC did trade regularly begin to filter through the insulating layers of difficult geography and hostile barbarians to begin creating a Eurasian-wide network. The key to the development of systematic trading contact between the east and west of Eurasia was the expansion of the Persian Empire during the sixth century BC. The Persians built and defended a system of roads and routes linking the Aegean ports of Anatolia via Mesopotamia and Persia to Central Asia and the Indus valley. The Persian Empire and its successors served as the keystone of the famous silk road caravan routes connecting China, South Asia, the Middle East and the Mediterranean. By the fifth century BC there was consequently knowledge of India in Greece, and it was no accident that Alexander the Great headed eastward in pursuit of conquests. The tariffs on the silk road trade were a valuable source of revenue for any empire that controlled them.

The silk road trade was mostly high value, low volume luxury goods (silk, spices, jewels) from east to west, and gold and silver from west to east. The West had little that it could sell to the East, but much that it wanted from it. This situation persisted almost to the nineteenth century, posing a continuous balance of payments problem, and sustained drainage of gold and silver from west to east. There was of course also extensive trade within the East, among China, India and the Middle East, and this continued after Europe became cut off.

From the first century BC, the land route was accompanied by an extensive sea trade between the Red Sea and the Gulf, and South Asia, and between China and the Indian Ocean. Around 120 BC, Ptolemaic Egypt pioneered coastal, and then, once the seasonal wind patterns were mastered, open-ocean sea routes to India, making Alexandria a key entrepôt for the eastern trade with the Mediterranean. At about the same time, Chinese ships reached the Bay of Bengal, meeting up with Indian traffic to Southeast Asia. By the second century AD, these developments had evolved into a regular sea route connecting the Middle East, South Asia and China (see map 5).

The fourth wave of barbarian assaults wrecked the Roman end of the Eurasian trading system, put severe pressure on the Byzantine and Sassanian Empires, and helped precipitate four centuries of weakness and division in China. The fifth and sixth waves effectively cut post-Roman Europe off from the rest of Eurasia. Further barbarian attacks on Europe during the ninth and tenth centuries AD (Vikings, Magyars, Saracens) disrupted the recovery of trade and settlement, destroyed ports and contributed to depopulation, although the Viking traders did open up the trade routes from the Baltic to the Black Sea. The Arab defeat of China in 751 pushed Chinese power out of Central Asia and broke the land routes to the west, though reviving trade between Asia and the Middle East. In the ninth century both Arabs and Persians were trading at Canton. In the east, maritime and overland contact between China and India continued unbroken. What little Asian trade remained with the Mediterranean was tightly, and expensively, filtered through the Islamic realms, whose central location in the Eurasian trading system was an important source of their wealth.

With the Crusades, Europe began to reassert its influence in the Mediterranean, and so re-link to Africa and the Middle East. But the revival in east–west trade on which Venice built its prosperity remained constricted by numerous middlemen and high cost, by the ideological hostility between Christianity and Islam, and by the old problem of a lack of anything other than gold and silver that the east wanted from Europe. In the meantime, late medieval Europe was rebuilding its regional trading network. The Hanseatic League linked all of northern Europe and Russia, while Venice and other Italian city-states re-established the Mediterranean and Black Sea sea-trading routes.

But the Islamic monopoly on east–west trade remained until the Europeans found the sea routes around Africa, and across the Atlantic and Pacific Oceans, that enabled them to bypass the Islamic wedge and open direct trade with Asia for the first time. These developments ended the linear pattern of the classical trading system, replacing it with direct contact between seller and buyer world-wide. Indeed, it was the desire to bypass the costs and restrictions of the overland trade with the east that was the principal motive for the European explorations of the fifteenth and sixteenth centuries. The Portuguese opening of the sea route around Africa to South and East Asia, and the Spanish opening of the sea routes across the Atlantic and the Pacific, greatly reduced costs and avoided constraints. They also tapped new supplies of gold and silver from Africa and the Americas with which to pay for the Asian goods (tea, silk, porcelain, spices) which Europeans desired, but for which they still had little that the Asians wanted to buy in return. These global routes resulted in a world-wide trade that rapidly diffused many crops (cotton, tobacco, bananas, sugar cane, maize, potato, rice, wheat, sweet potato), animals (horses, sheep, cattle), diseases (smallpox, measles, typhus, malaria, yellow fever) and peoples away from their points of origin. This diffusion had increasingly profound effects on the regions into which new foods, new export crops, new domesticated animals, new plagues, and new peoples were introduced, beginning the process that produced the global political economy in which we now live.

It is interesting to note, connecting this story to that of the era of European expansion, that the Europeans were unable to resolve their chronic trade imbalance with the east until the eighteenth century, when they took over most of India, and penetrated the Chinese market with opium. By that time Europe also had some comparative advantage in manufactured textiles and weapons. Not until the nineteenth century did the industrial revolution give them a genuine trading (and military) advantage over Asia, a temporary reversal which it would seem, on current evidence of East Asian trade surpluses, is about to be reversed after little more than two centuries.

THE STAGNATION OF TECHNOLOGY

The last pattern that defines ancient and classical history is the relative stagnation of technology. The era opens with a sustained burst of innovation, both technological and social, that marks a comprehensive break with the long era of human prehistory. Cities arise, and along with them come writing, metallurgy, the wheel, roads, sailing ships, monumental architecture, large-scale urban and agricultural engineering, astronomy, and the systematic domestication of animals. People concentrated into cities create elaborate divisions of labour and class structures, and serve as the power base for trade networks and empires. The first models of this development were firmly in place in Egypt and Mesopotamia by 2500 BC.

But after this foundational burst, very little occurred in either the social or the technological spheres that was genuinely new. Throughout the entire period history is dominated by the same set of players: city-states, empires and barbarians. These players remain recognisably similar from beginning to end. No fundamentally new developments occur to change the speed of transportation and communication. Weapons remain basically the same across huge periods of time, as do agricultural techniques.

This is not to say that there were no developments at all, for there was a considerable incremental improvement of existing techniques. Sailing ships became larger and more efficient, and navigational techniques made steady improvement. Metallurgy moved on from expensive bronze, to cheaper and more widely available iron. Wheels evolved from crude, heavy solid slabs to sophisticated light spoked constructions. Writing developed from complex cuneiform and pictogram systems to simpler and more versatile alphabets. Mathematical and astronomical knowledge accumulated. Horses were bred until they were strong enough to carry mounted warriors. As we have seen, it was also the case that bureaucracy and government became more sophisticated and effective. Notions of citizenship developed in Greece and Rome that were considerably more advanced than the forms of social organisation in earlier and more primitive empires. Any one of the late agrarian empires could, in principle, have overwhelmed the Incas and the Aztecs almost as easily as the Spaniards did.

But despite these improvements, there is still a stagnant, or at best very slow-moving, quality about this whole gigantic era. Some have argued that this technological inertia is a fundamental quality of agricultural societies. Perhaps the only area of real innovation during this time was religion. Classical civilisations invented nearly all of the world religions and ethical systems that still shape our time. But with this exception, technological and social change were incremental and slow during this huge era. For thousands of years no new breakthrough occurred that made much difference to the problems of distance, climate and geography that separated civilisations from each other. Not until the rise of Europe did a new burst of physical and social technological development begin that was comparable to that which opened the era of ancient and classical civilisation.

CONCLUSIONS

The ancient and classical world was, in a sense, a series of separate worlds. These worlds tended to expand over time, and as they did, contact amongst them (at least amongst the four civilisational cores in Eurasia) increased. In a few cases there was significant military rivalry, especially in the eastern Mediterranean. But mostly contacts were for trade, and these were not direct. This was less true within the east. Persians, and later Arabs, penetrated directly into South and East Asia, as did Chinese coming the other way. Even though trading contacts were very light by today's standards, they diffused ideas between civilisations. The heyday of the silk roads was also the period during which Buddhism spread north and east from India. Although they remained distinctive, the Eurasian civilisations steadily influenced each other by the exchange of technologies, arts, religions, and to a lesser extent, ideas about social organisation.

For all of this period most of Europe is either a barbarian backwater or a colonial periphery. Only its southern countries were main players in the classical age. Yet the classical era provided many of the key ingredients, both cultural and technological, that went into the making of the European miracle. When Europe finally emerged from its post-Roman barbarism of unstable petty kingdoms and warring barons, it found a world of ancient and still powerful civilisations. Connecting these was a well-developed pattern of trade which Europe was once again able to tap into, and which the West eventually came to dominate.

For all its apparent stagnation, the ancient and classical world nevertheless fits into a picture of overall human progress. Although technological innovation was slow after the initial burst, the range and depth of civilisation expanded quite steadily. Trading networks grew, and the political skills of humankind, among which one might count the development of universal religions, developed impressively. The human population expanded, and the long-standing threat from the barbarians was eventually contained and defeated. The ancient and classical world provided the foundation on which the European development was built.

If the rise of Europe had not intervened, it is easy to imagine that the process of slow expansion from several cores of civilisation might have continued. Trade and contact might have increased as the different zones of civilisation overlapped more with each other, eventually resulting in a global system. This system would have been quite different from that which the Europeans eventually created. The story in this chapter thus combines with the one told in chapter 2 about the rise of Europe, to reveal a turning point in the development of human civilisation. The momentum of the ancient and classical world was towards the eventual inter-linking of several different civilisations. But the momentum of Europe was a direct drive towards a single global system domi-nated by one civilisation. Once Europe had overwhelmed the two weakest of the old civilisations in the Americas, wiped out more than 90% of their population with imported diseases, and added two re-peopled continents to its power base, its world historical momentum was unstoppable. Europeans went on to create the West and two centuries of global control.

It is less clear how deep this change is, or how long-lasting it will be. Is there now in some sense a single, Western-based global civilisation, or do the older multicultural patterns from the ancient and classical era persist strongly enough to resurface? Remember that a thousand years of Græco-Roman-Byzantine colonisation did not eliminate Middle Eastern languages or civilisation. The question is whether some of these older pat-terns will re-emerge now that the relative power of the West is declining. Debates about 'Asian values', 'Islamic fundamental-ism', and 'Hindu nationalism' are all projections out of the ancient and classical era into what some perceive as a post-Western future. This thought is what underlies the fashionable speculation about a 'clash of civilisations' as the model for the twenty-first century. That may be one possibility, though we doubt it. More intriguing is to think about the multicultural possibilities that emerge as these two great historical momen-tums begin to fall into a more equal relationship with each other.

FROM PRE-HISTORY TO CIVILISATION

4

It was with the founding of cities that the ancient and classical period began. But cities did not just spring up from nowhere. They represented the culmination of a trend towards more dense and more settled human populations that was long in the making.

If one looks back to the end of the last ice age, some 15,000 years ago, the human species numbered only a few million people world-wide, hardly more than the current population of Berlin. It was thinly scattered, and there were no places where great concentrations of people existed. Humankind was everywhere organised as nomadic hunter-gatherer bands, typically composed of a few families totalling 25–60 people. These bands did not practise settled agriculture or herd domesticated animals. Having not yet mastered either the wheel or the horse they moved on foot and travelled light. Far-ranging migrations took place over long periods, but encounters between bands were probably quite infrequent. They lived by hunting, fishing and harvesting from the local vegetation. Their cultures had little social, political or economic differentiation, and therefore little rank, status or hierarchy. Everyone did much the same work, and if there was a leader he or she had little ability to order the people to do things against their will. If the group got too big for its environment to support, or if there were differences of opinion amongst its members, it split, and one fraction moved away to start up its own independent existence elsewhere. It should not be forgotten that this pre-civilisational mode of existence, though almost extinct by the late twentieth century, lasted in some places right through the ancient and classical era and into modern times. In Africa, the Americas and Australia, the expanding Europeans encountered whole continents still peopled by hunter-gatherers, whom the agricultural revolution, and the long struggle of civilisations and barbarians had left largely or completely untouched.

To move from this situation to one in which tens of thousands of people were concentrated into cities, and empires numbered their populations in millions, required a massive transformation in the human condition. Life in cities is the diametrical opposite of life in hunter-gatherer bands. It is the difference between high and low numbers of people, high and low densities of habitation, specialised versus unspecialised economic roles, and hierarchical versus egalitarian societies. In bands, people generally did not have to work too hard in order to live, they did not have to take orders from anyone, and they could move as the seasons and the food supply dictated. Learning, and the transmission of traditions were all done by word of mouth and memory. In cities, people might be imprisoned, conscripted, or worked to death as labourers or slaves. They could be commanded by priests, kings, bureaucrats, and soldiers. Their food supply depended on complex arrangements of local agriculture, centralised grain storage, and trade, and they were generally tied to both a particular place and a particular type of crop. Records were kept of production, trade and tax, and writing empowered a literate class against an illiterate mass.

The shift from hunter-gatherer to urban living marks one of the great transformations in the human condition. Since history is generally understood as the study of written records, this transformation is literally the beginning of history, perhaps the only moment in the life of our species to compare with the huge unleashing of human potential by the scientific, industrial and political revolutions in our own time. But history in this sense began at different times in different places: just before 3000 BC in the Middle East, around 2700 BC in South Asia, somewhere between 2700 and 1700 BC in China, 750 BC in the central Mediterranean, 55 BC in Britain, during the sixteenth century

AD for much of the Americas, and for parts of Africa not until the 1890s. To understand how this change came about we need to look at four inter-linked lines of development: the environmental changes that led to the ending of the ice age; the growth in the human population and its effect on the hunter-gatherer way of life; the invention of agriculture and its consequences; and the development of trade.

ENVIRONMENTAL CHANGE AND THE ICE AGE

Compared to the stories we have surveyed so far, the story of humankind before the rise of cities is very long. The modern period is at most a few centuries old. The ancient and classical period lasted five millennia. If one wanted to go right back to the origins of human culture in our first tool-making ancestors, then we would be looking at 2.5 million years of biological and cultural evolution, but we can start with the advent of the first biologically modern human beings, probably in Africa, some 100,000 years ago. By 35000 BC these people had occupied Asia and Europe, and were on their way to Australia (which means that they had developed seagoing boats). The Americas were probably colonised by modern humans towards the end of the ice age, about 15,000 years ago, though possibly rather earlier, completing the human occupation of the planet.

The point is that the entire early history of modern humanity, and indeed much of its biological evolution, took place during the ice age. Particularly for the last 700,000 years, humankind has evolved within a radically unstable environment, in which there were quite frequent and quite large swings in prevailing temperatures. These temperature swings produced dramatic effects on the conditions in which humans lived. Huge ice sheets advanced and retreated over most of Canada, northern Europe and Russia. As they did so, they transferred significant percentages of the world's water from sea to land and back again. Sea levels fluctuated by as much as 200 meters (perhaps creating the folk memories of great floods that have been absorbed into some religions). When the glaciers pulled enough water out of the oceans, people could walk from France to Britain and from Siberia to Alaska. The Persian Gulf and large parts of the Mediterranean basin became dry land, and Sri Lanka and much of Indonesia ceased to be islands and became parts of the Indian and Southeast Asian peninsulas. Local climates changed drastically. When the ice sheets advanced, they obliterated most of the plant and animal life in their path, and pushed the temperate zones southward. When they retreated, forests and tundra returned. Away from the ice sheets there were massive climate changes resulting from shifts in temperature and rainfall.

The last great advance of the glaciers was at its peak around 16000 BC. By 13000 BC the ice age was over, though substantial fluctuations in climate continued for several thousand years. The Sahara, for example, had extensive lakes and grasslands as recently as 6000 BC. Only when the climate had warmed and stabilised was it possible for human numbers to increase and for settled agriculture to develop. Only once these two developments were well underway did conditions exist in which cities and civilisations could emerge.

THE GROWTH IN HUMAN POPULATION AND ITS EFFECT

The absence of records in prehistory means that it is difficult to estimate early human numbers with any great accuracy. A reasonable calculation is that the total human population was about 4 million in 10000 BC, rising to 5 million by 5000 BC, and then accelerating more rapidly to 7 million by 4000 BC, 14 million by the beginning of civilisation in 3000 BC, reaching 50 million by 1000 BC (i.e. about the same as the current population of Britain or France). The warmer climate after the ice age meant that the planet could support larger numbers of people.

Hunter-gathering is an extremely inefficient way to support human life: large concentrations of people quickly exhaust the ability of their environment to support them. But past a certain point of population growth, hunter-gatherers effectively filled up the usable territories. This began to happen as soon as the post-ice age climate settled down and the numbers of humans began to rise.

When all of the territory was occupied, humans had to learn to live together in larger societies (whether by peaceful means or by conquest), and to do that they had to learn how to increase food production. Bands clustered together into tribes, and some of these developed into chiefdoms with populations of several

thousand people. Larger numbers restricted mobility, both because all habitable territory was occupied, and because bigger
groups are harder to move. As human communities became
larger, they began to lose the simple, egalitarian organisation
of bands, and acquire more specialisation, more differentiation
into social ranks, and more authoritative leadership. The early
city-states were the culmination of this process and represented
a shift from temporary to permanent institutions, and from
individuals or families being the ultimate repository of authority, to the state acquiring forms of centralised control over its
subjects. As human communities expanded in size, individuals
moved from the freedom of egalitarian societies to the servitude
of rank-differentiated societies.

THE INVENTION OF AGRICULTURE

As the post-ice age climate stabilised, it offered more opportunities for human habitation. In terms of sea level, temperature
and rainfall, the planet began to take on the features with which
we are familiar today. A variety of more or less stable environmental zones divided the land area of the planet into different
opportunities for human existence. These ranged from arctic
zones, where the harsh conditions of the ice age still ruled, and
northern forests (where hunter-gathering was still the only way
to earn a living), through grassy steppe lands and fertile river
valleys, to deserts and tropical forests. Within this more supportive ecological framework, human numbers increased, eventually to the point where the only alternative to starvation or
battles for control of territory was to find ways of increasing the
food supply.

Under these pressures, various human groups began to experiment with the deliberate growing of plants (especially grains)
that they had previously only gathered, and with the taming and
herding of animals that they had previously only hunted. From
around 8000 BC the human population began a long revolution in
its economic life from universal dependence on hunter-gathering
to nearly universal dependence on farming and herding. Only
fishing remained, as it still does today, a vestige of hunter-
gatherer culture. By the time the Roman and Han Empires were
at their height, this agricultural revolution was complete, with

only a small and mostly remote percentage of the human population still dependent on hunter-gathering. As the agricultural revolution unfolded, people learned more about how to breed plants and animals in order to improve their yield. They learned how to suit particular crops to particular types of land and climate. As productivity improved, population increased, creating continuous pressure for further improvements, or for opening up new lands to agriculture or pasture.

This economic transformation not only sustained the growth of the human population that followed the ice age, but also moved the bulk of humankind from a mobile to a sedentary way of life. Most forms of farming required investment in adapting and maintaining the land, and therefore encouraged settled communities. In some places, most notably in river valleys such as those of the Nile, the Euphrates and the Yellow, and on the Andean coastal plain, rich soil was combined with sparse rainfall. This meant that agriculture required irrigation. To extend irrigation any distance from the river banks required substantial engineering works and a high degree of organisation, but the rewards of productivity from doing so were great. From at least 5500 BC in Mesopotamia, this combination led to the formation of agricultural villages and towns, and eventually, by around 3500 BC, cities. Extensive irrigation and good soil provided the conditions for dense clusters of population to develop. They also encouraged the development of more centralised societies, able to maintain, extend, and defend the irrigation works, and defend the agricultural surpluses against raiders. It was in this way that the agricultural revolution generated the rise of the first states, and of civilisation.

Via the domestication of animals and the development of breeding and herding, it also led to the emergence of the nomadic barbarian cultures adapted to the steppe lands. The steppe lands were marginal for agriculture, but ideal for herding. The agricultural revolution thus branched into two lines of development that set the pattern for the whole of the ancient and classical era. The nomadic barbarians were mobile by definition, and they had every incentive to improve the breeding of horses, which once perfected provided them with the mounts that made them such a feared military force for thousands of years. Agrarian civilisations, by contrast, developed large populations, and become increasingly fixed in walled cities that served as centres for control over ever larger territories. Hunter-gatherers still existed in this scheme, but only on the margins, having been left behind by the economic revolution that transformed the condition of most of humankind.

THE DEVELOPMENT OF LONG-DISTANCE TRADE

Long-distance trade is a remarkably old institution in human affairs, long preceding anything that we might recognise as a state or a civilisation. There is archaeological evidence from as long as 40,000 years ago that Cro-Magnon people traded over long distances in the types of tool-making stone that were essential to their way of life. Similar evidence exists for trade in such luxury goods as sea shells and amber, which are found in association with human remains in places far removed from their point of origin.

But the real growth of trade begins after the ice age, when the human population begins to expand, and particularly after the agricultural revolution. The development of farming and herding not only meant that the human population increased and settled down, but also that it began to become specialised in what different communities produced. This specialisation was not a market-driven choice, but a product of the different ecological niches into which humans settled. Grain producers in the valleys could trade their surpluses with herdsmen in the steppes and mountains in exchange for their surpluses of livestock. Or as in western South America, fish producers on the coast could trade with potato growers in the highlands.

As agricultural communities became more territorially fixed, they needed to trade in order to provide themselves with the things that their own territory could not produce. And as human communities became larger, more diverse and more socially stratified, exotic luxury goods became important as a way of marking off priests and chiefs from the lower orders of society. For both of these reasons, long-distance trade is older and more significant than trade within a community. Within a prehistoric community most people produced the same goods, and there was therefore little reason to trade. It was the differences in the flora, fauna and mineral resources of different communities that stimulated trade. In part such exchange created a class of long-distance traders, but much of it was done by long chains of short-range exchanges. Goods passing from village to village could travel long distances without being carried by any single person.

The impetus for trade increased during the sixth millennium BC when farmers began to occupy and work river valleys like the Euphrates and the Nile. Once irrigation was mastered, these valleys yielded grain crops sufficient to support dense populations and to export surpluses. The rivers provided ready-made transportation systems suitable for moving bulk goods even with quite primitive boats. And although the valleys were rich farmlands, they were poorly provided with wood, stone and metal, and were not well-suited to raising livestock. As the populations and towns of the valleys expanded, they created a strong demand for these goods which necessarily had to be brought from afar. New technologies, especially the smelting of gold, copper and silver beginning around 5000 BC added further stimulus to trade, as did the later development of sailing ships and wheeled carts.

As the agricultural revolution deepened and spread, long-distance trade developed established patterns and routes. Trade routes stimulated the development of towns, and vice versa. Towns not only provided concentrated markets, security and diversified demand for goods, but also became production points for specialised craft goods (glass, pottery, fabrics, jewellery) that could be put into the trading network. In return, trade routes generated wealth which could be used to support and expand the town. Trade also stimulated the development of writing. Without quite sophisticated systems for record-keeping, large-scale commerce was too vulnerable to thievery and fraud. By 5000 BC the need for accounting systems was evolving towards writing, in the process producing bureaucratic techniques that were as valuable for political as for economic control. As we have seen, this same symbiotic relationship between political and economic developments marked the ancient and classical period, with city-states and empires both feeding and being fed by the trading networks that they often competed to control. Both trade and the development of towns and cities could and did exist independently of each other, but each was enormously stimulated and advanced by association with the other. By the dawn of civilisation in the middle of the fourth millennium BC, well-established trade routes stretched from the Mediterranean to the Gulf, linking Egypt, Anatolia and Mesopotamia.

CONCLUSIONS

The transformation from prehistory to history is mostly focused in the five thousand years preceding the first rise of civilisation. The background to it is the stabilisation of the climate after the ice age, and the consequent increase in human numbers. But the real key to human progress in this era is the agricultural revolution. It was the development of farming and herding that enabled the human population to grow and concentrate. Agriculture underpinned the creation of villages, towns and cities, and spurred the development of long-distance trade. The general process of the transition from prehistory to civilisation, and from hunter-gatherer bands to city-states, was broadly similar everywhere, though with significant differences of detail and timing.

This era is very remote from our own time, but by following the human story backwards one can see quite clearly that it connects to us in many ways. For one thing, it shows clearly how fundamental transformations (hunter-gatherer to agrarian, rural to urban, agrarian to industrial) are a repeating feature of human development. This pattern supports arguments about our modern times that there are broadly common processes of modernisation and development. All such transformations involve complex interplays between technological and social innovation, and in the ancient world seem to be separated by long periods of consolidation. Another obvious connection is that long-distance trade is a continuous part of the human story. And for another, it shows more clearly than any other era (except perhaps the one we are moving into), how dependent human civilisation is on the stability of the planetary climate.

LOOKING BACKWARD, LOOKING FORWARD

5

Having looked back from the end of the twentieth century to the dawn of civilisation, what lessons can we draw? We have already identified many linkages amongst the main eras of human history. We have seen how trade is a permanent feature of human development, and how main features such as religion and culture carry over from one era to the next. But what are the grand patterns in humankind's 12,000-year march from hunter-gathering to the dawn of the information age? What does this long look back tell us about the momentum of events coming out of the past into the future? Two patterns stand out: the making of the planet into a single human space, and uneven development.

THE MAKING OF A SINGLE HUMAN SPACE

In this gigantic perspective one pattern of progress that is crystal clear is the growth of an ever more dense, complicated and interconnected human occupation of the planet. This is not just a matter of more people, though rising human numbers have been a critical part of it. It also comes about as a result of

73

increasing levels of human activity, knowledge, organisation and interaction. Over the millennia, ever wider networks of human contact and organisation have been built up, culminating in our own century in the making, for the first time, of a single global space for humankind.

It is not clear what this single space should be called. Different names identify different aspects of a single reality. 'International system' emphasises the division of humankind into states and nations, and the fact that interactions amongst these, whether conflictual or co-operative, form a single system. 'International society' also emphasises states and nations, but puts more emphasis on the fact that relations amongst these are conducted according to generally accepted rules and norms. 'World society' emphasises what integrates rather than what divides. It puts the focus on world-wide communications, and the shared experience, and eventually shared identity, which they cultivate. 'Global market' gives a more economic picture, stressing the way in which many patterns of production, finance and trade have now become planetary in scale. The making of this single human space does not mean that human activity has become centrally controlled. What it means is that for better or worse, intentionally or unintentionally, and in conflict or cooperation, humans, especially of a wealthier sort, cannot avoid knowing more about each other and having their actions intersect with those of others in ever more complicated ways.

In retrospect, the forward march toward this global human system appears unstoppable. Despite the setbacks caused by wars, plagues, famines and environmental catastrophes, human populations have increased, although some have increased far more than others. Civilisation has proved similarly persistent, albeit uneven in its expansion. Since the first city-states precipitated out of the agricultural revolution more than 5,000 years ago, diverse civilisations have steadily extended their domain against simpler forms of human organisation. Countless empires have fallen, and whole peoples and languages have been obliterated. Even whole civilisations have disappeared, taking with them their language and writing. Where now are the culture and cuneiform script that included the Sumerians, Assyrians and Babylonians? Yet civilisations on the whole have spread until they dominated the whole planet.

With the expansion of human numbers, and their concentration into cities, trade and communication have spread ever wider networks of contact and exchange through the body of human-kind. The rise of civilisations brought both a rising need and increased incentives for trade in a more densely populated world. By the time of the Roman Empire, all of Eurasia and much of northern Africa were connected by trade, and similar processes were unfolding, albeit more slowly and with more primitive technology, in North and South America. Five hundred years ago the Europeans completed this development by creating the first global trading network, pulling the Americas, the rest of Africa, and later Australia into the Eurasian trading system. This march towards a global economy was not without setbacks. Sometimes barbarian incursions would cut land links and destroy production, and sometimes, most notably under the Mongols, they would open up and make secure the routes between Europe and Asia. But overall the trend towards an ever wider economic system is unmistakable.

This economic story could also be told as an intellectual and technological one, in which human ingenuity steadily over-comes the obstacles of distance and geography. Sometimes geography was an ally, especially where navigable rivers pro-vided natural highways. It is no accident that such rivers were often the cradles of civilisation. Mountains, deserts and seas were mostly obstacles, as was distance itself. The domestication of pack and riding animals and the development of wheeled carts enabled trade to break away from the rivers. Robust sailing vessels opened up the seas, and eventually the oceans, providing much the cheapest form of bulk transport over long distances. Once again the pattern is clear, leading up to the phenomenal expansion of shipping, railways, roads, air transport, and elec-tronic communications over the last two centuries.

The momentum behind this pattern is enormous. Human num-bers are still increasing at a prodigious rate, although the end may now be in sight as the growth rate has clearly begun to fall. Having achieved global dominion, civilisation is busily increas-ing the depth of its penetration across the planet, obliterating vestiges of other ways of life and sucking people into cities. The global economy is rapidly wiping out the remaining autonomy of local economies, creating global markets not only for resources and manufactures, but also for labour and capital. Technology has nearly achieved the death of distance in many aspects of human life. During the nineteenth and twentieth centuries, a huge drop in the cost of transportation transformed world trade and production. During the twentieth and twenty-first centuries a similarly huge drop in the cost of communication is transforming patterns of organisation, control and culture. It seems safe to assume that this pattern remains a dominating feature of the human condition. Not only is the momentum enormous, but humankind cannot undo its single global space without suffering catastrophe on an unprecedented scale. Billions of people are now dependent on the global economy for survival. Increasing specialisation and urbanisation mean that ever fewer people are in a position to feed and clothe themselves from locally available resources.

But there is one large question mark over this easy assumption. How will this project be changed now that the single human space has largely been achieved? Until now there has always been more room for everything. More people could be accommodated by rising productivity or migration to less populated areas. Civilisation still had frontiers against barbarians and 'empty' continents. Trade and communication networks spanned the planet, but did not yet penetrate into every corner. Now there is little unexplored territory (except under the oceans), and not many countries would claim to be under-populated (except underground).

The long phase of expansion that has dominated all of the history of civilisation may well be nearly over. The only way to continue it would be to extend the pattern off this planet, but the costs of doing that appear prohibitive. Although we might explore space and put colonies on the Moon and Mars, these will for a long time involve only tiny numbers of people and a few specialised economic, scientific and military activities. With existing and foreseeable technologies, space does not offer solutions to a potential problem of overpopulation. If the great mass of humankind is effectively sealed onto this planet, then expansion in the traditional way cannot continue. If it does, and if the growth rate in human numbers should begin to rise again, then major stress may well be placed on the carrying capacity of the planet.

UNEVEN DEVELOPMENT

Although it can be argued that the making of a single human space has been the principal pattern of history, an equally strong case can be made that development within this pattern has been strikingly and persistently uneven. Although it is true that development was often a 'two steps forward, one step back' affair, unevenness has also been a dominant feature of how, when and where development occurred. In no sense has the making of a single human space been a smooth or uniform progression, and this pattern is strongly present right down to our own time. Unevenness can be seen clearly in terms of both time (episodic progress rather than smooth lines), and space (different degrees or types of development in different places at the same time). There is every reason to expect that this pattern will continue to shape the future of human development.

Two examples demonstrate the uneven progress of human development in time: technology and the basic organisation of human society. It is easy to think of technology as a smooth linear development. This image hides a more complicated reality in which fundamental breakthroughs occur in bursts, separated by long periods of incremental improvement or stagnation. One such burst accompanied the beginnings of civilisation around 3000 BC. This outpouring of creativity established most of the technologies that shaped the progress of civilisation for the next four thousand years. Once ships, and scripts and wheels and weapons had settled into mature forms, there was little fundamental change for thousands of years. Another burst of technological innovation began in late medieval times. It reached a fierce pitch of intensity over the last two centuries, transforming the means of transportation, communication, production and war.

The second example concerns the basic organisation of human society, and shows a similar, and perhaps linked, pattern to that in technology. Again, it is easy to assume a smooth progression from stone-age savagery, through the glories and tyrannies of the ancient empires, to the modern-day welfare state. And again, this would be wrong. Rather than a smooth progression, there are two fundamental revolutions. The first marked the transition from pre-history to history, and from a political economy of hunter-gathering to a political economy based on agriculture. In that transition, the human condition was transformed. Except for the nomadic herdsmen that history renders as barbarians, flexible, small-scale, mobile human groups with minimal political structure gave way to rigid, large-scale, immobile ones in which individuals were subject to the authority of rulers and rules.

The second marked the transition from the civilisations of classical antiquity with their agrarian political economy, to the modern state and the political economy of industrial society. Again, the human condition was transformed. The bulk of the population moved from the land to the cities. Time and money became much more important in the lives of the common people, and both employment and leisure became much more specialised. Perhaps most important, the veneration of tradition and the wisdom of the old gave way to the veneration of the new, the technical and the style of the young. As the historian Marshall Hodgson has argued, each of these transformations had the effect of speeding up history. Once Europe had opened the door to industrialism it embraced much higher rates of innovation and change than those that prevailed in the classical world. This opened up a gap that has proved difficult to close. The West not only accelerated away from other civilisations, its pervasive influence prevented other civilisations both from evolving down their own path or copying the European model. Only by finding a faster route could they have any hope of closing the gap, and only a few societies have found such a route.

Many of those who study these transformations are puzzled that they occurred at all. How did the relatively free individuals of hunter-gathering society come to accept the relative imprisonment of agriculture and the city-state? How did the scientific, industrial and commercial revolutions ever escape from the fearful conservatism of agrarian elites? In both cases the answer is a unique combination of peculiar circumstances. Other things being equal, these revolutions should not have happened. That they did is partly because the people caught up in them did not realise what was happening. In the 1840s virtually no one in Britain understood that the country was in the middle of an industrial revolution that was about to transform its economy, politics and society. Thus many of the actions that help the transformation are taken unintentionally or for other reasons. Sometimes actions taken in an attempt to support the status quo help the transformation, as seen recently in Gorbachev's deployment of glasnost and perestroika in an attempt to save Soviet communism. Actions that might be taken against are not because the magnitude and nature of the changes in the offing are not seen. Only in a few times and places – the river valleys in ancient times, England in the eighteenth and nineteenth centuries – do things line up so as to allow these momentous developments to take place. This kind of social development is not only discontinuous – it is a minor miracle that it occurs at all.

This episodic rather than linear character of human development in both the technological and social spheres raises interesting questions about our future. Having grown up in the heart of one of the periods of rapid change, we easily assume that such change is normal, and now a permanent part of the human condition. The pattern of history should at least lead us to question this assumption. Some have argued that many of the technologies that have transformed transportation and communication – and in the process human society and history – are now mature. The argument is that although there is endless scope for incremental improvement, there is not much room for fundamental transformation in the speed and range of these technologies. Some think that the great project of physics is close to completion. Others argue that history has 'ended' in the sense that the major disputes about the best ways in which to organise the political economy of humankind are now known.

If these arguments are correct, perhaps we are on the brink of a new 'classical' era, in which progress in many key areas will be more incremental than transformational, and more within a stable pattern than continuously overthrowing existing paradigms. If so, such an era will be radically different from the classical era that preceded ours. It will still be driven by systematic scientific enquiry, and will not carry the burden of agrarian conservatism. But it will also be different from the pell-mell, across the board change of our era. Several major technological and social forms would become relatively stable, in the sense of making incremental progress within a given form. Radical change might be confined to fewer areas, making its social impact easier to handle. The long view of history gives us no reason to assume that our present notions of progress must define the entire future of humankind. Progress has always been an uneven process, varying in character from era to era. It would be vain to think that our civilisation had somehow found a way of breaking that rule.

The uneven progress of human development in space is clearer than that in time. There is little room for the illusion that human development has occurred evenly over the planet, either in the past or in the present. Uneven development in spatial terms can be looked at in two ways. The first is when unevenness is present in two different but related types of activity at the same time. The main example of this is the seemingly permanent mismatch between the scale of economic activity and the scope of political control. There is something like an iron law saying that for any civilisation or any point in history, the range of trade will far outdistance the range of any single political control. In other words, the creation of a single human space has always been more advanced in the economic sphere than it has in the realms of politics and society. The trading zone of human communities, whether Neolithic tribes or classical civilisations, has always been more extensive than their political boundaries. This remained true during the period of European expansion, and still holds today. Although virtually all of the territory on the planet is now politically organised, that organisation is fragmented into nearly 200 separately governed states. The UN is a global political forum, but it has relatively little power to govern in any sense. By contrast the international economy is much more powerfully organised globally, albeit in a decentralised fashion. Global markets determine the price of most commodities, the exchange rates of most currencies, the interest rates on capital, and increasingly, the price of labour. Lopsidedness in the development of the economic and political spheres is thus a feature in the making of a single human space that has persisted for many millennia, uninfluenced by revolutions in both technology and social organisation.

The second type of uneven development in spatial terms is when the human community can be classified into distinctly different zones of political economy. Our long look back provides many instances. The whole of the ancient and classical period, for example, was marked by radically different zones of development, each occupied by distinctive types of political economy. An initially small core of agrarian civilisation expanded steadily but never occupied as much as half the land area of the planet (though incorporating much more than half of the population). Around its fringes, the nomadic barbarians and their herds occupied the steppes and deserts, with the rest, perhaps half of the planet, thinly inhabited by hunter-gatherers and primitive agriculturists. An even more dramatic example of uneven development is provided by the rise of Europe. Here one civilisation made a number of breakthroughs that sharply differentiated its form of political economy from that of all the others. The resulting power advantage enabled it to expand to world-wide dimensions.

This kind of unevenness in the political economy of human development is still very visible today. During the 1970s it was fashionable to define it in terms of three 'worlds': the first world was Western and capitalist, and sometimes referred to as the 'core' or 'centre'; the second was communist, and sometimes referred to as the 'semi-periphery'; and the third was 'less developed', comprising much of Africa, Asia and Latin America, and sometimes referred to as the 'periphery'. Unlike in premodern times, the political structure of these three worlds was trying to be homogeneous – all of them were occupied by territorial states based on the European model. What differentiated them was their political economies. The first world was rich, industrialised, technologically advanced, mostly democratic and capitalist. The second world was less rich, still industrialising, mostly less advanced in technology, totalitarian, and organised as command economies. The third world was poor, mostly not industrialised (and therefore dependent on primary goods exports), had low levels of technology, and was mostly authoritarian. These were said to be its dominant features regardless of whether countries were attempting to follow capitalist or socialist roads to development.

An alternative view is that these three worlds exist not as distinct and separate territorial spaces, but as interleaved ways of living. Thus many cities in the West contain substantial bodies of second- and third-world populations, while cities in the third world contain elites living at first-world styles and standards.

Given the rapid rise of the East Asian economies, and then the implosion of most of the second world beginning in the late 1980s, after the Cold War it is now more common to speak of two worlds. Some of the older names are still used: North–South, centre–periphery, even third world despite the fragmentation of the third world and the vanishing of the second. Since the ideological divide has largely evaporated, the main distinction is in levels of development. Even most of those countries still clinging on to communist political systems (China, Vietnam) are hell-bent on marketising their economies, and most of the rest of the world is trying in one way or another to adopt the capitalist way. But despite the greater degree of ideological homogenisation, huge differences in levels of development still exist and seem likely to remain for the foreseeable future. While there is no simple division between rich and poor states, there is some truth to the notion that there are countries that are likely to remain poor or rich for some time to come.

A new and more ominous set of terms for characterising the two worlds is zone of peace versus zone of chaos. This is a more political way of looking at the divide, emphasising the different types of states within the two zones and the different rules of international relations prevailing in each. In the zone of peace (essentially the Western core), most of the states are defined by democracy, broad spectrum openness, and relatively high levels of socio-political cohesion (e.g. US, Britain, Germany, Japan). Their international relations are constrained by nuclear deterrence, by interdependence, and by populations now largely opposed to war for purposes of expansionism or empire building. In the zone of peace, states do not expect or prepare for war against each other, and since this zone contains most of the great powers this is a very significant development for the whole of humankind.

In most of the rest of the world, most of the states are either defined by strong government control over society and restrictive attitudes towards openness (e.g. Iran, Iraq, China, North Korea) – or defined by low levels of socio-political cohesion and poorly developed structures of government (e.g. Afghanistan, Somalia, Nigeria, Zaire). In this zone international relations operate by the traditional rules of power politics that prevailed all over the world up to 1945. States expect and prepare for the possibility of serious tension with their neighbours. Some restraint is provided by deterrence (in a few places nuclear deterrence) but economic interdependence between neighbours is generally low, and populations can often be easily mobilised for war. Even in the prospering states of East Asia where economic interdependence between neighbours is growing, the states are still often fragile and highly protective of sovereignty.

To divide the world in this way oversimplifies. Some places close to the core of the zone of peace behave like the zone of conflict (ex-Yugoslavia), and some ostensibly in the zone of conflict have managed to build substantial regional barriers against local wars (the Association of Southeast Asian Nations – ASEAN). The general distinction nevertheless seems valid. There are fundamental qualitative differences in the way in which the states of Europe, North America and Japan relate to each other, and the way in which states in the Middle East, South Asia, and many other places do so. These differences are rooted deeply in the form and character, and therefore also the history, of the states within the two zones. Thus the nature and shape of zones in the international system change over time, but the fact of them does not.

One of the main questions resulting is how the different zones or sectors relate to each other. Often this relationship is a central defining feature of the international system as a whole. How do political and economic structures relate to each other when the economic zone outreaches the political one? How do different zones of political economy relate to each other? In the premodern era, the relationship between the barbarian and civilised zones was crucial. Sometimes the barbarians were vital intermediaries in the long-distance trading networks, and at other times they were fearsome invaders. Again, during the European expansion, the relationship between the modernising European core and the premodern periphery was the defining feature of world history. In recent times, much attention has focused on the relationship between centre and periphery, and with the Cold War out of the way we can expect this to intensify. Will the core try to keep the periphery out or try to dominate it? How the zones of uneven development will relate to each other is one of the great unanswered questions for the twenty-first century. Uneven development seems likely to remain a persistent feature of the single human space.

CONCLUSIONS

On the basis of our long look back we can draw two compelling conclusions: first that the making of a single human space is a strong pattern, and second that uneven development is an equally strong and persistent feature of that pattern. From these conclusions, we can make two conjectures: (1) that a major transformation lies close ahead as the forces that have successfully created a single human space run up against the limits of the planetary carrying capacity; and (2) that uneven development will persist into the foreseeable future, and will play a large role in shaping the character of life within the human community.

On a more detailed level we also argued in chapter 1 that a number of Western ideas had become effectively universal (scientific method, the state, nationalism, the market, individual liberty) and would go forward strongly to shape the future. It was also the case, for a variety of compelling reasons ranging from nuclear deterrence, through economic interdependence and historical memory, to democratisation, that most of the great powers in the international system are no longer at risk of going to war with one another. The demise of the Soviet Union was, remarkably, achieved without war. This is not to say that war itself is at an end. Far from it. Minor powers in the zone of conflict may well resort to war against each other, and conflict is also possible between the great powers and minor powers (as in the Gulf in 1991). The rise of China will certainly cause much tension, and will put this theory to a serious test. But China, like the Soviet Union, may be constrained, and wars amongst the major powers of the type that have dominated much of history may well be a thing of the past. If this is true, then one of the major factors contributing to the historical instability in the organisation of the global political economy will not operate, or at least will do so at a much lower level, in the future. Although states, nations and civilisations will still face threats from economic and cultural competition, and from their own internal contradictions, they may be much less threatened by military obliteration in wars between the great powers.

It is also likely that the past will still play a major role in shaping the future. Many of the ideas going forward from modern history constitute a coherent package of practical and interlinked ideas about the organisation of the human political economy on a global scale. This package has been several centuries in the making, and it would require a transformation of truly astounding proportions for it to be quickly displaced. Not only are its individual components now deeply rooted in human society, but they are in many ways mutually supportive despite the tensions amongst them. The market needs a political framework. The state needs societal legitimacy. Societal legitimacy requires economic productivity. Both wealth and power require science and technology. The function of the whole, and indeed its survival, require that great powers avoid nuclear war with each other. It is not at all obvious how some or all parts of this package could be excised without threatening the overall function of the whole political economy. It is even less clear where the replacements would come from or what they might be. What we seem to be looking at is the culmination of a long process of working out the forms of an industrial, global-scale, human political economy, and there is every reason to think that this package will have a profound effect on the future.

PART II
THE HERE AND NOW

At this point we know roughly how we got to the end of the second millennium AD. We also have some sense of the historical stream within which our own time floats, and where it might be heading. Yet just as we cannot know what kind of adult a human child will become, so the future will unfold itself in ways that we cannot foresee. But we know that the future has to grow out of the present, just as the adult grows out of the child, so we cannot anticipate the future unless we understand its antecedents.

So now we need to change gear. Instead of sweeping across vast swathes of history at top speed, we will take a close hard look at our own time both as a product of that history and as the cradle of the future. Not everything that is happening in our lifetime is of epochal importance, even though it often seems that way. Our task in this section is to look at the main patterns of change and continuity that play through our own time. We want to see where these patterns came from, and whether they seem to be of long-term significance. And we want to begin examining claims that our time represents a historic turning point. The main features of the global forces now in play can be divided into seven sometimes overlapping categories: the planetary environment, population, identity, knowledge, capital, sovereignty, and military power.

THE PLANETARY ENVIRONMENT

6

Human beings are a tiny portion of the living things on our planet. Until recently we have paid little attention to the health of our planet and the rights of other living things with which we share the environment. Indeed, the relative stability of the environment has underpinned the whole story of human civilisation. During all of the ten millennia in which humankind has constructed civilisation, the climate has been remarkably stable. Although there have been some local changes, the sea level and the temperature range have remained broadly constant, and it has become easy to assume that it will remain so.

As the power of human beings to alter the environment has grown, we have also become more aware that although humankind is increasingly able to inflict significant changes on the environment, nature itself is still the biggest force for change in play. Those who recently watched the comet Schumacher-Levy 9 punch a string of earth-sized holes in Jupiter can have little doubt about nature's power. We are still learning how much we do not know about where and how we live. As we saw in chapter 4, the apparent stability of earth's environment is a mere blip when seen in a long perspective. For most of the period of human evolution, the climate has swung through dramatic changes, with the sea level oscillating by hundreds of meters. There is reason to think that humankind may not enjoy this stability for much longer, the catch being that nobody can yet say how long.

Schwartz on Connected Environments

Each of us should have a personal stake in the quality of the global environment, in the growth of the global economy, and in the increasing quality of education everywhere. Our fates are interconnected. People have had a very hard time grasping these connections because for most of human civilisation, the connection was not as important . . . Today the international economic relationships, our impact on the natural environment, and the globe-spanning technologies have made a tangible difference . . .

From Peter Schwartz, *The Art of the Long View*, pp. 217–8.

Change could come either from nature or from humankind. There could be a turn in the (as yet not very well understood) natural cycle, which would suggest a new ice age, and the relegation of human history to the status of an interglacial moment. Past patterns suggest that such a cooling turn should be due within the next 1000–2000 years. Or our own contributions to changing the composition of the planetary atmosphere (dust, CO_2 and other 'greenhouse' gasses) might lead to global warming. A new ice age would cause sea levels to drop, exposing more land, but it would wipe out many of the current main food producing areas, and move nearly all coastal cities tens or hundreds of kilometers inland. Global warming would raise sea levels, drowning most coastal cities and much agricultural land, though releasing into production much land now under permafrost. Even just the melting of the East Antarctic ice sheet would raise world sea levels by sixty meters.

Global near-surface temperatures difference in degrees Celsius from the average

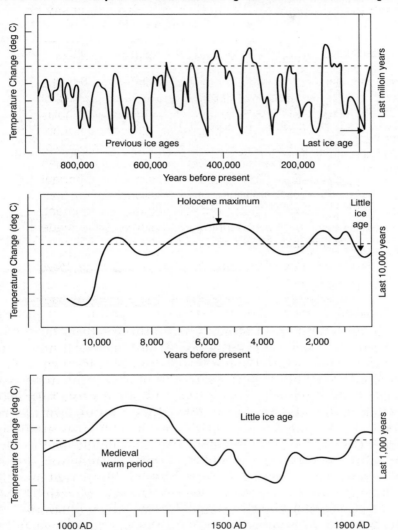

Schematic diagrams of global temperature variations since the Pleistocene on three time-scales. The dashed line nominally represents conditions near the beginning of the twentieth century.
Source: J. Jager and H.L. Fergusen (eds), *Climate Change*, Cambridge: Cambridge University Press, 1991.

Summary of key greenhouse gases affected by human activities

	Carbon Dioxide	Methane	CFC-11	CFC-12	Nitrous Oxide
Atmospheric concentration	ppmv	ppmv	pptv	pptv	ppbv
Pre-industrial (1750–1800)	280	0.8	0	0	288
Present day (1990)	353	1.72	280	484	310
Current rate of change per year	1.8 (0.5%)	0.015 (0.9%)	9.5 (4%)	17 (4%)	0.8 (0.25%)
Atmospheric lifetime (years)	(50–200)†	10	65	130	150

ppmv = parts per million by volume;
ppbv = parts per billion (thousand million) by volume;
pptv = parts per trillion (million million) by volume.
† The way in which CO_2 is absorbed by the oceans and biosphere is not simple and a single value cannot be given; refer to the main report for further discussion.
Source: J. Jager and H.L. Fergusen (eds), *Climate Change*, Cambridge: Cambridge University Press, 1991.

Those concerned about global warming, pollution of oceans or the reduction in the diversity of living species, like to claim that they take a long-term perspective about the state of the planet. But a perspective that is wider than just the effects of the industrial revolution may suggest that we are at a different stage of our development. It is strikingly significant that human impacts and nature's cycles seem to be pulling in opposite directions: warming versus cooling. A longer-term perspective thus suggests that perhaps for the first time in human history we have the opportunity to fundamentally manipulate how our environment shapes our lives. If nature takes a challenging turn with a new ice age or a massive meteor strike, we might have options about how to respond. Similarly, if human activity changes the environment, we can in principle do something about it. The possibility of 'geo-engineering', as some are beginning to call it, is new territory in the human experience. Looming in the future is the possibility of beginning to shape the planetary environment to our needs and preferences.

For much of human life we understood very little about nature's challenges, and had little ability to do anything about them. If a meteor struck or a volcano erupted, human beings just had to suffer the consequences. With the agricultural revolution and the rise of civilisation, the one-way domination of human life by the environment began to change. Humans developed knowledge and technology that enabled their collective action to change the world around them, both by design and by accident. They could change forests into farmland, change flows of water, breed plants and animals, and bring life and death to other species as well as themselves. But these blessings were characteristically mixed. Irrigation could feed more people, but also created environmental problems with salination. The industrial revolution reduced public health by polluting the environment, but increased health by laying sewers and improving medicine. Human endeavour was able to make people live longer and grow in number, undoubtedly key elements of human progress. And yet, as impressive as all this ingenuity undoubtedly was, it could do little or nothing against environmental disasters whether natural or human-made. During the fourteenth century, plague wiped out up to one-third of the population in many parts of Eurasia. In the seventeenth century, human ingenuity was responsible for carrying a variety of Eurasian diseases to the Americas, killing off more than 90% of the indigenous population. In South Asia, Central America and the Middle East, civilisations fell when either their own actions or nature's made the farmland unproductive.

It is only in this century, when we began to understand how the planet developed, and how life was created, that we began to understand how humankind was threatening the carrying capacity of the planet. Only recently have we made major efforts to think about and improve our environment. So far, most of the thought has been about immediate, short-term issues – pollution, disease, extinctions of species, deforestation, destruction of the ozone layer. Even in this respect we are only beginning to gather our thoughts and strategies in a sensible way. Our motive in doing so has a great deal to do with the gradual democratisation of human activity, and the consequent demand by people that their governments take action to improve their living space. Our ability to take positive action depends to a large extent on our wealth and technological capacity. In short, only the free and the rich can and do take an active interest in improving the planetary environment. But before the free and the rich take their virtue too seriously, they might reflect on the fact that they have done the most damage. Feelings of guilt apart, the free and the rich have begun to see the errors of their ways, and are urging those now aspiring to be free and rich to avoid the same mistakes.

Forested area in temperate regions, selected areas

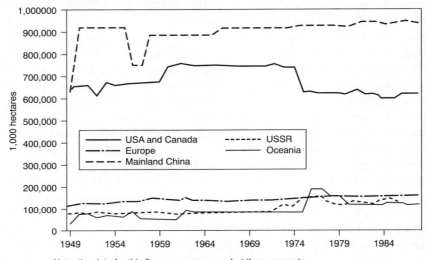

Note: the data for this figure are very poor, but they appear to be the best multi-decadal available

Notes: North America includes USA (including Alaska and Hawaii) and Canada. Forest data are collected and updated only intermittently. Extended periods in series without change reflect this procedure.
Source: United Nations Food and Agriculture Organization Production Yearbooks. The data given for a particular year are the data given for that particular yearbook; they are not the result of forest surveys taken in that particular year.

The litany of damage to the planet has been well rehearsed. Although nobody seriously contests the growing human impact on the ecosphere, there is much dispute about whether and how this matters. In comparison to the changes wrought by nature on nature (e.g. volcanoes), humans are still a relatively modest threat. Even though nature has wiped out far more species than humans have done, we have rightly grown more concerned about our own ability to kill other species as we destroy or alter their habitats. Specific practical debates rage about how much such lost species held the biological keys to medical and chemical breakthroughs, and more general ones about whether a narrowing of the ecological base puts the foundations of human civilisation at risk. Unresolvable moral debates surround the question of whether the loss of species diversity is damaging to the soul of humankind or the pleasures of life's rich tapestry. Does it matter if our children grow up in a world without elephants, rhinos and tigers? We do not know enough about the interconnectedness of complex biological systems to answer many of these questions. The difficulty is knowing when to make great efforts to preserve individual species. Complex human societies have no clear way of weighing the costs and benefits of such difficult choices. How is one to choose whether a bypass should be built to preserve the environment of a lovely village, when the result will mean the death of some seemingly obscure species in the woods outside town? Is money better spent lifting humans out of illiteracy and poverty or saving animal species from extinction?

Because of uncertainties about causes and effects, environmental debates throw up huge quandaries of cost-benefit analysis, not only about who pays the costs and who gets the benefits, but also about whether costs paid will produce the expected benefits, and whether the benefits will be worth having. This logic applies to individuals and to countries. Such choices are made when poor peasants are told, in effect, that they should starve instead of being allowed to cut down their forests or kill the game. They are told that the global commons needs the oxygen in those treetops, but all they know is that they need the land to keep their children alive and the firewood to cook their food. Similarly, poor countries are told they should not build dams – as in the Three Gorges Project in China – because there will be problems up and downstream as the environment is altered. But China needs electricity and wants to grow rich like the other great powers. The poor countries are not inclined to worry about damage to the ozone layer if remedial measures come at the cost of their own development opportunities. They are certainly not keen to go to the expense of replacing their refrigerators with ozone-friendly ones made in wealthy countries. They point to the devastation that Western countries inflicted on themselves during their processes of industrialisation, deforestation, 'satanic mills', and appalling conditions of labour.

Poor countries do understand that concern with the environment is in their interest. This is especially true for those such as Egypt, Bangladesh, the Maldives, and many others with low-lying lands that would be submerged by even quite small rises in sea level. These have already begun to organise politically. But in general, such countries see the costs and benefits in different ways. Polluted water from heedless factories kills poor peasants in India just as it kills rich industrial workers in Japan. But rich countries can afford to clean up and have industries that specialise in such technology. Developing countries can less afford to put economic growth at risk and life is often considered more cheaply in poor peasant societies. It is only when pollution in poor countries is seen to be benefiting local criminals or bloated bureaucrats that environmentalism is swept into the wider political movement for more democratic government. The misuse of the environment in the former Soviet Union and Eastern Europe led to the creation of green groups that helped form the backbone of the forces that overthrew communism in 1989–91.

As the poor resist what they see as trendy and self-serving environmental movements in the developed world, they have given pause to the rich and free who are asked to help pay the bills for preserving the global commons. There is nothing like being asked to open your wallet to make people consider the costs and benefits of good causes. In the 1990s, as the rich and free contemplated their minor economic recession, they found it easy to put aside their most grandiose environmental protection plans. As their populations aged and their healthcare systems became too expensive, the free and the rich began to see the similarities between healthcare and environmental protection – both were bottomless pits. No amount of money could purchase a perfect state of health for an individual or the planet. So how much was enough?

There can be no fixed answer to the question, and even within our own generation very different answers have been given. There are at least three questions under debate. First, we are trying to figure out if there really is an environmental crisis. Twenty years ago the expert testimony was of the risks of global cooling, and now some of the same scientists and institutions warn of the opposite. Given such an uncertain intellectual track record, it may be foolish to spend vast amounts of money to change the structure of industry and the global market economy on the off-chance that this time the scientists are correct. The costs of such action are much more certain and immediate than the benefits. If the scientists are right this time, and we have sat on the fence, then it will certainly cost more to put things right than if we had acted early. But future societies will probably be richer and more capable than ours, so why not leave the decision to them?

Some may benefit. Even if the Dutch have to build higher dikes, the Canadians (if there still is such a country) will become richer as their grain-growing zone is extended further north. For rich economies whose electorates and corporations have shorter-term priorities, it is hard to explain why present growth and welfare opportunities should be foregone. Try to explain to an American parent that there is no place in college for their kids because scientists think that it may be three degrees warmer in thirty years time.

If this tendency to discount the future seems short sighted, so too does the idea that the environmental crisis is mainly about the present impact of human activity on the planet. If we really are only in an inter-glacial period, and getting towards the end of it at that, then much larger questions loom about how to defend ourselves against turns in nature's cycles. On what is a very clear past record, the gift of environmental stability will not last forever. How we face that eventuality could make or break our civilisation.

A second feature of the debate is whether any steps we take to restrict damage to the environment should be undertaken with or against market forces. The economic forces that both inflicted the environmental damage, and produced the wealth to clean it up, are mostly derived from the power of the market economy. Command economies such as those in the former Soviet Union are also capable of massive damage to the environment. But such systems cannot produce long-term economic growth and there-fore cannot produce long-term wealth to provide for environ-mental protection. Thus it seems that any long-term solution will have to come along with the very market forces that created the problem in the first place.

It is not easy to find ways to persuade those whose job it is to make money that they should invest in seemingly uneconomic goals such as environmental protection. While there are indus-tries that are in business to clean up the environment, these are few and far between: much more common are firms that see a benefit from a green image as a marketing gimmick. Most companies need to be given a good reason, much like paying taxes, for reducing their environmental damage. If all their competitors face similar regulations, then they will be less resistant to the costs. But when competition comes from companies in countries where no or lower environmental costs are imposed, there will be calls for a level playing field. Hence the notion of negotiating, either on an industry-wide or an international basis, a system of quotas for pollution. Quotas can be traded, and they offer one possible way in which governmental and inter-governmental regulations can work with the grain of market forces to control damage to the environment. But the choices about what standards to set remain very tough, and the problems of achieving the necessary broad consensus in the cut-throat world of global market competition even tougher.

Ambient air pollutant concentrations, USA, 1976–90

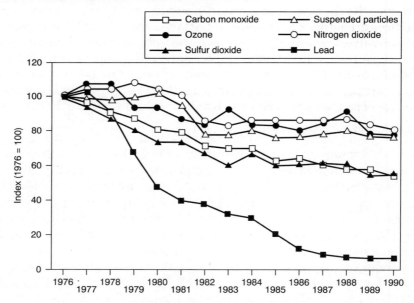

Source: US Environmental Protection Agency, National Air Quality and Emissions Trends Report, annual.

A third and related debate is how much the rich and free world should pay for the poor to help preserve the environment. The rich know that even if they did a magnificent job in cleaning up their own environment, they could do little more than they are already doing to halt damage to such global commons as the ozone layer, sea levels, air temperatures or air quality. Much current damage to our environment is the result of past actions by rich countries, but the problem in the future is mostly about the expected actions of the not-yet-developed. Poor but developing countries know that it is not in their interest to see the problems develop, but they see them as lesser problems compared to pursuing development. The poor might be persuaded to take some measures if they are provided with the money and technology – for example a Japan that is downwind of China's polluting industries is likely to provide environmental assistance to China. But that creates the problem of the rich countries subsidising their economic rivals. The scale of the potential growth in the developing world is such that unless the developing countries choose to take environmentalism seriously, it may be that there is little that is likely to be done to deal with the problem. Rather than paying off competitors, the rich may well see an increasing logic in staving off the effects of environmental deterioration by buying their own way out of trouble: providing free sunscreen lotion, using biotechnology to make new strains of food, or building more water purification plants.

Atmospheric pollution in the United Kingdom

SO_2 and smoke emission and concentration, United Kingdom, 1962–88

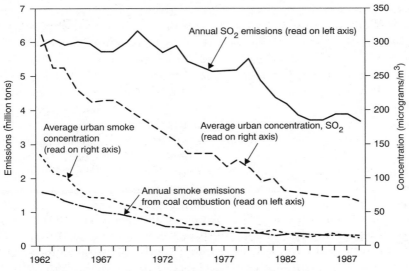

Note: SO_2 and smoke emission and concentration, United Kingdom, 1962–88

Source: Compiled from data presented by the UK Dept of Environment (1990).

Thus we stand at a turning point in human history, but one confused by numerous paradoxes. We have devised fiendishly clever ways to manipulate our environment, but we also have done serious damage to that same environment. There is good logic for finding global solutions to planetary problems, but we seem unlikely to act on this logic except in cases such as the deterioration of the ozone layer, or the threat of epidemic diseases, where the costs of a damaged environment have already become apparent. The market, to some extent like the environment itself, is a mostly self-regulating system whose operation we do not fully understand. There is a role for administrative means, whether at the level of firms, states or international institutions, but the main response to environmental crisis looks like being fragmented and market driven rather than co-ordinated and co-operative. From the selfish point of view of the rich states, it is not self-evident that it is better to pursue global collective action on this, the most quintessential of the global commons issues. The rich may well discount the future, refuse to aid the developing countries, and trust in the hopefully benign 'invisible hand' of market forces that produced their wealth in the first place. If and when the rich and free are forced to adapt to environmental crises in the short-term, they will hope to buy their way out of danger, creating new products and new markets for self-defence against the environment in the process. They will hope that when the poor grow richer, they will find reasons to change like the now rich and free did in their turn. On that basis they will gamble that a richer world will be more democratic and more environmentally sensitive, and that the market will eventually take care of the problem before any really big catastrophe occurs.

There are some grounds for optimism within this rather risky picture. The rich countries are becoming eco-realists and are cleaning up their own act, albeit sometimes cynically by exporting the dirtier industries. Second, despite all of the reasons for hesitation, the international community does appear able to act when problems become pressing, as in the case of the ozone layer. Third, wealth is growing very fast in the newly industrialising countries, and this may lead them to develop sensitivity to their own environmental problems sooner rather than later. Fourth, the more advanced countries, and particularly their pressure groups, have done a good job of raising awareness of environmental issues around the planet. They have also begun to develop technologies to reduce pollution and clean up its effects. It is easy, and up to a point appropriate, to view these developments with cynicism. Nevertheless, in the longer run they may make a difference to how soon and how thoroughly the newly rich begin to adopt more environmentally sustainable development policies.

But if we raise our gaze above the relatively small-scale issues of our immediate environment, we may see a very different picture. It may be that precisely because we have grown more aware of our ability to shape our environment, we will develop the tools necessary to meet the far larger challenges posed by nature to nature. As the next ice age looms in less than 2,000 years, or if a major comet should strike or a volcano erupt, humankind might be able to meet the challenge. Had the challenge come a generation or two earlier, we might not have been up to the task.

POPULATION

7

Throughout history, and since the dawn of the human species itself, populations have enjoyed (or simply taken) both the right to increase, and the right of mobility. Both of these features of human behaviour have played a huge role in shaping history. The steady increase in population provided the essential motor without which the creation of a single human space would not have occurred. Until very recently in the human story, the rise and fall of population was essentially a local matter. Populations could be sustained depending on the good sense of local leaders, the good luck of climate, and the impact of disease. When conditions changed and the given space could no longer support the population, then people migrated. Small groups slipped away from tribes as people spread out from Africa to populate the world.

Migration has played a complex role. Initially, it was the key to getting humans distributed around the planet. After that, its main role was in mixing races and cultures all over the world. For example, the surges of migrating barbarians that eventually overwhelmed the Western Roman Empire had come far from the east. They mixed with or displaced the indigenous Celtic populations and laid the foundations for most of the modern European nations. These modern Europeans in their turn surged outward in search of a better life, transplanting more than 30 million people to the Americas, Australia, South Africa and Siberia, and, in their colonial heyday, moving millions more

Africans, Indians and Chinese from their native lands to other continents. Similar stories could be told of Arab, Turkish and Chinese expansions. Until the twentieth century, the world was more or less seen as an open system where pressures of population growth could be relieved by just going somewhere else. But in the modern world it is becoming clear that neither population growth nor migration will be allowed anything like the free scope they have had in the past.

Growth in world population		
DATE	(HISTORICAL MILESTONES)	WORLD POPULATION (millions)
10000 BC	(HUNTER-GATHERERS)	4.0
9000 BC		4.18
8000 BC	(AGRICULTURE BEGINS)	4.37
7000 BC		4.57
6000 BC		4.78
5000 BC		5.0
4000 BC		7.0
3000 BC	(CIVILISATION BEGINS)	14.0
2000 BC		27.0
1000 BC		50.0
500 BC		100.0
0	(ROME, HAN CHINA)	170.0
500 AD		195.0
1000 AD	(MEDIEVAL EUROPE)	300.0
1500 AD	(GREAT VOYAGES)	510.0
1600 AD		545.0
1700 AD		679.0
1800 AD	(INDUSTRIAL REVOLUTION)	957.0
1900 AD		1,650.0
1950 AD		2,516.2
2000 AD	(WHERE WE ARE NOW)	6,228.3
2025 AD		8,472.5
2050 AD	(HUMAN POPULATION STABILISES?)	12,000??

Let us start with numbers. It is said that while the death of an individual is a tragedy, the death of millions is a mere statistic. One reason for such callousness is the difficulty in making sense of massive numbers of people, whereas we all know individuals.

Perhaps this is also a reason why we have such difficulty in understanding the implications of the recent geometric growth trends in the number of people who inhabit this planet. Just as we are learning to understand the scale of population growth, awareness is growing that we are probably quite close to the time when human numbers will stop rising. There has already been a decrease in the rate at which the population is growing. On most projections, the total human population will peak some time between 50 and 100 years from now at a figure somewhere between 12 and 15 billion people. For the few remaining generations of expanding human numbers there will continue to be major differences in the rate of population growth. In some countries population is already static, and in a few declining. In others (e.g. China, India, Bangladesh, Egypt, Algeria) it is rising sharply. These different growth rates mean that in the next few decades major shifts will occur in where the bulk of the human population is located. North America, Europe and Japan will become a rather small proportion of humankind, perhaps one-tenth. Asia will be more than half. How will human horizons change as our numbers level off and redistribute?

Many of the mechanisms that reduce family size (prosperity, social security, education of women) are quite well understood, though some are contested. As Europe and North America grew richer, their population growth slowed without government attempts to impose curbs, and sometimes in the face of policies designed to encourage larger families. In recent years the booming economies of East Asia have shown a similar trend. Other Asian states, most notably China and states in South Asia, have shown that government campaigns, some coercive and some more educational, can make progress in slowing population growth.

The motives for having children vary enormously. Some parents have a vague desire for immortality. In conditions of high infant mortality there is often a more concrete concern about having sufficient hands to till the fields. In many places, offspring provide security in old age. Wealthier people choose to have fewer children. In part they do so because they know that their future prosperity is based on having time to make their own fate, and in part because they have a state or private pensions to give them self-reliance in old age. More systematic research suggests that the key to making possible a shift to smaller families also depends on the education of women, and their ability to make their own choices about whether to bear children.

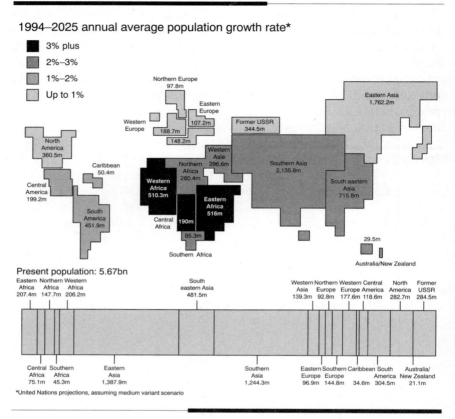

1994–2025 annual average population growth rate*

- 3% plus
- 2%–3%
- 1%–2%
- Up to 1%

Northern Europe 97.8m

Eastern Europe 107.2m

Western Europe 188.7m

148.2m

Eastern Asia 1,762.2m

Former USSR 344.5m

North America 360.5m

Caribbean 50.4m

Central America 199.2m

Western Asia 296.6m

Northern Africa 280.4m

Western Africa 510.3m

Eastern Africa 516m

Southern Asia 2,135.8m

South eastern Asia 715.8m

South America 451.9m

Central Africa 190m

85.3m

Southern Africa

29.5m

Australia/New Zealand

Present population: 5.67bn

Eastern Africa 207.4m	Northern Africa 147.7m	Western Africa 206.2m	South eastern Asia 481.5m	Western Asia 139.3m	Northern Europe 92.8m	Western Europe 177.6m	Central America 118.6m	North America 282.7m	Former USSR 284.5m

Central Africa 75.1m	Southern Africa 45.3m	Eastern Asia 1,387.9m	Southern Asia 1,244.3m	Eastern Europe 96.9m	Southern Europe 144.8m	Caribbean 34.6m	South America 304.5m	Australia/ New Zealand 21.1m

*United Nations projections, assuming medium variant scenario

Political perceptions of population growth have also changed. Whereas it used to be common for states to encourage population growth, policy has changed sharply. Recent attempts to seek power through population growth in China, Romania and Iran already seem bizarre, and most political leaders now understand that past a certain point rising population is more a liability than an asset. In the agricultural and early industrial ages a large population was seen as economically and militarily beneficial. Population meant power. But in the capital-intensive late- and post-industrial world, the attraction of reducing population growth became obvious. Such states no longer need huge armies, and they cannot find employment for large numbers. For some less developed states the question is a more basic one of inability to feed and house rising numbers. What is now most important for economic growth and individual prosperity is the quality of populations in terms of education and training, not their number. If a state's economy manages to grow 5% each year but its population grows at a similar rate, then there is no real increase in prosperity. For individuals, as for states, smaller families mean a higher standard of living. By the end of the twentieth century, at least in rich, and near-rich countries, it is understood that human aspiration has undergone a massive psychological shift – it is no longer necessarily good to have more people.

The world's rising food productivity

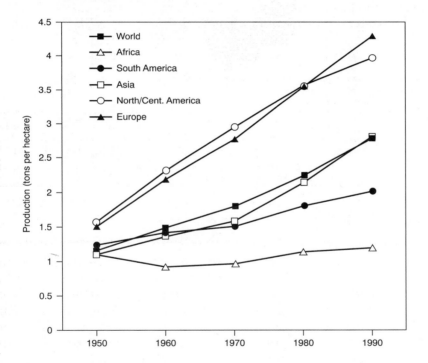

Source: FAO.

Knowledge about the possibilities for control, the apparent success in reducing population growth in much of Asia, and the benefits to those who no longer have to feed more mouths, points to the conclusion that the number of people on this planet will begin to level off in two or three generations. Perhaps. But whether or not this happens is largely a matter of complex choices determined by individuals and markets. There can be relative confidence that the levels of population in the rich world will remain stable. The key uncertainty is whether most of the rest of the world will achieve sufficient education and wealth for their populations also to stabilise. Most governments realise the need to curb population size, but the desire for large families is still deeply embedded in many cultures. And relying on the market mechanism involves hazards similar to those experienced in relation to the environment. Will the same logic work for the rest of the world? Will market forces make the problem worse before they make it better (in this case by higher birth survival rates and lower death rates)? Will they work quickly enough to avoid a really big crisis? Can the rich world insulate itself from the poor world during the transition process?

Food production and population

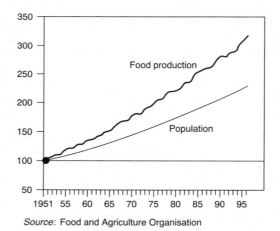

Source: Food and Agriculture Organisation

The transition from growth to stasis will not be made without some disasters, but a general Malthusian crisis of starvation seems highly unlikely. As a result of revolutions in the science of food production, there has been no 'population bomb' as predicted some thirty years ago. In an age of food surpluses and payments to farmers not to produce food in the developed world, it is absurd to talk of a global scarcity of food. To be sure, some food will be scarce, for example due to drastic over-fishing. But virtually all cases of starvation have local causes – climate change and local crop failure, or local wars and destruction of markets. It is reasonable to suggest that the revolution in food production can continue to keep ahead of population growth, at least until the projected plateau in the world's population. If starvation persists, it will continue to be a local phenomenon with local causes. Where this occurs it will be difficult to create local conditions for the generation of wealth and a reduction in population growth. In short, the market 'solution' may leave an enduring gap between a wealthy, educated and small population in many parts of the world and a poor and struggling remainder of the world where cycles of starvation become endemic.

The effect of disease is even harder to calculate. Despite the astonishing progress of medical science, humankind is not free from the threat of major plagues. Bacteria and viruses mutate and evolve with terrifying speed. Various cancers have been known for ages, but as better public health allowed more people to live longer, cancer has become a higher profile and far more complex killer than many had previously thought. New and incurable diseases such as AIDS may be less lethal than cancer, but like older ones, such as malaria and tuberculosis, are evolving superbug strains that may outrun the development of new drugs. It is not yet clear how far or fast new diseases will run, or whether some of the main lines of medical defence against more familiar diseases are about to give way. The poor may be more vulnerable, but some plagues are blind to wealth. Disease remains a player that could, as it has done in the past, have a big impact on human numbers.

Despite their relative advantages of population stability, the rich have no reason to grow complacent about demography, even within their own societies. The demographics of stable or declining populations pose fundamental, albeit very different challenges. Rich countries can already see that they will face a major challenge to their comfy social security systems as their population ages. There will obviously be difficult choices about ages of retirement, support for healthcare and the nature of pension contributions. The role of women is changing again as it becomes all the more clear how the 'wife as housewife' model of the rich countries in the 1950s and 1960s was an exception rather than the rule. As women return to the workplace, this time increasingly in more senior positions, family structures change. In rich countries we have already seen a shift from wider families, through nuclear families to a more atomised society. But in most rich countries the rate of increase in divorces has peaked and children are growing up knowing that it is normal to have a mother working outside the home. Societies with fewer children are also more reluctant to send them to war or to bear the costs of bloody engagements. These are societies that wish to take fewer risks and carry fewer responsibilities abroad. We should not be surprised if they wish to build up barriers against a seemingly hostile, teeming and problem-ridden world outside.

One reason for contemplating such barriers is the fear that drastic differentials in population growth and levels of welfare will trigger migration from the poor world to the rich one. For most of the last two centuries, the dominant issue in migration was the outflow of European settlers to other continents. With the dramatic increase in European prosperity, and with the de-colonisation of empires, this flow has largely dried up. It has been replaced by rising pressures both within the poor world, and from the ex-colonial world in the direction of Europe, North America and Australia. The urge for conquest has perhaps faded as a major motive for migration, but environmental disruption, war, over-population and hope for economic gain remain strong motives, as does desire to escape from oppressive political systems. Thousands of people already die annually trying to make risky journeys from poor and/or oppressed areas either to richer and freer ones, or simply to somewhere nearby where the chances of being killed or starved are a bit lower. The relative poverty and high population growth of the periphery in relation to the core suggest an historic role reversal, with Europe becoming a prime destination for migrants rather than, as for the past half-millennium, its principal source of them. But there is also huge scope for migrations within the poor world, as for example the present surge towards South Africa. Are the fears of the rich world real, or is the main force of migration now largely contained within regions?

The vast majority of flows of people are within the frontiers of individual states or to neighbouring states. To the extent that there are flows of people between regions, they are reversing the past practice and now are moving from poor to rich countries. But most population movement is within regions. The wars in the Caucasus displace people in this regional sense, where in earlier centuries they might have fled across the Atlantic. The last major global move, by refugees from the Vietnam war, was only possible because of the direct involvement of the United

States in the conflict. There are some 60,000 people a year leaving Hong Kong for distant parts, but this is a short-term problem where the people are more 'yacht people' than desperate 'boat people'.

This clear shift to the regionalisation of migration is masked by other trends. The influence of global communications makes people more aware of human tragedies around the world. Thus it seems as if the associated refugee problems are a problem for us all. But in reality the problems remain local and few people move outside their home region. When Pakistan fell apart in 1971, the Bangladeshi millions fled to India and very few came to England. In Rwanda, the refugees went next door to Zaire and Tanzania, not to France. Sudanese fled to Ethiopia, Afghans to Iran and Pakistan, and Cubans and Haitians to the US. Most refugees do not go far, and the strategy of the rich is to keep people in their home region so that they can be more quickly resettled.

The misleading sense that migration problems are global is also enhanced by the anecdotal sense of the rich that they are now able to travel so much further with so much more ease. That so many Europeans took holidays in the former Yugoslavia had a great deal to do with the fact that Europeans felt that the conflict that broke out in the 1990s created a problem for all Europeans. In reality, and certainly this was the case for the flows of refugees, the population was largely confined to neighbouring states. It may be ironic, but it is nonetheless true, that despite the fact that so many more people travel around the globe as tourists and on business, the flow of people making a new life on new continents is much reduced.

Would-be migrants face a more rigorously demarcated world than ever before. They are subject to more official control, and increasingly that control is unwelcoming or even hostile. Established communities, whether correctly or not, increasingly tend to see migrants as a threat to their welfare, their identity and their political and social stability. In the densely populated, territorially organised and unevenly developed world of the present and near future, it is clear that migration will not be allowed anything like the scope it has had in the past. From our generation onward, the spread of population in the numbers typical of the past will be fiercely resisted. The countries of the periphery will be unable to enjoy the safety valve of migration that Europe enjoyed during its process of modernisation. How

Places of asylum

	Places of Asylum	Mostly from /Number
Total Africa		**5,880,000**
Algeria	Western Sahara, Mali, Niger	[1]130,000
Burundi	Rwanda, Zaire	[1]165,000
	Côte d'Ivoire, Liberia	320,000
Ethiopia	Somalia, Sudan, Djibouti	[1]250,000
Ghana	Togo, Liberia	110,000
Guinea	Liberia, Sierra Leone	[1]580,000
Kenya	Somalia, Sudan, Ethiopia	[1]257,000
Liberia	Sierra Leone	[1]100,000
Malawi	Mozambique	70,000
South Africa	Mozambique	[1]200,000
Sudan	Eritrea, Ethiopia, Chad	[1]550,000
Tanzania	Rwanda, Burundi, Mozambique	[1]752,000
Uganda	Sudan, Zaire, Rwanda	323,000
Zaire	Rwanda, Angola, Burundi,	
	Sudan, Uganda	[1]1,527,000
Zambia	Angola, Zaire	123,000
Total East Asia/Pacific		**444,000**
China	Vietnam, Myanmar	[1]297,100
Thailand	Myanmar, Laos	83,050
Total Europe & No. America		**2,625,000**
Armenia	Azerbaijan	[1]295,800
Azerbaijan	Armenia, Uzbekistan	[1]279,000
Croatia	Bosnia and Herzegovina, other	188,000
Germany	Bosnia and Herzegovina,	
	Croatia, other	[1]430,000
Russia	Former USSR, other	[1]451,000
United States	Cuba, Haiti, other	181,700
Yugoslavia[2]	Croatia, Bosnia and Herzegovina	[1]300,000
Total Latin America/Caribbean		**94,000**
Total Middle East		**5,448,000**
Gaza Strip	Palestinians	644,000
Iran	Afghanistan, Iraq	[1]2,220,000
Iraq	Palestinians, Iran, Turkey	120,500
Jordan	Palestinians	1,232,150
Lebanon	Palestinians	338,200
Syria	Palestinians, Iraq	332,900
West Bank	Palestinians	504,000

Places of asylum (contd)		
Total South & Central Asia		**1,776,000**
Bangladesh	Myanmar	116,200
India	Tibet, Sri Lanka, Bangladesh,	
	Bhutan, Afghanistan	[1]327,850
Nepal	Bhutan, Tibet	104,600
Pakistan	Afghanistan	[1]1,202,650
Total Refugees		**16,267,000**

(1) Significant variance among sources in number reported. (2) Serbia/Montenegro. *Source: World Refugee Survey 1995*, U.S. Committee for Refugees, a nonprofit corp. The refugees in this table include only those who are in need of protection and/or assistance and do not include refugees who have permanently settled in other countries (as of 31 Dec. 1994).

effectively the forces pushing migration can be contained remains to be seen, but there is no doubt that the attempt will be made, both between the rich and poor worlds, and within the poor world. To the extent that it succeeds, it will create a future in which people's place of residence will change less often, as travel for business and pleasure becomes much easier.

The implications of the regional containment of population movement mesh with the prospect for highly uneven population growth between the rich and poor worlds. Some trends are already fairly clear. The balance of the world's population will shift very sharply. Cities will grow vastly larger in places such as Nigeria and China, while they shrink in Europe. The creation of large urban populations was a key part of the transformation of European countries into major powers with great wealth, but the prospects for that happening in the currently poor parts of the world depend on a wide range of other factors. There is no guarantee of a trend to power and wealth. There will be little or no opportunity for areas of high population growth to shift their surplus overseas, and attempts to do so locally will easily generate conflict. Conflict may reduce population size by slaughter, as in Rwanda and Cambodia, but it is unlikely to produce the conditions for economic growth that have made permanent population reduction possible elsewhere. Massive demographic changes tend to be accompanied by social change and even revolution, but the crises that result are essentially local and do not necessarily draw the active involvement of distant and richer states apart from partial attempts at humanitarian relief.

The rich will try to build walls against the teeming masses and developmental crises of the poor, while hoping that the market will eventually solve the problem. Perhaps some of the effects of high populations contained within their states and regions can be offset by the onrushing of globalised communications. Will opportunities for communication, work and leisure eventually undermine the motives for migration?

Drawing defensive lines will have costs, just as it does within individual societies. Victorian Europe and North America also tried to build high walls and offer their poor charity. Social order began to collapse and the ruling elite then developed a social market to provide basic support for the poor and enhance opportunity for the wider population. In most cases the changes came in time and major revolutions were avoided. Does the analogy hold for international society?

Perhaps. It is not that the rich must allow the poor to move into their house – that was not the Victorian solution either. But the rich did have to restrain, or at least compensate for, the unrestrained operation of market forces. They had to provide a basic standard of living through social security payments and to provide more equal opportunity to become educated and wealthy. The analogy is thus not only the provision of food aid, but also support for education for women, family planning and food production. If the new biotechnology has the answers, then they may have to be given away rather than sold. More controversially, if good government cannot be provided by poor states, then the international community might have to experiment with international trusteeships of the kind already tried in Cambodia, Haiti and Bosnia, and tried but failed in Somalia and Liberia, even though these look much like a form of neo-colonialism. But the basic approach of the rich looks like being a strategy of self-protection and market forces. The *nouveaux riches* of East Asia are certainly less likely to support social welfare schemes in poor countries – preferring to proffer their own recent lessons of hard work, firm government, mass education and market forces. East Asians' relative 'compassion deficit' may well encourage the '*ancien riches*' to believe that they too need not make vast sacrifices for the poor of the planet.

IDENTITY

8

All human beings carry multiple identities, and these identities are all defined in relation to the surrounding society. Hence the expression, 'no man is an island'. Even the sense of being a distinctive individual depends on having others from whom to differentiate oneself. The sets of identities carried by individuals can range from quite simple (self, family, clan) to extremely complicated (self, family, gender, profession, interest group, nation, religion, civilisation, humankind). Just how multiple and complex people's identities become depends heavily on what kind of society they live in. Members of remote hunter-gatherer bands may live their whole lives in a social universe defined by a few dozen others. Their identity will be correspondingly simple. People who live in wealthy, cosmopolitan, techno-logically sophisticated societies have in some important senses the whole of humankind as their social universe. They may well generate many layers and types of identity in response, though some will shrink from such complexity, and seek refuge in some simplifying, overriding identity such as religion or nationalism. Society both makes individual identity and is made (and un-made) by it. Shared identities are crucial to social cohesion, and rival identities are the foundation of conflict. This double-edged quality of identity – unifying on the one hand, dividing on the other – has been central to the making and breaking of human civilisation throughout history, and seems certain to remain so.

> ## Rethinking Identity
>
> Not only is the population of the earth growing, but its remarkable diversity will be an intimate part of your life – as it was not part of mine. Today, I have Thai, Turkish or Mexican restaurants on my street. In your world, Thais, Turks and Mexicans will be your neighbours . . . You will probably spend time in cities like San Francisco, London and Bombay – sources of new ideas, invention and tastes, because the new cultures will intersect there.
>
> From Peter Schwartz, *The Art of the Long View*, p. 223.
>
> It is always the same: once you are liberated, you are forced to ask who you are.
>
> **Jean Baudrillard**, *America*, 'Astral America' (1986; tr. 1988).

Looking at identity in the light of the story told in Part I, it seems obvious that there is an historical trend towards the creation of societies on an ever-larger scale. Only a tiny proportion of humanity now lives in hunter-gatherer bands, and even those are mostly exposed to knowledge of a much wider world. The bulk of humankind, even if they still live within distinctive cultures and civilisations, is now in some degree part of a global society. This widening social universe should mean that individual identities are becoming more multiple and complex. But it also has to mean that in some senses identities are becoming more uniform, because wider societies cannot exist without some foundations in shared identity. The question is how these atomising versus integrating imperatives are reconciled. Do some identities become collectively more important than others, and if so which ones, how, and with what effect?

The oldest identity, and the only one with any foundation in genetics, is gender. There have always been males and females of the species. Only a tiny proportion of the world's population define themselves as homosexuals and there is incomplete evidence about whether there is a genetic basis for such identity. Males and females have mostly been parents (85–90% of all humans are parents at one time or another) and this means that family has been one of the keystones of social identity. The blood bonds of family define relatively small social groups, but can be successfully extended into progressively larger scales of bands, tribes and clans. For much of human history these were the dominant forms of collective identity, and they remain active in the present day. Family ties play a big role in some business cultures, and clan structures still dominate political life in much of the Middle East and Central Asia. There are even widespread calls for the restoration of 'family values' in the West, where the pursuit of individualism and the operation of the market have done most to erode the family unit.

Ties of kith and kin quite quickly run into limits of scale, and to transcend these limits requires forms of identity that depend on shared values and/or behaviours. Perhaps the oldest, and still highly robust, of these transcendent identities is religion. The earliest civilisations were built around commonly held religions, and the most powerful and successful religions have aspired to embrace the whole of humankind. None has achieved this goal, but several world religions – Islam, Christianity, Hinduism, Buddhism – have lasted for millennia, and have a world-wide distribution of followers numbered in hundreds of millions. All of these, however, have subdivided into sects, which despite common roots have often fallen into fierce internecine conflict: Catholic against Protestant, Shi'ia against Sunni. Indeed, conflict within religions is at least as important in human history as conflict between them. Catholics sacked Orthodox Constantinople long before the forces of Islam managed to do so, and the interminable wars between the Ottoman and Persian empires were much inspired by the Sunni–Shi'ia divide.

By the late twentieth century religion remained an important and widespread form of identification despite being under sustained assault by both the secular truth of science, and the individualism and materialism of capitalist society. Partly as a result of this assault, the global force of religious identity has become very unevenly distributed. In some cultures, most notably the Islamic and Hindu, religion remains the main form of identity, dominating political and social life. But in the secularised West, it is a decreasing, though still formidable, force. Having suffered decades of terrible religious wars, Europeans began to reject the mixing of religion and politics during the seventeenth century. In the new United States of America, with its increasingly complex

Adherents of all religions by seven continental areas, mid-1994

	Africa	Asia	Europe	Latin America	Northern America	Oceania	Eurasia	World
Christians	351,682,000	304,887,000	422,159,000	422,140,000	246,319,000	23,240,000	109,747,000	1,900,174,000
Roman Catholics	132,102,000	132,053,000	267,972,000	411,514,000	100,386,000	8,427,000	5,615,000	1,058,069,000
Protestants	93,865,000	87,051,000	75,441,000	17,513,000	99,652,000	7,718,000	9,903,000	391,143,000
Orthodox	30,685,000	3,904,000	36,869,000	1,789,000	6,217,000	591,000	94,129,000	174,184,000
Anglicans	28,873,000	755,000	33,625,000	1,319,000	7,593,000	5,872,000	1,000	78,038,000
Other Christians	66,158,000	81,125,000	8,252,000	10,004,000	33,445,000	623,000	100,000	199,707,000
Muslims	293,993,000	675,297,000	13,194,000	1,395,000	5,500,000	107,000	43,967,000	1,033,453,000
Hindus	1,608,000	759,059,000	725,000	912,000	1,315,000	379,000	2,000	764,000,000
Buddhists	23,000	336,755,000	279,000	559,000	578,000	26,000	401,000	338,621,000
Chinese folk religionists	14,000	149,037,000	61,000	76,000	126,000	21,000	1,000	149,336,000
New-Religionists	23,000	126,869,000	51,000	548,000	1,473,000	10,000	1,000	128,975,000
Tribal religionists	69,872,000	28,197,000	1,000	967,000	42,000	71,000	0	99,150,000
Sikhs	29,000	19,557,000	237,000	8,000	363,000	9,000	1,000	20,204,000
Jews	128,000	4,289,000	1,761,000	458,000	5,907,000	95,000	813,000	13,451,000
Shamanists	1,000	10,754,000	2,000	1,000	1,000	1,000	250,000	11,010,000
Confucians	1,000	6,300,000	2,000	2,000	26,000	1,000	2,000	6,334,000
Baha'is	1,631,000	2,817,000	93,000	827,000	379,000	81,000	7,000	5,835,000
Jains	57,000	3,906,000	15,000	4,000	4,000	1,000	0	3,987,000
Shintoists	0	3,383,000	1,000	1,000	1,000	1,000	0	3,387,000
Other religionists	472,000	12,912,000	1,513,00	3,686,000	1,503,000	4,000	329,000	20,419,000
Nonreligious	2,936,000	733,740,000	58,199,000	19,327,000	23,884,000	3,756,000	82,236,000	924,078,000
Atheists	344,000	167,739,000	16,362,000	3,329,000	1,367,000	563,000	49,407,000	239,111,000
Total Population	**722,814,000**	**3,345,498,000**	**514,655,000**	**474,240,000**	**288,788,000**	**28,366,000**	**287,164,000**	**5,661,525,000**

Source: 1995 Encyclopaedia Britannica Book of the Year.

mix of ethnicities, religion and the state were formally kept apart. In the more developed parts of the Western world, religion was gradually moved into the private sphere. Science has delivered a powerful alternative to understanding the universe, and the attractions of materialism have undermined concern with other gods. But even in the West religion still has deep roots. Many decades of atheistic communist rule failed to extinguish Christianity in Central and Eastern Europe, and religion remains an important political force in the United States.

The mixture of religion and politics has by no means been universally abandoned, and conflicts within and between religions from Ireland and India to Bosnia, Sudan, the Caucasus and the Philippines are a salutary reminder of the reasons for separating them. It may be the case that a new gap is opening up between secular societies, and those in which religion still remains at the centre of social and political life. To the secular mind, it remains a source of amazement that the religious legacy of classical agrarian society remains so powerful two centuries into the industrial revolution.

A much more recent, and also highly successful, form of collective identity is that built around the idea of national identity rooted in the idea of shared ethnicity (and so having some tenuous links to the blood claims of clans). Of course there are no ethnically pure groups because the human population is the result of mass migrations and interbreeding over millennia. Much more important to national identity is that people should share a language, a culture, and a sense of common history. The political version of such national identity is known as nationalism, although nationalism also can be based either on common ethnicity (mythical or otherwise), or on a civic nationalism as in the United States or Australia. Nationalism is the doctrine that political legitimacy should be based on nations, and that each nation should have its own state. Nationalism feels like an old idea (that is part of its myth), but in fact is a political invention of the past two and half centuries. Nationalism can be seen as a tool of European governing elites looking for ways to restore social cohesion in the face of the deep class divisions created by the industrial and capitalist revolutions. It was also, in a sense, the answer to Marx, and one that proved so successful that it has now become a universal idea.

National identity can be created on a huge scale. The sociologist Benedict Anderson calls these 'imagined communities', where vast numbers of people share an identity despite never having met more than a tiny fraction of the other members. Nationalism was never designed to unify all of humanity and does not have the universalist potential that exists in some religions. But once implanted, nationalism is a harder identity to lose. People can convert into and out of most religions fairly easily, but it is more difficult (though not impossible) to change national identity. Its very definition presupposes exclusive groups, each bound together by deeply rooted cultural traditions and historical perceptions, things that automatically and strongly differentiate insiders from outsiders, us from them. It was this sense of exclusiveness that fascism amplified into claims of racial superiority, and the right of one nation to dominate others. In its heyday, nationalism was (and in many places still is) a dominant identity, claiming priority over all others in shaping individual behaviour. Millions have died in its name. Where nationalism could be fused with the state it created great political strength, as in France, Germany and Japan, albeit at the cost of fuelling wars between states for top nation status. But where states contained more than one nation it often sowed dragon's teeth, creating harvests like those reaped recently in the former Yugoslavia and in Sri Lanka.

Languages spoken by more than 100,000,000 people		
	Speakers (millions) **Native**	**Total**
Mandarin	844	975
Hindi	340	437
Spanish	339	392
English	326	478
Bengali	193	200
Arabic	190	225
Russian	169	284
Portuguese	172	184
Japanese	125	126
German	98	123
French	73	125
Malay-Indonesian	52	159

Nationalism is unquestionably one of the great social forces of modern times. It has transcended all cultural boundaries, and it remains a crucial tool of many governments. The disjuncture between 200 states and 5,000 nations defines many of the ongoing troubles of our time, from Liberia to Lebanon, and from Russia to Rwanda. For a while, nation-states were even seen as self-contained economies, and competition for markets was seen for a long time (and in some places still is) as one between the capitalists of individual states. It was only in the twentieth century that capitalism broke free from the interests of individual nations. As it did so, the notion of a global economy began to play a larger part in the lives of the richer world, so beginning to erode the importance of nation and state as dominant elements of identity. Increasing economic globalism, with its cosmopolitan cultural baggage, is steadily undermining the foundations of nationalism. At current rates of extinction, the 5,000 currently spoken human languages that define nations will be reduced to fewer than 600 within a century. Nationalism is an identity with a great deal of force still left in it, but one that, at least in the rich world, no longer commands the absolute priority that it enjoyed only a few decades ago. In other places, however, nationalism of the old school still rules. In the Balkans and the Caucasus and in some parts of Africa and Asia, it sustains old hatreds, armed rivalries and vicious wars.

In the rich world extremes of nationalism have been softened by new trends in increasingly pluralist political systems. In such systems people accept the multiplicity of their own and others' identities. The United States was perhaps the first state to adopt this notion in a major way, although even in its case there were bloody struggles between North and South, and black and white, before pluralism firmly took hold. In many ways the United States remains the most pluralist of the wealthy states at the end of the millennium. Canada, with its unresolved problem of Quebec, is another wealthy pluralist country, but also a warning that nationalism is not just a concern for the poor and uneducated.

Modern pluralist systems accept the notion of 'hyphenated' citizens – those such as Hispanic-Americans who see their Spanish origin as a major feature of their sub-identity within the American melting pot. Not surprisingly, pluralist societies have vigorous debates about multiculturalism and the extent to which the society as a whole makes compromises for sub-groups. Should Canadians in northern Alberta learn French because their vast country is composed of French-speakers in distant parts? Should schools in France tolerate discrimination against women just because it is said to be a feature of the sub-identity of their Islamic citizens? Can Singapore limit free speech for the supposed sake of ensuring racial harmony? In complex pluralist societies, identity is also a matter of class, level of education, profession, sexual preference, interest in sports and other activities, and style. Consumer capitalism encourages individuals to differentiate themselves by style and possessions, so creating an endlessly diversifying market for all manner of personal products. The cosmopolitan culture of the global market economy adds strong elements of world identity to this mix. English and Japanese children think that McDonalds is a local restaurant and it takes them a while to learn that Disney films come from the USA. In short, modern societies have multiple identities and cannot easily slip back into the simplistic definitions of nationalism.

There are many benefits to be had from societies with complex mixtures of identity. The 'spice of life' comes in part from being able to learn from others, let alone to taste their food or to enjoy their games, arts, sports, music and festivals. In many ways such societies fulfil the liberal dream. Individuals and groups are free to develop according to their own choices in an environment of mutual tolerance. Diversity expands markets and increases competition, so increasing the prosperity of all. Familiarity with other cultures reduces the fears and hatreds that fuelled wars in the past, and opens the prospect for cultural syntheses in the arts. It can also be argued that the increasingly complex identities of people in a sophisticated world create so many layers of identity that the importance of any one of them is reduced. As a result, societies are protected against the totalitarian extremes of fascism, ultra-nationalism and communism that caused so much misery and violence in this century. The much-made point that democracies don't go to war with each other reflects these benefits.

But it is worth re-stating the apparent conclusion that complex identity seems to be linked to the ability to develop and sustain economic prosperity. No society that is at war with itself can provide the conditions conducive to growth. Some states, such as Japan, seem to be able to sustain elements of pluralism within more ethnically homogeneous societies. And the move away from single-minded nationalism towards pluralism and multiculturalism is not without costs, some of them serious. It raises again basic questions about the balance between integration and fragmentation in the complex equations of identity. If too much fragmentation occurs societies may become ungovernable and states unstable. One can see signs of this in Canada, where the sense that 'Canadianness' is worth having is evaporating in the heat of more parochial identities, and in Italy, where parts of the country seem to be slipping outside the framework of government. A desire within many of the peoples of the EU to limit federalism and retain elements of national government may yet wreck the integration project and push Europe back towards its old ways of balance of power politics.

Democracy requires a measure of shared values. Without such common bonds, there is insufficient social cohesion to sustain the give and take, and wins and losses, of representative government. Diversity needs to be contained within a framework of rules – formally encoded in law or not – which are seen to be implemented through impartial justice. Societies which lack such mechanisms for settling disputes will often find that differences over identity get out of control. All of the most successful and stable economies in the world have such dispute-settlement mechanisms, although they vary in their formality and the myopia of their justice. The existence of rules to govern political and economic systems is not always enough to ensure basic stability and prosperity. It is said that when there are high levels of interdependence between groups, then they have a greater propensity to work together. But this is only true when there are few conflicts over basic values, resources and interests. As it turns out, these are often matters of dispute and therefore tension arises within and between societies and states. American blacks rioted because they felt they were being denied access to the fruits of their society. Thievery and corruption are often symptoms of a system with major inequalities or rapid social change.

In the more atomised society of rich countries, it is sometimes said that 'direct democracy' through new information technology can help build a new from of society. But leaving aside the need for a time for reflection in mature democratic deliberations, the notion of 'direct democracy' and 'virtual society' does not provide for the deeper essentials of stable democracy. Democracy and law cannot work if society is fragmented into individuals and groups all of whom put their own interests and values ahead of any sense of shared community. Shared identity is part of what motivates people to make sacrifices for others and to co-operate within wider society. It is a necessary counterweight to the economic and political conflicts of interest that can tear society to pieces. The ghosts of class war, religious intolerance, racism and ethnic hatred still roam. It is still true that no man is an island.

National identity is a challenge for the international system as well as the state. How are relations among individuals and their larger identities to be managed when they lack means of settling disputes short of force? As interdependence grows, the potential frictions within the system also grow; over trade, aid, interest rates, investment, migration, human rights and all of the other points of contact in an increasingly global political economy. These frictions feed on continuing and even growing inequalities between actors. The rich grow richer and only a few states – such as in East Asia – are able to join the prosperity. Amongst the richer states the older problems with conflicting identities seem to fade, but for those societies on the fringes, and especially for those societies outside the circle of prosperity, the conflicts over identity remain of major importance. Even some of the largest states, such as China, have yet to sort out basic elements of their identity in the modern world. Until they do so, a major challenge for the international system will be how to manage the risks of such massive social change.

But perhaps the main international problem is that patterns of identity evolve at different rates and in different directions. Some parts of the world have pluralist political systems while others are still in the grip of religion, ultra-nationalism or clans. There is a three-tiered generation gap between societies separating the West, the newly industrialising countries (NICs), and those still locked into premodern ways. The West sees itself as mature and advanced, the NICs as blindly about to repeat its mistakes of pollution, exploitation and hyper-nationalism, and the premoderns as childishly primitive. The NICs see themselves as the wave of the future, and the West as decadent, effete, and past its prime. The premoderns cling to the virtues of their indigenous cultures, but also fear being left behind by the NICs and the West. Clearly in this one globe with multiple worlds, it is hard to find a common language and rules. One recalls the Japanese Admiral Yamamoto's remarks when faced with criticism of Japanese occupation of Manchuria – 'the Western powers taught us how to play poker, now that they have all the chips, they have taken up contract bridge'. A modern Chinese admiral no doubt feels the same way.

Hence the fashionable talk in the late twentieth century of a coming clash of civilisations. Of course the thought that civilisations or religions (as in a new Cold War with Islam) could become dominant, unifying identities powerful enough to overcome all others and shape a new pattern of international affairs, is seriously open to question. It presupposes that civilisational identity will be a successor to nationalism on a grander scale. This ignores the strong drive towards more complex and multilayered identities in the rich world. Equally, anyone who knows Japan and China will know that there is no such thing as a Confucian world, and anyone who knows the Middle East can see that Islam is much more strongly divided within itself than it is united against the perfidious West. In Europe, the sense of common civilisation is so weak that it poses major problems for the EU, which struggles to find a strong enough shared identity to support its integration project.

But the clash of civilisations idea does usefully remind us that for many people, identity is still seen in relatively simplistic terms. This is especially so for those who feel that their main identity is insufficiently considered in the modern world. For Chinese nationalists or Islamic radicals, or African-Americans this sense of civilisational identity remains important. It also highlights the fact that humankind does not yet fully understand, and certainly has not yet come to terms with, the double edged quality of identity – fragmenting and integrating. Multicultural pluralists have not solved the problem of how to mix diversity of identity with stable and democratic government within their own societies. Neither have they developed a coherent way of managing a multicultural planet, and they are at risk of underestimating the power of older ideas about identity. On the other side, old-fashioned religious and nationalist enthusiasts have not found ways of addressing human rights and global markets, or of avoiding wars, both domestic and international. The mixture of such diverse societies brings international society itself into question. When social and political cultures are so different, and gaps in level of development so large, where are the shared identities to be found on which the norms and rules of international order can be built? The collective sense of being human is so far vastly weaker than the many sub-identities that divide our species. Perhaps only when the whole of humankind is challenged from outside will it be possible to construct an 'imagined community' on a planetary scale.

KNOWLEDGE

9

If 'knowledge is power', then in the late twentieth century knowing how to get and advance knowledge seems to be the key to power. The ability to build nuclear weapons provides huge power to destroy and coerce. Making tanks fire farther and more accurately, or making silicon chips hold more information and process it faster, leads to battlefield or commercial success, or both. 'Insider' knowledge can make (illegal) fortunes on the stock exchanges and money markets. More generally, developing or exploiting new knowledge is the key to achieving power and wealth. Less obvious, but perhaps of more than equal significance is the kind of knowledge necessary to produce new popular entertainment that is broadcast around the globe and reshapes the values of other societies. There is certainly a strong belief in Western societies that they need to rely more on inspiration than perspiration. Knowledge is the key to their power, even if they do not fully understand the processes of innovative thinking that produce knowledge.

All men by nature desire knowledge.

Aristotle, *Metaphysics*, bk. 1, ch. 1.

It was not always so. Until the scientific and industrial revolutions, holding power often seemed to depend on suppressing new knowledge that might upset the existing social order. Only when European societies embraced the pursuit of knowledge was this pattern decisively broken. The pursuit of knowledge, and the development of systematic scientific methods, helped to give Europe such a gigantic advantage that it was able to take over the rest of the world. Once decolonisation had restored political independence to most of the planet's people, the pursuit of knowledge became an almost universal human goal, virtually a condition of political independence.

Acquiring Knowledge

There are three principal means of acquiring knowledge available to us: observation of nature, reflection, and experimentation. Observation collects facts; reflection combines them; experimentation verifies the result of that combination. Our observation of nature must be diligent, our reflection profound, and our experiments exact. We rarely see these three means combined; and for this reason, creative geniuses are not common.

Denis Diderot, *On the Interpretation of Nature*, no. 15 (1753; repr. in *Selected Writings*, ed. by Lester G. Crocker, 1966).

But what is knowledge? The term covers everything from mathematics and physics, through economics and the social sciences, to moral philosophy and the arts. It ranges from how to build a space shuttle or play chess, to how to govern mass societies or raise children. In some senses our ability to know has improved vastly, for we did not even dream of a space shuttle several hundred years ago. Arguably for some, we have even made progress in how we govern ourselves. But in other areas our knowledge seems not much improved. It is not at all obvious that we know more about happiness or right and wrong than did the ancient Greeks or Chinese. This disparity between huge progress in knowledge about the physical world, and seemingly much less progress in knowledge about the social world, reflects the diverse quality of knowledge. Indeed, it is fair to say that the concept of knowledge itself is hotly contested. Some focus on the kind of knowledge produced by systematic observation and experiment, others on the social construction of knowledge arising out of shared understandings of things, and yet others on the intuition or insight of individual minds. These kinds of 'knowledge' don't necessarily add up. Different methods tell us different things, but none of them seems to stretch convincingly across the physical, social, spiritual and ethical worlds, and there is a lot of room for argument about what can really be called knowledge. Considering how important knowledge is to power, this is not a trivial problem.

> ### Animals and Knowledge
>
> Man is distinguished, not only by his reason; but also by this singular passion from other animals . . . which is a lust of the mind, that by a perseverance of delight in the continual and indefatigable generation of knowledge, exceeds the short vehemence of any carnal pleasure.
>
> **Thomas Hobbes**, *Leviathan*, pt. 1, ch. 6 (1651).

If we ignore the more difficult philosophical and religious fringes of knowledge, the big contrast is between knowledge of the physical and of the social worlds. The gigantic material progress and 'knowledge explosion' of the last two centuries has been carried on the back of the natural sciences' unprecedented accumulation of facts and theories about the physical world. But the process is neither smooth nor inexorable. Scientific enquiry may exhaust certain avenues, and technologies become mature. Physics, for example may soon come to a kind of completion in a unified theory of matter and energy, and mature technologies such as cars and aircraft subside into incremental improvements on basically familiar designs. But innovators soon uncover new paths to be explored, with current prospects in biochemistry and material sciences looking particularly bright. Ours is an age of rapid, and apparently never-ending scientific and technological advance. The impact of scientific progress extends all through society, bringing with it massive social, political and economic change. Sometimes the process has unintended effects, but on balance there can be no question that knowledge in this sense is advancing. Nevertheless, there is much room for debate about whether the effects of this knowledge promote progress when applied in the social world. Nuclear energy is undoubtedly a triumph of knowledge, but many feel that both its civil and military applications have been dangerous and undesirable. There would have been no industrial revolution without the new science and technology, nor could there have been the fundamental change in women's roles without modern contraceptives. For better or for worse, Western civilisation has opened itself, and the rest of the world, to an apparently unending social revolution fed by continuous changes in the material conditions of human existence. Whereas we tend to resist the imposition of social change by foreigners or reformers, we tend to allow it if it comes as a consequence of new technologies.

Knowing and Not Knowing

To know yet to think that one does not know is best; Not to know yet to think that one knows will lead to difficulty.

Lao-Tzu, *Tao-te-ching*, bk. 2, ch. 71 (tr. by T.C. Lau, 1963).

We have not the reverent feeling for the rainbow that a savage has, because we know how it is made. We have lost as much as we gained by prying into that matter.

Mark Twain, *A Tramp Abroad*, vol. 2, ch. 11 (1879).

But in relation to the social world, the advance in knowledge is much less impressive. Many aspects of the social world do not yield to the same methodologies that generate knowledge about the physical one. Core ideas such as power, justice and security do not have the same fixed and measurable qualities as mass, velocity, and electrical charge. Unlike matter and energy, the ingredients in the social world do not reliably produce the same results when mixed in the same way. Full-scale scientific experimentation with social theory would be prohibitively expensive and morally unacceptable, though much of public policy has qualities of (unsystematic) experiment about it. Some scientific advance has been made in economics and psychology – for we do understand much more about how markets work or the mind functions. But the progress has not been such that economists or political scientists have any consensus about predicting the future. Indeed, if social science could predict, that knowledge itself would undo the theories that generated it. Atoms do not reflect on their behaviour, but humans do, and they would very quickly learn to evade, or profit by, expectations about behaviour. Matters are not helped by the continuous revolution in social affairs that is driven along by advances in the natural sciences. Where basic conditions are in such continuous upheaval, it is difficult to establish any foundation for understanding.

Nevertheless, social knowledge does accumulate in a slow and difficult manner. Our understanding of our own and our planet's history improves steadily. We also learn lessons about better and worse forms of government and economy. We have invented complex markets and political systems such as federalism. In this century we have learned that absolute monarchy is not a sensible form of government for advanced industrial states, and that communism is less effective in producing prosperity and happiness than liberal market economies. We know that democracies seldom go to war with each other. We are currently experimenting to find the best balance between market logic and social welfare.

But for all its ambiguities, knowledge is still one of the sought-after keys to power, both within and between societies. There is thus an abiding interest in how to create knowledge, and how to shape societies so that they can not only use, reproduce and improve the knowledge they contain, but pass that growing legacy on to future generations. These imperatives often pull in opposing directions. Creating, using, reproducing, improving and passing on knowledge are best done in open societies. But exploiting knowledge for commercial, military or political power frequently requires secrecy. The battle over private versus public knowledge is endemic to contemporary society, both domestic and international. Within states it takes the form of struggles over freedom of information, between states it gives rise to vast intelligence services whose job is to probe the strategic secrets of other states while protecting the strategic knowledge of their own. The contradiction is that private knowledge can enhance the short-term power of those who hold it, but societies that exercise too much control over knowledge tend to be outperformed in the long run by those that are more open.

Because knowledge is one of the keys to power, all contemporary societies have to relate to it in three fundamental ways: (1) they have to preserve accumulated knowledge, disseminate it to the population, and pass it on to future generations; (2) they have to create and/or absorb new knowledge; and (3) they have to apply knowledge to the pursuit of goals such as welfare, security, justice and power.

The preservation and transmission of knowledge is rooted in language. Ever since the invention of language, there has been an accelerating improvement in the means with which humans can preserve and transmit knowledge, and as methods of communicating changed, so did power relationships. Originally, and for tens of thousands of years, there was only spoken language and human memory. Then, around five thousand years ago, when writing was developed, knowledge could be more effectively preserved, communicated, and passed through the generations. Those who could read and write had power. The spread of printing from the fifteenth century onward made possible a much wider distribution of knowledge, and laid the foundations for today's literate mass societies. During the twentieth century, a virtual explosion of recording and transmission technologies enabled speech, sound and pictures to be accumulated and broadcast on a gigantic scale. Control of such media – radio, cinema, television, and now the internet – conferred power, and became intimately bound up with the political life of modern mass societies, both democratic and totalitarian. The 'global village' was now a reality. In 1969 much of the world was able to watch, in real time, when humans first set foot on the moon. Yet it is not good enough simply to have the physical means of communication such as satellites or mobile phones. There also need to be appropriate institutions and a climate of thinking conducive to openness. Authoritarian systems that manage the media too strictly, end up limiting the flow of new ideas.

The babel of human languages has always been an obstruction to wider communities of communication, and lingua francas have been a common solution. These are languages – usually, but not always, those of the present or immediately past dominant power – that get taken up to make communication across cultures easier. In their times and places, Akkadian, Chinese, Swahili, Greek, Latin, and French have all played this role. Lingua francas have often been driven by the needs of commerce, but now science and entertainment are equally important. For various reasons the language in which this book was written has become the most important language to learn in the late twentieth century. Such primacy is not due to its superior qualities as much as because it is used by the two greatest powers of the past 250 years, Great Britain and the United States. The power of these two countries was not based on English, but because the countries were powerful, use of English has become a tool of power.

All modern societies seek to disseminate knowledge into their populations through formal processes of education. Unless they do so successfully, they will lose out in the competition for wealth and power. Ideally, education is not just about learning facts, for in a fast-moving knowledge environment, facts change. What is more essential is to teach people how to find the facts they need, how to evaluate information, and how to think – in short, teaching them how to use fully the remarkable instrument that lies between their ears. The most powerful and successful societies have been those that maximised the skills and opportunities of their citizens.

Many obstacles intervene to obstruct this ideal, and despite the potential rewards, it is seldom achieved on any large scale. One problem is that mass education has other functions, not least to socialise citizens into the norms of society. Those norms often restrict and distort what can be taught – look for example, at the national bias in almost any school history text book. Because knowledge is power, its open dissemination easily threatens the foundations of existing authority. It may even be rejected, whether valid or not, because of its association with authority. And then there are the debates about methods of education and about how much society can afford to spend on it. There is also a deluge of rival information, often of dubious quality, that saturates society via the media and the internet. Success in education remains a key to current and future power of both people and states. Yet this apparently obvious self-interest has not been able to transcend the struggle between openness and secrecy even in the societies where openness is most strongly prized. What are we to make of the weakening of literacy in some of our most advanced societies?

As well as being able to preserve and transmit knowledge, societies also need to be able to create new knowledge, or failing that absorb it from the places where it is being created. New knowledge is essential to maintain the cycle of product innovation and growth on which the political stability of capitalism rests. Without it, growth would stagnate. Then the relatively benign politics of dealing with inequalities of distribution when the pie is expanding, would be replaced by the much nastier business of fighting over the distribution of a static or shrinking pie.

Nobel prizes by year, 1991–95	
Nobel Prize for Physics, 1965–95	
1965	Richard Feynman, Tomonaga Shinichiro, and Julian Seymour Schwinger
1966	Alfred Kastler
1967	Hans Albrecht Bethe
1968	Luis W. Alvarez
1969	Murray Gell-Mann
1970	Louis Eugene Neel and Hans Olof Alfven
1971	Dennis Gabor
1972	John Bardeen, Leon N. Cooper, and John Robert Schreiffer
1973	Leo Esaki, Ivar Giaever, and Brian D. Josephson
1974	Martin Ryle and Antony Hewish
1975	Aage N. Bohr, Ben Roy Mottelson, and James Rainwater
1976	Burton Richter and Samuel Chao Chung Ting
1977	Philip W. Anderson, Sir Nevill F. Mott, and John H. Van Vleck
1978	Peter Kapitza, Amo A. Penzias, and Robert W. Wilson
1979	Steven Weinberg, Sheldon L. Glashow, and Abdus Salam
1980	James W. Cronin and Val L. Fitch
1981	Nicolaas Bloembergen, Arthur Schawlow, and Kai M. Siegbahn
1982	Kenneth G. Wilson
1983	Subrahmanyan Chandrasekhar and William A. Fowler
1984	Carlo Rubbia and Simon van der Meere
1985	Klaus von Klitzing
1986	Emest Ruska, Gerd Binnig, and Heinrich Rohrer
1987	K. Alex Muller and J. Georg Bednorz
1988	Leon M. Lederman, Melvin Schwartz, and Jack Steinberger
1989	Norman F. Ramsey, Hans G. Dehmelt, and Wolfgang Paul
1990	Richard E. Taylor, Jerome I. Friedman, and Henry W. Kendall
1991	Pierre-Gilles de Gennes
1992	Georges Charpak
1993	Russell A. Hulse and Joseph H. Taylor, Jr.
1994	Clifford G. Shull and Bertram N. Brockhouse
1995	Martin L. Perl and Frederick Reines

Nobel Prize for Chemistry, 1965–95	
1965	Robert Burns Woodward
1966	Robert S. Milliken
1967	Manfred Eigen, Ronald George Wreyford Norrish, and George Porter
1968	Lars Onsager
1969	Derek H.R. Barton and Odd Hassel
1970	Luis Federico Leloir
1971	Gerhard Herzberg
1972	Stanford Moore, William Howard Stein, and Christian B. Anfinsen
1973	Ernst Otto Fischer and Geoffrey Wilkinson
1974	Paul J. Flory
1975	John Warcup Cornforth and Vladimir Prelog
1976	William Nunn Lipscomb
1977	Ilya Prigogine
1978	Peter Mitchell
1979	Herbert C. Brown and Georg Wittig
1980	Paul Berg, Walter Gilbert, and Frederick Sanger
1981	Kenichi Fukui and Roald Hoffman
1982	Aaron Klug
1983	Henry Taube
1984	R. Bruce Merrifield
1985	Herbert A. Hauptman and Jerome Karle
1986	Dudley R. Herschbach, Yuan T. Lee, and John C. Polanyi
1987	Donald J. Cram, Charles J. Pedersen, and Jean-Marie Lehn
1988	Johann Deisenhofer, Robert Huber, and Hartmut Michel
1989	Thomas R. Cech and Sidney Altman
1990	Elias James Corey
1991	Richard R. Ernst
1992	Rudolph A. Marcus
1993	Kary B. Mullis and Michael Smith
1994	George A. Olah
1995	Paul Crutzen, F. Sherwood Rowland, and Mario Molina

Despite their critical role, the sources of innovation are not well understood. In pursuit of it, societies support the often seemingly fruitless form of thinking known as research, usually embedded in the higher ranks of the education system. That is often the rationale for arcane theory or expensive laboratories, whose success is difficult to measure but is often trumpeted in the form of Nobel prizes. It is the nature of innovation that one does not know where it will come from, but in recent centuries it has come overwhelmingly from the Atlantic world. Yet a successful economic and political system at the end of the millennium is one that delivers constant innovation and effective transmission of knowledge. Despite its obvious inefficiencies and idiocies, a system that allows individuals maximum freedom to produce ideas seems to work better than one which attempts to order the creation of knowledge. Innovation springs from the constant challenge of ideas in competitive debate. Communism and various forms of authoritarian government that suppressed such debate largely failed to sustain themselves in the long-term competition, even though they achieved some success. Innovation could be 'planned' only in short bursts and only in specific fields. In order to generate new knowledge over the long haul, systems and opportunities need to be open. Gains from knowledge had to reward the innovator so as to stimulate further ambition. Innovation is by definition an open process, and closed systems cannot compete in its production, at least for any length of time. Neither can they absorb knowledge from outside without threatening their system of authority.

No society has yet found an ideal way to support effective research. As with education, the same questions about threats to authority and limits to resources arise. So too do the questions about openness versus secrecy, and free versus 'policy-relevant' research. Openness works best to generate new knowledge, but secrecy is often the key to extracting the rewards of power or wealth that new knowledge offers. Innovators dare not let others steal a march, yet they also dare not restrict knowledge too tightly, lest they kill off the innovative spirit that lays the golden eggs. The difficulty of these choices is reflected in the peculiar sight of some of the most liberal governments imposing increasingly tight control on the direction of research in the name of economic efficiency.

As well as being able to preserve, transmit and create knowledge, societies need to be able to use it in pursuit of social goals. As with the creation of knowledge, how this is best done is a bit of a mystery. Open societies seem to be generally better at it, but closed ones can successfully focus on particular developments, particularly military ones, for sustained periods. To be good at creating knowledge is not necessarily to be good at utilising it, as the oft-cited case of Britain illustrates. Even among open societies it is not clear how best to exploit knowledge. The liberal panacea of leaving it to the market discriminates in favour of projects with short-term returns, and may ignore

13-year-olds' average score in TIMSS* (Int average = 500)

	Maths		Science	
1	Singapore	643	Singapore	607
2	South Korea	607	Czech Republic	574
3	Japan	605	Japan	571
4	Hong Kong	588	South Korea	565
5	Belgium (F†)	565	Bulgaria	565
6	Czech Republic	564	Netherlands	560
7	Slovakia	547	Slovenia	560
8	Switzerland	545	Austria	558
9	Netherlands	541	Hungary	554
10	Slovenia	541	England	552
11	Bulgaria	540	Belgium (F†)	550
12	Austria	539	Australia	545
13	France	538	Slovakia	544
14	Hungary	537	Russia	538
15	Russia	535	Ireland	538
16	Australia	530	Sweden	535
17	Ireland	527	United States	534
18	Canada	527	Canada	531
19	Belgium (W‡)	526	Germany	531
20	Thailand	522	Norway	527
21	Israel	522	Thailand	525
22	Sweden	519	New Zealand	525
23	Germany	509	Israel	524
24	New Zealand	508	Hong Kong	522
25	England	506	Switzerland	522
26	Norway	503	Scotland	517
27	Denmark	502	Spain	517
28	United States	500	France	498
29	Scotland	498	Greece	497
30	Latvia	493	Iceland	494
31	Spain	487	Romania	486
32	Iceland	487	Latvia	485
33	Greece	484	Portugal	480
34	Romania	482	Denmark	478
35	Lithuania	477	Lithuania	476
36	Cyprus	474	Belgium (W‡)	471
37	Portugal	454	Iran	470
38	Iran	428	Cyprus	463
39	Kuwait	392	Kuwait	430
40	Colombia	385	Colombia	411
41	South Africa	354	South Africa	326

*Third International Maths and Science Study †Flanders ‡Wallonia
Source: TIMSS.

Maths: teaching hours per year v TIMSS score

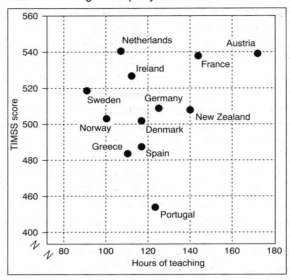

Sources: TIMSS; OECD

State spending per pupil*, $'000 PPP 1993

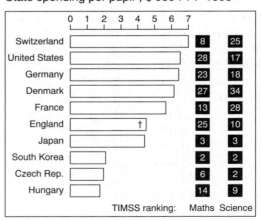

Sources: TIMSS; OECD
*Secondary
† Average for whole of Britain

socially or militarily important opportunities. Given the great costs of high-technology development, even the governments of market economies are keen to 'pick winners' among national companies in the hope that they can save money. But while such national champions may have the odd success, it is unlikely to be sustained over time. Large and coddled companies of this sort lose their competitive edge. Bright entrepreneurs attack them from the outside and innovation develops outside the planned market. In such a system, many small companies fail, but some, such as Microsoft, soar past state-directed companies or even large behemoths such as IBM.

Those societies that are most successful at exploiting knowledge (even if they didn't create it) become relatively rich and powerful. But as new scientific knowledge reshapes both the economy and society, the conditions necessary to get the most out of the most advanced knowledge change. Societies that once had a successful formula (Britain, again) lose headway, and societies that are better adapted to the new conditions surge forward, sometimes, like Korea and Taiwan, from a low starting base. Although the industrial revolution is too young for us to know for sure, it seems that no state, or even collection of states, manages to stay permanently on top, though some, like the United States and Germany, do seem remarkably capable of staying in the top rank for many decades, and perhaps centuries. As other states in the northern hemisphere have also found, success increases their ability to continue to invest in education and systems that will keep them ahead in the knowledge business. For that reason alone, the gap with most of the poorer world is likely to grow. Societies which cannot afford the latest means of transmission will not only be less effective places to do business, but they will also be less effective places for the learning and transmission of new knowledge. Scholars not wired to the internet suffer from a lack of information and speed of exchange, as do unwired companies or even governments. Some poor countries can buy cellular phone systems and skip the wiring phase. Most can buy modern libraries, but there seems to be no way to stop the best innovators in poor countries migrating to richer states where opportunities are greater, and knowledge networks more dense. In a liberalised world, where the skilled and the wealthy have almost limitless mobility, it may be difficult to balance the extremely uneven distribution of knowledge and power that history has bequeathed us.

But there are also costs to success. Knowledge-driven societies expose themselves to relentless forces of change. New ideas breed new technologies. These change lifestyles, educational needs, employment prospects and social relations. They may virtually eliminate whole classes (and class cultures) just as the industrial revolution did to the peasantry, and as the information revolution is doing to many unskilled and semi-skilled workers. Changes in production, transportation and markets kill some towns and cities and breathe new life into others. The individual and social stress caused by life in a knowledge-driven market leave some people hankering after a simpler and more stable life, often envisaged as the supposed pastoral bliss of peasant societies. It is sometimes disorienting to live in a society, as in much of Western Europe, where agricultural economies were replaced by industrial and then by service-oriented economies in less than a lifetime. But these transitions have been the key to maintaining prosperity. In the late twentieth century, it is the service sector, whether it be education or software programmers, that will produce the innovation, the new knowledge, the power and the prosperity for most people.

But before the rich countries become too sanguine about their lead in innovation, it is worth reflecting on just how little we know about knowledge and its effects. We have no idea whether progress is linear. We can recognise great breakthroughs in the past – the wheel or writing – but these have been exploited unevenly depending on other forces at work. The invention of steam power is generally recognised as a great breakthrough, but it was known by the ancient Greeks and only really exploited in the eighteenth century. We do not know enough about the surrounding forces that made it possible for innovation to be fully exploited, but such knowledge about knowledge is vital. Neither do we know how well social and political structures will be able to withstand the constant battering of change. Will open societies succeed in creating and applying new knowledge only to find that they have undermined their own internal stability, or will the fruits of change be able to buy off the stress that it causes? Will opening societies to the fruits of knowledge expose them to dangerous developments? Some would argue that nuclear technology has already done this. Will genetic engineering be a monstrous transformation or open a vast new potential for human happiness? Will the market-dominated social forces we have set in play make us make the wrong choice about what knowledge to unleash into our societies?

CAPITAL

10

The use of capital[1] affects the whole of society. If capital is efficient, then societies can grow and prosper. If it is inefficient, societies stagnate and have to struggle over the distribution of scarce resources. If capital is closely tied to society in the form of national economies, then distinctive development projects (like those in mercantilist and totalitarian states) are possible. If capital is largely detached from particular societies, operating in an open international system, the picture is quite different. Distinctive national development projects become impossible, the pressure for uniform rules between and within states rises, and the capacity of governments to manage their societies becomes much weaker. These two issues intersect when the requirements for efficiency dictate the scale on which capital operates, for example whether on the scale of states, regions and empires, as during the 1930s, or globally, as at the end of the twentieth century. The relationship between capital, the state system and society is what analysts call the international political economy.

Economists assume that people are motivated by the desire for wealth, and this half truth does indeed tell us a lot about society. Although some people seek happiness through virtue, most seem

[1] By *capital* we mean generally the material wealth of society, and especially the wealth available for, or capable of, use in the production of further wealth, and the class of people who own and/or control it.

to associate it with prosperity. Individuals in their collective form of states are even more pragmatic, tending to seek prosperity and its associated goal of power, to the exclusion of nearly everything else. It may seem paradoxical to some that truly prosperous modern societies chose to spend some of their capital cleaning up the natural resources that they once polluted in search of a narrow definition of wealth. Putting salmon back in the Thames river or restoring the incomparable beauty that once was Japan's Inland Sea are cases in point. They also result in an increase in Gross National Product, but their value is very different from that derived from the once bellowing petrochemical plants.

GNP of Canada, USA, Australia, Sweden, UK (Constant US $)

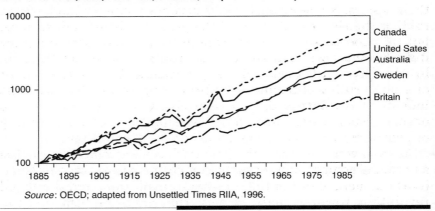

Source: OECD; adapted from Unsettled Times RIIA, 1996.

Thus at the end of the fifth millennium of civilisation, we are not only still learning about the meaning of prosperity, we are also still learning about how prosperity is obtained. The recipe for prosperity, like virtue, has many elements that have to be carefully blended. Economic power requires the effective marshalling of the talents of people, old and new knowledge, technology and resources, all within the context of social order and international security (which traditionally has meant deploying military power). The historical record on prosperity has been very uneven. Many paths have been tried with varying degrees of success and longevity, but there is no questioning the extraordinary overall increases of the last five hundred, and especially of the last two hundred years. These increases have not been universal, and have been unevenly distributed even where they are strongest. But by historical standards a truly remarkable number of people (both absolutely and relative to the total of humankind) now live in conditions of unprecedented material welfare. Two things seem clear. First is that the paths to prosperity will undoubtedly continue to evolve. Second is that, unless there is a major environmental catastrophe, there is little reason to believe that humankind will abandon its search for continuing economic growth.

Historically, there were two great pathways to prosperity: trading and raiding. Most of the great city-states and empires of premodern times accumulated wealth through combining both. Their control of trade routes for luxury goods provided a flow of taxes, and their military ability to raid neighbours and extract loot or tribute was an additional way of replenishing their coffers. Nomadic barbarians perhaps put more emphasis on raiding the rich storehouses of the great agrarian civilisations, but they too played a crucial role in trade, often providing key links in the trans-Eurasian trade routes known as the Silk Roads. This wealth was generally concentrated for the benefit of a small ruling elite, and its military apparatus. Only with the industrial revolution did mass production of goods begin to occur on such a scale as to make possible progressive widening of prosperity to larger proportions of the population.

As we saw in chapter 1, the twentieth century can be viewed as a period of struggle amongst the competing pathways to prosperity that emerged out of the industrial revolution, and the social revolution towards mass society that industrialism created. Traditional autocracies, as in Russia, were too slow to redistribute wealth and power, and were quickly eliminated. Two varieties of totalitarianism, which sought to fuse capital and state in ambitious and often expansionist development models, had a brief but spectacular run. Fascism tied national capital to ultra-nationalist ideology in a bid to create top nations. Communism tried to eliminate the capitalist classes altogether, subordinating everything to the state in a bid for an egalitarian and cosmopolitan development model. Both experiments succumbed to militarism, fascism so much so that it had to be crushed by a coalition of liberal-democratic and communist states. Communism lasted a few decades longer. Its attraction to those badly exploited by rapacious elites was obvious, but it failed both on grounds of economic inefficiency, and because it replaced one exploitative elite with another. It failed to stimulate individuals

Growth of real GDP, 1966–2005
(current 1994 dollars and 1987 prices and exchange rates–average annual percentage growth)

	1994 GDP (US$ billions)	1966–73	1974–90	1991–94	1994	1995 estimate	1996–2005 forecast
World	**25,677**	**5.1**	**3.0**	**1.5**	**2.9**	**2.8**	**3.5**
High-income	**20,397**	**4.8**	**2.8**	**1.7**	**3.0**	**2.5**	**2.9**
Industrial countries	19,677	4.7	2.7	1.6	2.9	2.4	2.8
G-7 countries	17,174	4.7	2.8	1.6	2.9	2.3	2.8
United States	6,738	3.0	2.6	2.5	4.1	3.2	–
Japan	4,590	10.0	4.0	1.2	0.5	0.4	–
G-4 Europe	5,296	4.4	2.3	0.9	2.9	2.5	–
Germany[a]	1,835	4.3	2.0	1.3	2.9	2.1	–
Other industrial	2,500	4.9	2.3	1.2	3.1	3.2	2.7
Other high-income	720	8.8	5.6	6.2	5.9	5.5	5.5
Low- and middle-income	**5,280**	**6.9**	**3.6**	**1.0**	**2.5**	**3.9**	**5.3**
Excluding Eastern Europe and former Soviet Union	4,490	6.2	3.8	5.0	5.5	4.9	5.4
Asia	1,910	5.9	6.8	7.7	8.5	8.2	7.2
East Asia and Pacific	1,520	7.9	7.9	9.4	9.7	9.2	7.9
China	520	8.5	8.7	12.9	12.2	10.2	–
Korea, Rep. of	380	11.2	8.5	6.6	8.0	9.3	–
Indonesia	175	6.4	6.7	7.6	7.3	7.5	–
South Asia	395	3.7	4.9	3.9	5.7	5.5	5.4
India	295	3.7	4.8	3.8	6.1	5.8	–
Latin America and the Caribbean	1,627	6.4	2.6	3.6	4.9	0.9	3.8
Brazil	555	9.8	3.6	2.2	5.8	4.2	–
Mexico	380	6.8	3.4	2.5	3.6	–6.9	–
Argentina	280	4.3	0.5	7.6	7.4	–3.2	–
Europe and Central Asia	1,030	6.9	3.3	–9.0	–8.4	–0.7	4.3
Russian Federation[b]	380	6.9	3.6	–10.6	–12.6	–4.0	–
Turkey	130	6.1	4.5	3.2	–5.3	5.3	–
Poland	90	7.3	0.2	1.8	5.2	7.0	–
Middle East and North Africa	510	8.6	1.4	2.4	2.1	2.5	2.9
Iran, Islamic Rep.	65	10.2	–0.3	5.2	2.4	2.7	–
Algeria	42	6.3	4.4	–0.6	–1.0	3.5	–
Egypt	43	3.8	7.3	1.1	2.0	2.5	–
Sub-Saharan Africa	278	4.7	2.2	0.7	1.7	3.8	3.8
South Africa	120	4.7	2.1	–0.1	2.4	3.4	–
Nigeria	35	6.5	1.1	2.8	2.5	0.5	–

Note: Growth rates over intervals are computed using least squares method.
a. Data prior to 1991 cover Federal Republic of Germany.
b. Data prior to 1992 cover former Soviet Union.
Source: World Bank data and staff estimates.

through an appeal to their desire for prosperity, and beyond the early stages of industrialisation it failed to generate enough wealth to redistribute effectively.

Liberal democracy was the great winner in this competition. It drew its sustenance from the Enlightenment's notion of the rights of the individual. It nurtured political revolutions in Great Britain and most notably in its offshoot, the United States of America. These states found that prosperity was best achieved when individuals were freer to choose how they should become more prosperous and were less subject to arbitrary elites who took away the fruits of their skills and labours. Thus was born the liberal market economy. The defeat of communism through economic competition was only possible because the liberal market economy also learned to adapt. It borrowed the essential notion that there needed to be at least a modicum of redistribution of wealth in order to avoid the worst aspects of class warfare. Some class rivalry was deemed necessary to stimulate competition and a will to succeed, but the process required benign government management. The right balance between government and the private sector – the idea of a social market economy – remains subject to debate, with the intellectual pendulum swinging back and forth between market liberalism and more communitarian, social democratic values. To date this remains the most efficient, and thus the most powerful, way to generate and use capital.

With the death of 'really existing socialism', the wiping out of totalitarian capitalism, and the near extinction of monarchical capitalism (except in the Gulf), by the end of the twentieth century much more attention began to be focused on the myriad forms of modern market economies. Within this system, the relative degree of state intervention or authoritarian government can vary a great deal, as can levels of development, natural resources, and political culture, though there was increasing pressure on authoritarian capitalism in Latin America, Africa and Asia. There was a hope, and in some places a contested assumption, that market economies would tend to generate democratic, or at least pluralist societies. Teachers at business schools and management gurus love to offer typologies of market economies, but the fact is that the economic systems keep changing. In any case the range of factors that make up economic success in a market economy are far too large to fit into a single theory of competitiveness or success. The search for a single model of success in this tapestry of economic systems is also pointless because people choose different governments in order to experiment with new (and sometimes old) ideas. Under such circumstances, what generates comparative economic advantage differs from society to society, and is constantly changing everywhere.

By the late twentieth century it was possible to declare that there is at least one consistent process at work. Nearly all economies that generate substantial prosperity inevitably make a transition from predominantly agricultural production to one based on industry, and then eventually to one where the service sector dominates. Not all peoples have moved very far along this track, but it is worth noting, especially for those who doubt that there is something called 'progress', that no state ever goes backwards (unless it is destroyed in war). It is also worth noting that 'service' is not just changing sheets in hotels. Service sector workers include the authors of this book, software writers or brain surgeons. Most of the price of a car is for services (software for robots, healthcare for workers), not steel or assembly.

The law of comparative advantage has ensured that nearly all developed economies are increasingly service economies, because it is cheaper to buy labour-intensive agricultural and industrial (and even service) products from poorer countries where labour costs are lower. Even in rich parts of the world such as Canada and Australia where food and raw material exports are significant, the economy is still overwhelmingly dominated by the service sector. These trends have been made possible, and accelerated, by the much noted globalisation of economic forces. When a Canadian's car comes from Korea, the mortgage is owed to a Japanese bank, and the fruit on the table comes from New Zealand, it is clear that competition is more intense, and product standards generally higher, than ever before. The aggregation of firms and markets makes the defences of individuals, trade unions, firms or even countries mostly fruitless in face of the powerful waves in the global market economy.

The emergence of a global economy, at least for the powerful rich states, seems to have occurred in two stages. In the late nineteenth and early twentieth century there was talk of a global economy, and in many senses it was only in the late twentieth century that the degree of interdependence among the major market economies returned to the levels reached early in the twentieth century. The economic depression of the 1930s had revealed deep flaws in the management of global capital and trade policies, and the damage done to the world economy lasted for decades. It was not until the sustained growth starting in the 1950s that global interdependence grew back in strength. In its late twentieth-century variant the extent of the globalisation was far greater, even if the ratios of trade to GDP were not very different from eighty years earlier. Both private sector organisation (in the form of tens of thousands of multinational firms), and state-led organisation (in the form of numerous international economic rules, regimes and intergovernmental institutions such as the WTO, the World Bank and the IMF), were far more extensively developed and deeply rooted than in the earlier phase of globalisation.

As the apparent 'golden age' of capitalism gathered pace, the beneficiaries began to sing the praises of these global forces. Governments found it harder to buck the market. A new socialist government in France in the early 1980s had to abandon out-dated ideas about massive state spending in a matter of months because the international money markets doubted the good sense of the French government. Interest rates are now set more by global trends than national ones. The absence of most currency controls made business and travel much easier and more efficient. Companies, many of whom now seek funds on global markets and are often taken over in complex international mergers and cross-ownerships, are forced to adapt faster to new ideas. Entrepreneurs and intrapreneurs are made more powerful and effective by the easier access to money and other factors of production.

Liberal enthusiasts argued that as global openness made markets larger and more accessible, and economies everywhere more efficient, so more people could be added to the circle of prosperity. Individuals can be appealed to as consumers having the right to maximise their choices and advantages. Why should they accept a government that tells them they must pay more for food, fuel, clothes or electronic gadgets, or accept lower quality goods, just because local workers want higher pay or secure jobs? It is one thing for people to permit protectionism to remain in place when they have known little else – viz. Japan – but quite another matter to ask people to go back to a less efficient system when they have experienced the consumer benefits of economic openness. And now that the ideological confrontation with totalitarianism is over, the need for the state as a military protector is much reduced. As a consequence, the state, with all of its inefficiencies and constraints on market forces, can be rolled back, allowing global market forces a much larger role in shaping society. The momentum behind this liberal revolution, flush with victory over its rivals, is truly formidable, and there is little doubt that it will be the main shaper of the political agenda for decades to come.

And yet there are also reasons to be wary of unbounded liberal optimism. As we have already suggested, there is something intuitively simplistic about simply totting up higher GDP figures and suggesting people are more prosperous. If American streets are unsafe and private law enforcement agencies contribute to GDP, does that make the United States a richer place than a country with a less divided society? What is the value of clean air? If a bridge collapses because of poor workmanship, does it make sense to count the rebuilding costs as increased GDP? These questions are now asked more often in rich countries who are developing more nuanced views of prosperity. But for poor countries still climbing the GDP ladder, such nit-picking is pointless.

More importantly, modern capitalism has important flaws, and in its new global form constitutes a vast social experiment whose outcome is far from certain. Concern focuses on two questions: what happens to society when the state is hollowed out by exposure to unrestrained market forces? And how stable are the globalised economic arrangements in their own right?

The rolling back of the state is a direct consequence of the globalisation of capital. As capital has sought greater efficiency by increasing the scale of its operations, it has become increasingly de-linked both from labour and national society. Capital now moves freely in search of the cheapest labour and resources and the highest returns on investment. Unlike in the past, it shares no identity with the societies in which it operates, and has little reason to invest for social purposes. The implications of this for workers and their companies are far-reaching. Competitiveness is now much more between firms than between countries. The firms compete within their own country, but more importantly with firms in other parts of the world. They seek capital and labour on a global scale, and not surprisingly more than 50% of trade among developed states takes place within single firms. The value of factories and subsidiaries owned by companies outside their home countries is growing at twice the rate of world trade and nearly ten times the rate of growth in the world economy. In order to sell something in a foreign country companies are more likely to make it there than to send it there. One-fifth of the entire world economy is made up of sales by foreign factories and subsidiaries. Skills and pay scales have to increase or decrease depending on how they compare with those in other countries, widening the income gap between elites and the bulk of the population. Production shifts more rapidly as firms are bought out on world stock markets and their futures are traded forward on world futures markets. The ability of national governments to legislate for individuals and companies is restricted by the concern that they will move elsewhere.

The upside of this divorce between capital and society is that it makes any return to fascism or communism almost impossible. The downside is that it separates elites from the general population, and leaves a weakened state to deal with the consequences of ever more intense competition and rapid change. In the global markets there is surplus production capacity in almost every product, from cars to clothes, from aircraft to apples, and from weapons to wheat. Although some countries win, many must lose, watching their previous sources of prosperity go down the drain. It is not clear that the socio-political side of this economic equation can remain stable even in the rich world. As the welfare state unravels, and some 10–12% of the society remains in seemingly permanent unemployment, the appeal of consumer logic weakens. To be more than a subsistence consumer, one has also to be part of the production process. Even the viability of democracy might be questioned if a substantial proportion of society becomes permanently alienated from the economy. The problem has many similarities to that discussed above under knowledge: how can societies adapt to relentless and fundamental pressures for change without losing their cohesion, and therefore their political stability? It is not clear how government is to function when capital goes international but societies and their politics remain firmly rooted on a more local scale. It seems entirely possible for capital to flourish, while significant sections of the population even in core countries do badly. One symptom of this growing mismatch is the way in which economic statistics are still collected and presented on a national basis even though most economic activity has long since gone global.

Such practices distort both our understanding and our political perception of what is going on.

Concern about the stability of the global market has resonances from the unbounded optimism of the 1920s and the crash that followed. Many lessons have been learned from that experience, and many barriers erected to prevent its recurrence. But it would be foolish to suggest that people fully understand the continuing risks in the fluidity, openness and intense competition of the new global economy. This is especially so in the fast-moving world of finance. Poorly understood derivatives markets can bring rapid ruin even to large companies, and huge speculative financial flows can wreck national currencies. Easy money can mean quick and deep debt. Credit risks are calculated on shorter terms, making firms subject to whims of confidence. Longer-term prospects may be missed. Being subject to global forces undermines a clear sense of accountability and damages the sense of belonging that often stimulates greater effort. And of course, fluidity in the factors of production also makes possible the dark side of the open economy: organised international criminal mafias with annual turnovers well in excess of that of many countries, trading in socially destructive goods ranging from drugs and slaves, through refugees, endangered species, and banned chemicals, to armaments and nuclear technology.

These problems notwithstanding, the trend towards an increasingly global economy is probably irreversible. Short of some major catastrophe or breakdown, the liberal momentum is too strong. The persistent return to the challenge of building a global economy suggests that it is an inherent part of the logic of capitalism. The 1930s reminds us that the process is sometimes dangerous, but there does seem to be a long-term trend towards globalisation. Such a development is in keeping with the late stages of the process of making a single human space. After a false dawn at the start of century, we seem to have reached a point where trade is likely to remain global. This is not a picture of a confident global economy full of self-assured companies and secure individuals. The system is in fact based on competition and insecurity, though now the threat is much less of nuclear obliteration, and much more of economic immiseration. It would be foolish to suppose that unrestrained market principles will engender international co-operation. And even if somehow the richest states could get together and manage their competition, they would soon find themselves challenged by new firms and states unbound by cartel conditions.

Hence despite the bluster of liberal triumphalism, there remains the fear that global economic interdependence is a fragile idea. It depends on sufficient common good being generated by a mass of competing individual interests. It requires the maintenance of an open trading system with a high degree of transparency despite the costs that this imposes on participating societies – even winning ones like Japan and South Korea. The World Trade Organisation (WTO) was established in 1995 in order to help entrench this open system and establish an agreed method of dispute settlement. At the same time, many of the states who set up the WTO formed increasingly coherent regional trading units. They are not yet blocs and for the most part not yet closed, but the existence of the European Union (EU) and the North American Free Trade Area (NAFTA) suggests that the building blocs are available for a more closed and hostile trading system. Those likely to be outside the core blocs (Russia, Central and Southern Asia, the Middle East and Africa) would find life difficult even if they formed regional blocs of their own. The tension between the globalising thrust of capital and the regionalising response of many states is captured in moves towards super-regional blocs such as Asia-Pacific Economic Co-operation (APEC) and the mooted Transatlantic Free Trade Area. Such super-blocs would almost recreate the WTO, and are seen by some as US-inspired attempts to undermine regionalist tendencies in Europe and East Asia, and to remain a central player in the global political economy.

It is logical more than ironic that as national protectionism becomes less likely (because the costs in loss of efficiency and welfare would be too high, and because national capital, with its protectionist instincts, is now much weaker than international capital, with its liberal ones), inter-bloc protectionism grows more likely. For all the reasons that people seek a sense of belonging but find they damage their prosperity by doing so on a national basis, so they may find some comfort in a larger unit that is something less than global, but better able to compete in a tough market system. Regional blocs offer both the possibility of a stronger operating base in an open world economy, and a relatively secure bastion into which to retreat should the global economy once again fall into crisis. For these reasons government officials and managers of firms may accept or even demand some form of regionalism. They will accept the restraint this imposes on their powers and prerogatives in return for the insurance and reassurance that it gives them.

The logic of regionalism does not mean that the laws of comparative advantage and the competitive system will fade away. It means that within blocs the calculations between countries will change, for example when high-priced Dutch managers can draw on cheap Polish labour instead of finding themselves in competition with it. One might expect new regional business cultures to develop, replacing national ones and becoming part of the global competition. Regional blocs may provide some solution to the demographic challenges facing some rich societies where there is a small pool of young labour supporting the pensions of a larger number of elderly retirees. Migration can take place within blocs with less damaging consequences than if the national interests of individual states were at stake. The creation of such regions may also help ease some of the problems of disparities of wealth, for the poor peasants of Ukraine may be within an EU just as Mexican labourers will be members of NAFTA.

At the end of the twentieth century, it is clear that economic nationalism at the level of the state carries too great a cost of inefficiency and loss of power and prosperity to be a viable option for major societies. The choice for organising the political economy of the coming century seems to lie between the regional and the global scales. Most likely is some mixture of the two, with the debate about the degrees of mixture between private sector and social market being steadily pushed upward from the state to the regional and global levels. Regions will flourish to the extent that the global system proves unstable, and that individual states prove unable to handle the social and political consequences of exposure to the forces of global capital.

SOVEREIGNTY

11

The main unit in international affairs is still an odd thing called a sovereign state. Sovereignty formally means the claim to self-government covering a specific territory and its inhabitants, and that the state recognises no political authority higher than itself. In practice the state is far from having absolute autonomy. A small country squeezed between two larger neighbours, such as Nepal or Finland, may have to exercise its sovereignty under highly constrained conditions. Thus the fact that sovereignty is both claimed by a state, and that the claim is recognised and accepted by other sovereign states tells us only a limited number of things about how states actually operate in the real world. Nevertheless, the fact that states recognise each other as similar types of entity with the same formal legal status and rights, is the foundation of international society. Beyond such legal formality, differences in power, ideology and interest will determine how states relate to each other. Yet a large degree of erosion in real state sovereignty has taken place in the last part of the twentieth century.

Ideally, sovereignty should be both internally established and externally recognised. That is to say, a state's right to govern should be accepted both by its population and by other states. In some cases these two things do not line up. Taiwan, for example has a firmly established internal sovereignty, but is not formally recognised by many other states because of its unresolved sovereignty claims with China. Somalia, Lebanon and Liberia, on the other hand, hardly exist as states from an internal perspective, but are generally accepted as sovereign by the rest of the international community. In principle, sovereignty means that states have the right to construct whatever form of government best suits them. Whether a state is a democracy (Denmark), a dictatorship (Iraq), a monarchy (Saudi Arabia) or a theocracy (Iran) should not affect its status as sovereign.

This type of decentralised, international political order is usually called 'anarchy'. International anarchy means the absence of world government. It does not mean chaos, for the world is divided into chunks (states) and the more powerful among them order relations among states. Sometimes this system collapses into chaos and war, but often it is quite peaceful and orderly. There has, for example, been no threat of war amongst the Nordic countries for nearly a century, and relations amongst them have been open and friendly. As we saw in Part I the sovereign state is a European invention which has been imposed on the rest of the world. For better or worse, the principle of sovereignty is an important part of international political order.

Regional distribution of locations with at least one major armed conflict, 1989–95

Region[a]	1989	1990	1991	1992	1993	1994	1995
Africa	9	10	10	7	7	7	6
Asia	11	10	8	11	9	9	9
Central and South America	5	5	4	3	3	3	3
Europe	2	1	2	4	5	4	3
Middle East	5	5	5	4	4	5	4
Total	32	31	29	29	28	28	25

[a] Only those regions of the world in which a conflict was recorded for the period 1989–95 are included here.

Source: Uppsala Conflict Data Project.

It was not always so. Before the rise of civilisation, humans lived in bands and tribes. There were no separate political structures, and no political leaders in the modern sense. Nobody held the right to rule, or even to speak for, the rest of the group. One of the frustrations of European empire builders in the Americas and Africa was that they often could not find anyone with sufficient authority to make a treaty on behalf of a tribe. The great empires of the ancient and classical world might superficially look like modern states, but they were not. Such empires were usually collections of city-states, kingdoms and other territories that were held in varying degrees of subordination to an imperial centre ruled by a great king.

Europe's innovation was to invent a political form, the state, in which political authority was highly concentrated, and the territorial domain of that authority was clearly demarcated. To this was added the idea of mutual recognition among states. Inherent in the idea was the principle that by recognising each other, states undertook not to intervene in each other's internal affairs. The right to self-government meant the right to conduct one's domestic business in one's own way. By accepting each other as legally equal entities of the same type, the European states laid down the foundations for international order, and for systematic practices of international law and diplomacy. Mutual recognition among legal equals was, on balance, an advance over relations governed merely by relative power. Although power considerations could and did overwhelm diplomacy and recognition, the aspiration was that there should be a stable system of international relations in which states could regulate their relations by treaty. Within this framework, the European states evolved internally from absolutist autocracy, to modern pluralist democracy. Sovereignty became 'popular' – that is, seen as vested in the population as a whole rather than in the ruler.

Formal sovereignty remains a much sought-after status. Separatists (Quebecois) and exiles (Palestinians) seek recognition for their claim to sovereignty. The rise of nationalism strengthened sovereignty by making legitimate the idea that different cultures should have the right to self-government. Leaders as diverse as Saddam Hussein and Margaret Thatcher argue their respective cases (against the UN, against the EU) in terms of sovereignty. Even communist governments, who might in principle have objected to sovereignty as a false division of the working class, quickly adopted it as a crucial defence of their rights to pursue a different form of government and society from the West. For better or worse, there are no other ideas around to define both the rules about how peoples will relate to their own government, and how those governments will relate to each other.

Sovereignty is nevertheless under serious question. If sovereignty is (mis)understood as an autonomous ability to determine one's own behaviour, then it looks like an idea already half dead. States are so enmeshed in global markets, international rules, regimes, and treaties, and relations of unequal power and influence, to make any pretence of autonomy absurd.

There are three related hard questions about the relevance of sovereignty. First, in a world that is being reshaped by international capital, global knowledge, and rising awareness of collective environmental issues of planetary scale, how long can the idea of having hundreds of self-governing islands of territory survive? What should, and indeed can, the function of sovereign governments be when capital is hollowing out the state?

Second, what is to be done about the inability of some, mostly third world, states to live up to the internal requirements of sovereignty? A not inconsiderable number of post-colonial states have failed to take root, and show few if any signs of being capable of self-government in any meaningful or civilised sense. Rather than earning their recognition as a result of demonstrating a capacity for self-government, as European and some Asian states had to do, these states were given recognition as part of decolonisation in the hope that they would grow into it. For a whole range of reasons, from the poisonous legacies of colonialism to the character of indigenous cultures, some of these states have not worked. Should they still be treated as sovereign by the rest of the international community, or should they be downgraded into some kind of mandate or protectorate status? Should they be allowed to disintegrate and re-form as happened with the former Yugoslavia and Soviet Union?

Third, in an increasingly open and interdependent world, in which a global economy is a ubiquitous driving force, is there any point in trying to claim the continuing relevance of one of the keystones of sovereignty, the principle of non-intervention? The triumph of liberal democracy has already created a new 'standard of civilisation', like that which the imperial European states once used to deny recognition as equals to non-European countries and peoples. This standard is being relentlessly imposed on a wide range of states. Aid, trade, and even diplomatic recognition are made conditional on domestic reforms towards Western-style laws on property rights, human rights, and pluralism. Iraq, which tried to extinguish a neighbouring state, is denied a whole range of military rights. Attempts are made to cut Iran out of the global economy because of its support for Islamic extremists. Trade negotiations often engage directly with distinctive aspects of local cultures.

One way of thinking about these three questions is to look at sovereignty in terms of the three different types of states that currently inhabit the international system. We can call these 'closed', 'open' and 'weak/failed' states. Closed states dominated the international political landscape until quite recently. They represent the classical archetype of a European state right up to the end of the Second World War. They take their sovereignty and their territory seriously, and see themselves as independent, self-reliant and culturally unique entities. They often have distinctive national development policies, and try to keep control over a broad industrial base and an independent set of armed forces. They cultivate dominant identities, often, but not always, nationalist ones, as a means of unifying their populations. Their borders mark real lines of closure against outside economic, political and cultural influences, and their sovereignty is sacrosanct. Closed states take non-intervention very seriously, and typically define a wide range of military, political, economic and cultural factors as threats to national security. Such states shaped our understanding of what it means to be a great power. They still exist. The Soviet Union was a closed great power, and China is evidently trying to become one. Iran and Iraq are closed states aspiring to be powers in their regions. For closed states, sovereignty remains the central principle of existence.

The leading states, and all of the great capitalist powers, have now evolved beyond the closed model. In pursuit of wealth, democracy and individual rights they have taken on an open form. They still retain the trappings of closure such as borders and sovereignty and national identity, but don't take them nearly so seriously as before. Open states have a much more tolerant attitude towards cultural, economic and political interaction. Their borders are more porous and they define a much narrower range of things as threats to national security. In open states civil society has as much or more influence than government. Open states are democratic, but that may matter less than their relentless pluralism and individualism. Citizens focus much more on their individual and collective rights against the state, than they do on their individual and collective responsibilities to it. In many cases the social cohesion of a single overriding national identity has given way to multiculturalism and multiple identities of all sorts, whether to do with gender, culture, sport, work or style. Civil society no longer wants to be contained by the state either economically or socially, though it does still look to the state for some forms of security. Open societies are prosperous and educated, and this has both driven down the size of families, and shrunk the size of the younger generation in relation to those above it. For open states, sovereignty is problematic. In some ways it seems out of date, and even an encumbrance needing to be transcended or replaced. But in other ways it remains an essential foundation, difficult to abandon, or even to ignore, without undercutting the pillars of domestic and international political order.

Weak/failed states are those that have yet to establish, or have lost, effective self-government. They may seem to have strong (in the sense of brutal and dictatorial) governments but these govern by force more than by consent, and their rule often does not extend far beyond the major towns. Society is deeply divided over how and by whom it should be governed, and the right to govern is often contested internally by force. To the extent that government does exist, it fails to penetrate into large sections of society and cannot either extract taxes or impose administration effectively. In other words, weak/failed states have not established internal sovereignty, regardless of whether or not they enjoy external recognition.

Open states hold the major concentrations of power, wealth and organisation in the international system, and it has been their civil societies that have created, and been the main beneficiaries of, the global market. They are the ones pushing against the restraints of sovereignty, yet they are also the ones that invented the system of sovereign states and imposed it on the rest of the world. These states are steadily enmeshing themselves in a thick web of agreements and complex interdependencies that constrain their behaviour. They are participating in the construction of a single economy that contains them all, and which requires that they both open their borders, and substantially harmonise their political, economic and social policies. They are even dependent on each other even for supplies of weapons or strategically crucial components. These states no longer comprise self-contained economies capable of supporting national military mobilisations (as they were less than fifty years ago), and it is not surprising that their military actions are increasingly undertaken jointly.

They remain technically sovereign, but since they share a single economy, and increasingly a single security regime, a single elite culture and a style of government, much of the practical significance of sovereignty is no longer relevant. The richest states in the world are formally sovereign, but they have voluntarily given up elements of sovereignty for the sake of other goods (stability, security, wealth). Citizens of the United States of America carry an American passport, but the key features of their lives are increasingly determined outside the nation's capital. Interest rates are the result of global flows of capital. Rates of taxation cannot be too far out of line with other states in the global market economy or else the USA will lose skilled people and market share. Even high policy questions such as nuclear weapons do not escape, as France discovered with the world-wide reaction to its nuclear tests in 1995.

Increasingly, these states are confused about how to organise their government. On the one hand, it seems clear that most economic issues, and increasingly also many environmental, cultural and political ones, have outgrown the boundaries of single states. For many purposes, the old state is no longer an effective administrative unit. This type of thinking underlies the integration process of the EU, which can be seen as an attempt to create a significant layer of government above the state. On the other hand, even the most open societies still retain strong attachments to their states, and resist attempts to construct wider forms of government. This is most clearly illustrated in the EU, where the process of integration is effectively stalled by the unwillingness of peoples to see their states dissolved into a wider union. The sovereignty of their state may effectively be hollowed out, but still they do not want to abandon it.

Thus, the question remains unanswered: what form of government should open states have, reflecting what distribution of sovereignty? Only extreme liberals believe that markets can be left to run nearly everything, making government redundant. Most believe that political order and security are prior conditions for allowing markets to generate economic prosperity, and that providing them is the function of government. At the moment, we have a mixture of gutted national governments; shaky, half formed and stalled federalist projects; and a variety of weak intergovernmental organisations and regimes such as the WTO, IMF and G7. We are clearly in the presence of an old system breaking down and transforming itself into something new. But at the end of the century, the process of breakdown is much more clearly visible than the 'something new'.

For many weak/failed states, the question is when, or in some cases whether, they will be able to consolidate themselves sufficiently to function as states, both domestically and internationally. Where decolonisation has produced failed states, what should be done? How are peoples to be treated who are not yet apparently capable of self-government to an acceptable 'standard of civilisation'? The post-colonial strategy, supported both by the West and by nearly all the ex-colonial states, was to freeze the colonial boundaries regardless of the mix of peoples they might contain, and try to make workable states within them. This may succeed in some places (South Africa, India) but seems a recipe for disaster in others (Sudan, much of Africa, Pakistan, Afghanistan).

The dilemma is acute. If the existing framework of sovereignty cannot produce stable governments it is far from clear what the best choice is. Pursuing nationalist principles would fragment Africa into some 900 states, creating minority problems that would make the former Yugoslavia look like Switzerland. Despite the rhetoric of Pan-Africanism, there are no political resources that could make federations of the present states any more promising, although this idea might work better in the Arab world, which does have traditions of imperial unity.

Should the rich world intervene to re-colonise failed states in some polite form? Any attempt at re-colonisation would be resisted by both sides: rich states unwilling to take responsibility for expensive, long-term problems with no clear solutions (and no obvious profit), and poor ones desperate to avoid having their dignity once again trampled upon. Or should the rich world say that weak/failed states will have to go through the same process that made the original states in Europe – i.e. nearly a thousand years of shifting boundaries, wars both civil and international, and a long process of violent identity formation and stabilisation of territorial claims? If this choice is made, does the rich world simply stand aside, and coexist with a mirror image of its own earlier savagery, aggression and carnage? Does it try to experiment with various degrees of humanitarian aid and political intervention?

It is sometimes possible to persuade people in an open country that it is in their interest to defend the right of people in a small country to remain free, especially when their freedom helps ensure lower oil prices or a more open global economy. When a conflict is seen to be murderously complex and few vital interests are at stake (as in the Balkans, Afghanistan, the Caucasus or Central Africa, and potentially in many other weak/failed states), it is harder to persuade free and rich people that they should become directly involved. Notionally sovereign governments in the rich world are, on the one hand, pressed by their people to 'do something' about the atrocities they see on their television sets, but on the other hand find that the same people want both a clear sense of limits on costs, and of how bearing burdens will defend or improve their own life or liberty. Some open states are also strongly constrained by the old principle of non-intervention. Although they will happily try to manipulate the governments of other countries, they are much more uncertain about either their rights or their responsibilities when sovereignty itself fails in other countries.

Closed states hang between the weak/failed and open dilemmas. They risk both falling back into weak/failed chaos, and being pulled into the open world before their societies and economies are ready to take the strain. The open world threatens closed states with both inclusion and exclusion. If it includes them, then they are admitted as weak members, and their distinctive development projects are subjected to the homogenising pressures of level playing fields. This is the dilemma of Latin American aspirants to NAFTA, Eastern European and Turkey in relation to the EU, and China in the international economy. If it excludes them, then the closed states are outside the magic circles of development and prosperity, and are faced with the prospect of permanent economic marginalisation. If the open world perceives an ideological or military challenge from a closed state, it can close ranks and squeeze it to death, as was done with the Soviet Union, and as conceivably could be the case with China. By their nature, closed states fear intervention and define a wide range of things as threatening (think of Iranian, Soviet, Saudi and Chinese reactions to penetration by Western styles and media). Also by their nature closed states prize military self-reliance, and are more willing to use force in pursuit of their goals. Saddam did not hesitate to attack Iran or seize Kuwait; India and Pakistan regularly rattle, and occasionally use, sabres against each other, and China apparently thinks nothing of threatening to invade Taiwan and publicly displaying its capability to do so.

This old-fashioned military quality of closed states raises vital questions about how the closed and open worlds relate to each other. The open states have superior military technology, skills and resources, but have abandoned the use of force amongst themselves. They are afraid of costs and casualties, inhibited by the moral dilemmas of using force (even worrying about their opponent's casualties!), disinterested in reviving old-fashioned types of imperialism; and reluctant to get involved unless their interests are directly engaged. The closed states have fewer inhibitions about fighting, and may command considerable military power in their own area.

As noted in chapter 5, some have argued that this is a recipe for two or more worlds of international relations. There may be an open zone of peace, characterised by blurred and hollowed-out sovereignty; and a zone of conflict (or perhaps two zones), containing closed and weak/failed states, which still operate on old rules. What remains unclear is how these three worlds will relate to each other. Will they evolve largely separately, with the open world trying to keep the rest at arms length? Will the open powers be drawn into the old game in the periphery that they have abandoned at the core?

MILITARY POWER

12

Marvel for a moment at the fecundity of the human imagination when it comes to inflicting violence on each other. In the beginning there were just fists, feet and teeth, and simple sticks and stones. Then we developed more sophisticated weapons such as knives, clubs, spears and swords, and soon weapons for striking at a distance, such as slings, javelins, and bows and arrows. Blades got stronger and sharper as metallurgy improved, and bows became more powerful. As early as classical times we bred horses to become cavalry, made fighting ships, invented incendiaries such as Greek fire, and developed heavy throwing weapons for hurling stones against walls. We learned drill, so that large groups of men could fight as a single unit rather than as a rabble of individuals. With the application of gunpowder to the arts of destruction starting in the fourteenth century, we began a process of developing guns, explosives and chemicals that seemed to culminate in the apparent perfection of mass slaughter in the trenches of the First World War, and the carpet bombing of the Second. Then in 1945 we invented the atomic bomb and found we could, for the first time, destroy life on earth. Although nothing could be more catastrophic, we continue to refine ever more accurate, stealthy and compact weapons, and to seek new means of destruction in areas such as biology and directed energy weapons.

As weapons and military organisation have evolved, so too has the style of warfare. Before the widespread use of guns, much combat was man-to-man. Warrior skills and virtues were highly prized. As guns made war more industrial, the emphasis shifted to weapons technology, mass production, and the skills of command and control over larger and widely distributed forces. At the end of the twentieth century, we seem to be moving into information warfare, where elaborate and pervasive surveillance technologies are married to accurate, high-tech means of destruction. High-performance aircraft use laser-guided weapons, cruise missiles follow computer maps to precise locations, and troops are positioned by use of satellites. Such warfare was used on a small scale in the Balkans in 1995, and earlier on a far larger scale in the Gulf in 1991. The trend at the leading edge is towards ever more capital-intensive types of war in which machines play more of the roles, and humans are increasingly insulated from the destruction they inflict.

Acquiring capabilities for mass destruction does not mean that such weapons will be used. The paradox was that even though we invented ever more effective weapons of mass destruction, some of the most effective of these were rarely used, even in an age when we killed more human beings in war than ever before. Knives, guns and bombs remain the most used killing tools even in the last years of the twentieth century. Only relatively small numbers of people have been killed by chemical weapons, and nuclear weapons have only been used twice. By international standards, there are fairly serious institutions in place to try to block, or at least slow down, the spread of weapons of mass destruction.

Perhaps even more significant is that a substantial group of the most advanced states seem to have abandoned war amongst themselves. War, in Clausewitz's famous dictum, is a continuation of politics by other means. This used to be unproblematic. States resorted to war fairly easily and regularly, and for a wide range of reasons, some of them quite trivial. But in the late twentieth century, and especially in open societies, war is increasingly viewed not as a continuation of politics, but as a last resort, to be used sparingly, reluctantly, and only when all other means have failed. This is qualitatively different from earlier types of restraint on the use of force such as those practised by feudal warriors in Europe or Japan, or the aristocratic codes of

International comparisons of defence expenditure and military manpower in 1985, 1994 and 1995

(1995 constant prices)	Defence Expenditure US$m			US$ per capita			% of GDP			Numbers in Armed Forces (000)		Estimated Reservists (000)	Para-military (000)
	1985	1994	1995	1985	1994	1995	1985	1994	1995	1985	1995	1995	1995
Canada	10,688	9,695	9,004	421	345	320	2.2	1.7	1.6	83.0	70.5	37.7	5.2
US	352,551	293,214	277,834	1,473	1,130	1,056	6.5	4.2	3.8	2,151.6	1,547.3	2,045.0	88.3
France	44,604	45,184	48,002	808	781	826	4.0	3.3	3.1	464.3	409.0	337.0	93.4
Germany	48,149	36,965	41,815	634	454	509	3.2	2.0	2.0	478.0	339.9	414.7	25.1
United Kingdom	43,536	35,409	34,154	770	609	586	5.2	3.4	3.1	327.1	239.6	260.3	n.a.
Russia	n.a.	96,693	82,000	n.a.	649	551	n.a.	8.5	7.4	n.a.	1,520.0	2,400.0	280.0
Japan	29350	46639	50219	243	372	401	1.0	1.0	1.1	243.0	239.5	47.9	12.0
China	27107	28945	31731	26	24	26	7.9	5.6	5.7	3900.0	2930.0	1200.0	1200.0
Global Totals[a]													
NATO	560,777	479,044	473,279	496	448	396	3.3	2.4	2.5	5,378.0	4,059.8	5,711.9	811.4
Non-NATO Europe	45,694	28,072	30,840	309	153	167	4.3	4.2	4.6	1,449.1	2,158.0	7,295.6	395.9
Middle East and North Africa	91,937	44,243	43,04	739	449	428	12.3	6.8	6.5	2,530.7	2,871.7	2,772.7	684.3
Central and South Asia	14,127	15,078	16,013	15	17	19	4.6	3.6	3.8	2,113.7	2,627.8	1,467.2	1,608.2
East Asia and Australasia	102,018	129,730	140,909	234	237	260	6.5	4.6	4.5	8,057.7	6,912.3	16,306.4	2,162.2
Caribbean, Central and Latin America	19,130	20,045	20,176	54	39	39	3.0	1.7	1.7	1,344.2	1,325.7	2,607.3	769.0
Sub-Saharan Africa	10,308	8,673	8,224	29	21	20	3.6	3.0	2.8	958.5	1,077.9	717.0	378.3
Global totals[b]	1,173,441	821,578	814,481	383	252	235	6.7	4.4	4.2	27,131.9	22,553.2	39,278.1	7,089.3

Source: IISS, *Military Balance* (1996).

eighteenth-century war in Europe. It is not about rules by which war is conducted, but about the social legitimacy of war itself. The capitalist countries of the West, including Japan, form what is called a 'security community': they neither expect nor prepare to use force against each other. This reluctance to use force also extends to their relations with the rest of the world, but not so strongly. It stems both from their understanding that all-out war between advanced powers would be suicidal, and from their collective interest in sustaining their common economy. It is reinforced by various domestic features of these states, such as the possibilities for opposition to any use of force in complex democracies, and the fact that rich societies with small families are reluctant to risk their children in war. This security community is the basis of the idea that the international system is dividing into a zone of peace and a zone of conflict. Thus the end of the twentieth century is a new peak not only for humankind's ingenuity and inhumanity, but in some senses also for the development of its restraint in the use of military power.

Despite the availability of ever more exotic and destructive weapons, and the potential for information-age capital-intensive warfare, in practice war is dominated by mixtures of old and new features. Much of the killing in Africa, the Middle East, Central Asia and the Balkans is done with quite simple technologies and face-to-face fighting. Indeed, the pervasive, and often illegal, trade in small arms that feeds these conflicts plays no small role in the political difficulties of many of these states. This trade is even threatening the ability of some Western governments to keep their own populations disarmed. The Iran–Iraq war during the 1980s, with its trenches, bombardments and mass infantry assaults was eerily reminiscent of the First World War. Sometimes these conflicts draw in the more modern forces of today's rich powers. In the Gulf War such technology helped ensure quick victory, but in the Balkans it was sometimes used without fierce political will and was often foxed by such basic obstacles as cloud and trees.

The rich states are likely to see new technology as a way of coping with their smaller number of troops, but for most of the conflicts that are currently envisaged, high technology is not necessarily effective technology. These societies are moving towards capital-intensive, all-volunteer, professional armed forces which may make for a better fighting force, but also a more expensive one with smaller numbers of troops, and therefore greater reluctance to be engaged in several small conflicts or one large one. There is much talk about the new battlefield being one of information and high technology, but so far there is little evidence that such notions have much impact on the nasty little wars that are killing most people today. Superior fire-power is useful, but may not be sufficient to outweigh superior numbers, superior motivation and simply clever strategies. Even the most modern and efficient societies can lose wars. Fighting on distant soil, fighting for dubious causes, or fighting while handicapped by a divided society may mean that seemingly inferior forces triumph. Indeed the risk must be that high-technology armed forces that rely too much on their hardware and practise less the mundane business of managing guerrilla war, will be less prepared for most conflicts that are actually fought. The nature of war today, as in the past, depends to a great degree on the particular circumstances of the case. There is no general pattern, and therefore military systems tailored exclusively for modern war will always risk being unsuited to the specific conditions that might arise. High technology helps, but flexibility in doctrine, training and deployment is absolutely essential. In short, there are no absolute rules about who wins wars because military power is a combination of so many factors.

The recent ending of the Cold War has helped transform the role of military power. The nuclear paralysis that had developed between the Soviet Union and the United States by the 1960s made wars amongst the great powers seem highly unlikely and undesirable. As a consequence, concern with military power already began to fade during the Cold War, much helped by rising concerns about the development of a global economy. With the end of the Cold War the need for sustained military vigilance between the great powers dropped to very low levels. None of the great powers perceived military threats from any of the others in either the short- or the medium-term, and it became unclear just what, if any, role military power would play in the absence of a single, dominant great power conflict.

Between 1947 and 1989 it made sense for the great powers to deploy major military forces to wage what turned out to remain a Cold War. The two superpowers, and to a much lesser extent the two fading powers Britain and France, deployed and used armed forces in pursuit of security and advantage in their global ideological rivalry. But apart from these four states, all other military power was regional or even local. The Cold War marked an important change in the use of military power in the sense that for the first time such large forces could be maintained at high levels of alert for such a long time, and no war broke out. There were secondary conflicts in Africa, Asia and the Middle East, where the East–West rivalry intersected with local ones, but the global powers did not fight directly. Even more remarkable was the fact that over-arching these local and regional confrontations was a global risk of nuclear war. The nuclear weapons revolution meant that the superpowers risked destroying life on the planet through nuclear war – an unprecedented state of affairs for humankind.

With the ending of the Cold War, military power reverted almost to the premodern, pre-European-imperialism pattern of a militarily more decentralised world. This meant both a weakening of the state's monopoly on the means of force, and a shift to more self-contained regional patterns of military relations. The state of course never had an absolute internal monopoly on the use of force. It claimed a monopoly on the _legitimate_ use of force, and in some places succeeded in disarming most of the citizenry, but never eliminated every vestige of armed criminal or political behaviour. In many weak/failed states the government cannot even pretend to be the only legitimate, or even the strongest, wielder of force. But in the open world both the practical and the legal monopoly of the state have been eroded. Economic liberalisation has significantly privatised many aspects of the use of force formerly run by the state. Prisons are often run privately, and in many places private security firms outnumber police forces. The legal and illegal trade in weapons make it easy for any citizen to acquire arms, and international mafias can afford to field considerable military force. Although open societies are seldom plagued by armed assaults on the government, their openness makes them vulnerable to terrorism. Terrorists have easy access both to innumerable targets and to the weapons needed to damage them spectacularly. The fragmented identities of such societies make it easy for terrorists to operate within them. Taking serious preventive measures threatens the very openness by which such societies define themselves. But allowing terrorists to operate erodes the civility of society, encourages further privatisation of violence, and disrupts the economy.

Externally regions and sub-regions, and even factions within states, increasingly shape their own military affairs, albeit fed by the global arms trade, both legal and illegal. There are now no

truly global military rivalries, and only the United States retains
the capability for world-wide military operations. Whether it
retains the will is a contested question. All hot wars are local,
and most of them are internal to particular states. They sometimes involve powers with regional interests, but no power sees a
local conflict as crucial to a global balance. To the extent that
great powers with distant but less than vital interests get
involved in a local war, it is because they provide troops for
United Nations efforts to bring peace. The UN factor is relatively new. It reflects a change of motive from seeking advantage
in imperial rivalries to helping cultivate sufficient levels of
world order to allow the international economy to get on with
its business.

In this modern world of regionalised conflict, it is not surprising that even the threat of nuclear war has faded. It is now hard
to imagine circumstances under which any of the nuclear powers
would unleash a sufficient part of their arsenal to threaten life
on earth. Of course there are worries about the risks of nuclear
proliferation, but these all concern specific local conditions. It is
not immediately obvious that if North Korea acquires nuclear
weapons, Ukraine or Nigeria will feel compelled to respond.
Should nuclear weapons spread, even local wars could become
more devastating, but the risk of wars being waged on a global
scale is much diminished. In this sense, we seem to have taken a
step backwards in time.

As already noted, one major cause of the downgrading and
localising of military power is the extent to which the richest
states are constrained by their openness. Rich democratic states
seem to have solved the problem of war amongst themselves, but
they do still sometimes go to war with non-democratic countries.
What remains unclear is precisely the kinds of causes that will
trigger the wealthy, developed states to use force. The war in the
Gulf in 1990–91 suggested intervention. It concerned the right of
sovereign states not to be annexed by their neighbours (a
principle not widely violated since the end of the Second World
War), the price of and access to oil (one of the key natural
resources for the global economy), and the notion that bully-boy
states should not be allowed to use force at will. The handling of
the much more complex questions surrounding the civil war in
Bosnia also suggests intervention, but with much more hesitation, and without the economic motive. It is not clear how many
of those values are transferable to other contexts. But what is

relatively clear is that the rich and free states are reluctant to use much power for the sake of mainly humanitarian causes or where local combatants have little will to strike a local deal (as in Somalia, Rwanda, Sri Lanka, Sudan). In short, the rich and free states are less prepared than before to go to war, but there are very specific circumstances under which war still remains an option for them.

Looking at this the other way around, from the perspective of those outside the core of rich states, there seem to be few constraints on the use of force. Arms are in plentiful supply, and modern and premodern societies generate few restrictions on the use of force. There is no shortage of territorial and political disputes amenable to resolution by military force in the traditional manner both within and between states. From this point of view, the big question is how much local states or feuding factions will be allowed to settle their own affairs by whatever method, or how much the rich world will continue to intervene either by taking sides or by seeking to dampen and contain the use of force. In other words, will deterrence operate locally, or will it continue to have a significant global dimension? Will ruthless authoritarian governments like those in Iraq or China be able to invade or bully weaker neighbours with some confidence that the soft democratic states will not intervene? Iraq discovered that it miscalculated the softness of wealthy democracies. China sees the South China Sea and Taiwan as its own, but often finds it hard to figure out what is really the American policy towards these local conflicts. It is not clear whether deterrence will be enhanced or weakened by the uncertainty and capriciousness of politics in open states.

There is only one power on the horizon that has the potential to shift the current diffuse and decentralised pattern of military power in any significant way – China. This is not the place to discuss the bases and prospects of Chinese military power. But it is the place to note that China is the only state that could bring the world back to a notion of global military power by engaging the current great powers in a major confrontation. Given its size and economic potential, China may well be set to become the world's largest power and it certainly already operates as the major regional power in one of the key areas of economic growth. China already has nuclear weapons and a booming economy. It is the only

non-status-quo power and the only one which is in the dangerous state of transition from poverty to prosperity, and from
communism to pluralism. Whether China rises or falters is the
single most important unknown about the global future of
military power.

WHERE ARE WE NOW?

13

We have clustered our assessment of the state of the world at the end of the millennium under seven categories. But as the reader who has stayed the course will know, the issues raised in the seven categories are intertwined. What remains to be done is to assess whether the events of the last few years really deserve the era-defining status they have been given. We think they do, and on a much larger scale than is generally realised. Humankind is not just at the end of the Cold War and the 'short' twentieth century, but it may also be at the end of what is known as the Western era. We believe there is much confusion about the notion of 'the decline of the West', but the issue deserves careful debate. Perhaps of even greater importance is that as population peaks, and globalisation penetrates to all corners of the planet, we seem to be near to the end of the era of making a single human space on this planet. We also appear to be on the verge of being able to remake our bodies, opening the possibility that the physical evolution of the human species is about to resume. These eras can be viewed like Russian dolls, with the smaller ones nesting successively inside the larger: the forty years of the Cold War inside the seventy years of the twentieth century, both inside the five hundred years of the Western era, and all three inside the fifty millennia of the making of a single human space. What makes our own time unusually significant is that so many large-scale historical patterns seem to be culminating together.

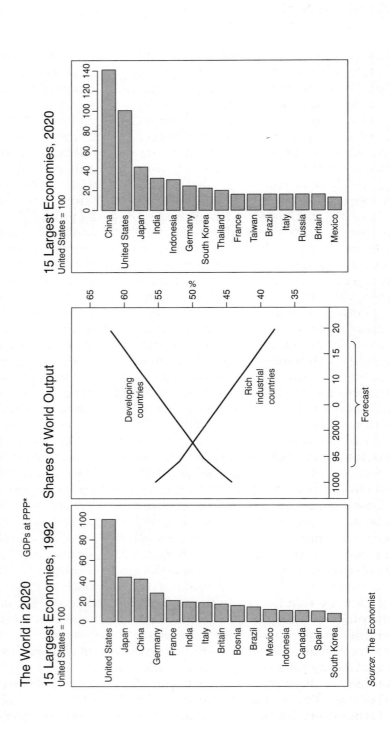

The World in 2020   GDPs at PPP*

15 Largest Economies, 1992
United States = 100

Shares of World Output

15 Largest Economies, 2020
United States = 100

Source: The Economist

What does it mean when we say that an era has ended? Obviously not everything is different on either side of a watershed. As we have seen, human history is the result of myriad flows of ideas and actions. Some flow faster and some blend in different ways under different circumstances. Most change is the result of a complex interaction of forces. Hence the notion of change as the result of chaos – the by now proverbial idea that the fluttering of a butterfly's wings in Belize can cause a typhoon in Tokyo. There are no wholesale transformations, only changes of greater and lesser significance within ongoing flows of events, and there can be no simple model to describe this process. Eras are easiest to see when looking backwards. It is almost impossible to predict the changing of eras, but we can make some decent guesses about claims relating to our own time.

There is a fashion for thinking that the present moment in history is somehow peculiarly significant. In part this is driven by the entirely arbitrary fact that in the most widely used (i.e. Western) of our calendars we are approaching the end of both a century and a millennium. There is no intrinsic reason to invest the millennium with much significance, although the idea that this is a time of historic transformation is supported by the concentration of great events during the past few years: the ending of the Cold War and its associated arms race, the collapse of communism, the implosion of the Soviet Union, and the rise of China.

Eras can be quite short (the forty-two years of the Cold War era), or very long (the 5,000 years of the ancient and classical era). By choosing shorter or longer periods, and by emphasising some criteria over others, history can be reshaped to fit a large number of different purposes. A particular choice of era not only bundles the past into a specific perspective, but since the end of one era has to be the beginning of another, it also shapes how one sees the future. As such, the idea can easily be hijacked either by those wanting to promote a particular idea (the death of capitalism, the end of history, the Age of Aquarius . . .), or by those wanting to exaggerate the significance of the contemporary. Pretending that our own day-to-day experience is located at a key juncture within a larger historical process is a human weakness as well as an attractive promotional strategy. And sometimes, of course, it will be true. History does contain big turning points.

In thinking about eras, what matters is a sense of the different levels of time. The business cycle, or cycles of political leadership may change every few years. Great powers, specific technologies, or ideologies may last decades or even a century or two. Probably the deepest sense of time is the pace at which our planetary environment changes. In this perspective the millennium is of little importance. Earthquakes still happen, volcanoes still erupt and we may still be struck by a meteor. The ice age is still due to return.

Variable Progress		
GDP per head, $*	**1900**	**1995**
Britain	4,200	18,900
Canada	3,000	19,200
Italy	1,400	19,000
United States	4,500	26,700
Educational enrolments '000	**1900**	**1995**
France		
Secondary	98	5,822
Higher	30	1,526
Japan		
Secondary	121	11,288[d]
Higher	25	2,139[d]
United States		
Secondary	519	17,117‡
Higher	238	14,210‡
Savings per head, $*	**1930**	**1995**
Britain	170	1,500
United States	140	950
Working hours per week, manufacturing	**1900**	**1994**
Britain	54	43
Canada	57	39
United States	53	42
Internet – number of connected networks**	**1988**	**1996‡**
United States	301	104,000
Non-US	33	91,000

*1995 prices and exchange rates †1992 ‡Projected
**Separate groups of linked computers that can share information
Sources: *The Economist*, International Labour Organisation; Internet Society; national statistics; OECD.

But we are at a turning point in the sense that we can now, for the first time, begin to manipulate some of the more basic features of our own bodies and the planetary environment in which we live. We are unsure just how much we can and are doing to the environment, but we know we do have a noticeable impact. For well over two thousand years we have been able to poison water and atmosphere and destroy forests. But now we can do so in a way that forces change on much of the world. We know we can destroy the ozone layer and that we need to stop doing so. We think we know we can warm the planet, and some think we need to stop doing so. This is an unquestionably epoch-defining event. Our relationship to the planet has changed from being passive recipients of its hospitality and its assaults, to being players in its evolution.

Our new ability to understand how our bodies function, and to change key features, is not just a matter of cosmetic surgery or changing gender. Our knowledge derived from genetics and science in general holds out the prospect of moving beyond organ transplants to even more basic manipulation of the human form and its abilities.

The extent to which we have gained control over aspects of the personal and planetary environment depends to a large extent on another sense of time – scientific time. There is a deplorable tendency in analysis of global trends to talk in terms of social and political factors and to relegate the sciences to the category of stage props. But in many ways the priority is reversed: social and political processes follow changes made possible by science. Scientific change is not linear, but it does seem inexorable. What is significant about our current scientific time is not just the pace of change, but the recent nature of change. For the first time we have tapped the deeper wells of physics and found sources of power sufficient to destroy life on the planet. We are building computers already capable of beating us at many of our own games, and just beginning to show potential as a new type of intelligence. We are on the brink of commanding knowledge about the biological essence of life and how to control it. As we write, the first steps are being taken to create direct links between brain cells and computer chips. These are god-like powers, giving humankind the possibility, for better or worse, of starting to take control not only of its own evolution, but that of the ecosphere as well. There are still species-threatening plagues such as Ebola lurking on the planet, but we are mostly confident about our scientific ability to cope, although possibly only after major loss of life. As is usually the case at the cusp of new knowledge, we know very little about how much we are about to learn. But the turning point seems clear enough. The relentless drive of scientific knowledge is opening up transformations in the human condition that we can only half imagine.

The Changing Quality of Life

The maps on p. 181 show the Physical Quality of Life Index (PQLI), developed by Morris David Morris of Brown University to measure progress among the poorer countries. The PQLI is based on life expectancy at age one and rates of literacy and infant mortality. Values range from a low of 6.3 in the West African nation of the Gambia in 1960 to a high of 94 in Japan in 1990. Because the PQLI is based on end results, it has advantages over other methods. Per capita gross national product in Iran, for example, is less than one third that of Saudi Arabia, yet the 1990 PQLI scores of the two countries are identical, indicating that income and wealth are more evenly distributed in Iran.

The historical record has registered a more or less steady improvement in the PQLI. Other countries that once had scores as low as those in the sub-Saharan region have shown remarkable change: Sri Lanka had a score of only 19 in 1921, but by 1993 it had reached 85. And 100 years ago the US had about the same PQLI score as the sub-Saharan countries do today.

In the social world, in terms of the ideas about how to organise human life, there is a strong sense of a transformation just made – strong enough, indeed, to trigger talk of the 'end of history'. As argued in chapter 1, the Cold War was not a self-contained event, but part of a larger twentieth-century process of wars about industrial ideology. It was the Third World War in a round of struggles to see whether monarchism, communism, fascism or liberal democracy would shape the future of industrial society. We expect that as a result of this process, the basic direction of human economic and political affairs is probably set for at least several decades to come. As well as entrenching global markets and social pluralism, this transformation also carries with it the apparent abandonment of war between the leading powers in the system.

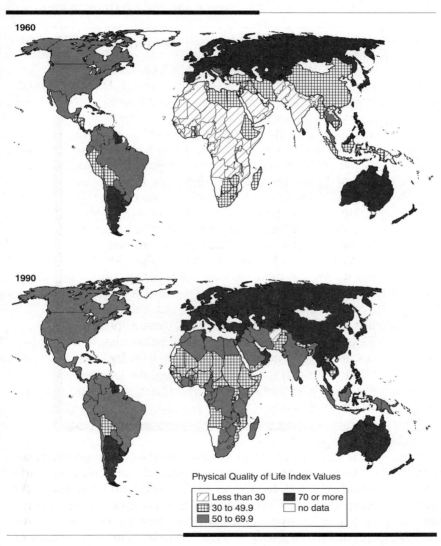

Physical Quality of Life Index Values

Less than 30	70 or more
30 to 49.9	no data
50 to 69.9	

Because of these transformations, there is much less feeling than in the scientific domain of an endless string of imminent revolutions stretching into the future. Some of the key patterns in the social world seem relatively set. Wars can be fought with far more violence, but if anything we seem to have stepped back from what was a revolution in military power – the ability to use weapons of mass destruction and destroy life on this planet. That potential still exists, but recent history reminds us that it is by no means inevitable that we use all our capabilities to their full extent. Humans can choose to restrain themselves. Neither is much basic change now likely in the way we use capital. There will be far more of it as the world grows more prosperous, but the essentials of trade, investment and financial exchange look relatively stable. Nor is there much sense that the capitalist system is driving towards an inevitable crisis any deeper than those it has experienced in the past. Capitalism is a turbulent and adventurous system, and periodic crises and collapses are part of its development. But it is also the system that has defied a thousand predictions of its demise, and there is every reason to think that its adaptability will enable it to continue doing so in the future.

The globalisation of capital and the fragmentation of collective identities have both gone some way to weakening the state as the main framework of political order, but even if it should shrink to some extent, there is little sign that it is about to disappear. The character of the state has already evolved considerably, and unevenly, over the last five hundred years. For those people who live in the most developed parts of the world, the retreat of war may make the state seem less important, yet the role of the state in people's individual lives is actually larger. Measuring this trend is difficult, but the fact that state spending as a percentage of total GDP is more or less at an all time high in most developed states, suggests that even a fairly sharp reduction in the role of the state will still leave a force that is far from dead. In short, even though we can expect a reduction in the role of the state in open societies, this is not a new era in the way in which political units are organised. Much more likely is the continued evolution of the state in response to economic, social and technological change.

The dynamism of science, and the prospective stability of the main ideas about how to organise society, all suggest a triumph of the West. There are undoubtedly features of what we glibly refer to as 'Westernisation' that require reform. Some ideas of relatively short duration – such as communism – are clearly dead. But other important ideas such as nationalism remain powerful, and fascism still lurks in the wings. The principles of the Enlightenment have triumphed but have also changed as they matured. The current search for communitarian values to further modify market liberalism suggests that ideas keep flowing, and that we are not particularly at a point of intellectual breakthrough. Indeed, some of the discussion of communitarianism suggests a throw-back to older ideas, and there may be grounds for worrying about the dearth of new ideas for dealing with the ever-unfolding problem of organising peaceful, prosperous, stable and sustainable human societies.

An argument can be made that the three world wars in the twentieth century constitute the period of Western decline. They weakened the global grip of the European powers, and opened the way for decolonization. The first two wars sapped the economic and military strength of Europe, undercut their myths of white superiority, and speeded their democratisation, so bringing the imperial role increasingly into contradiction with domestic values. Decolonization marked a decisive end to the direct political and military control by the West of most of the planet's territory and people. It also accelerated the diffusion to many parts of the planet of the key factors that had for over four hundred years given the West a huge power advantage over other societies: science, liberalism, statehood, industrialisation, and modern weapons. These developments meant that the West's exclusive control over industrial power was steadily replaced by a more multicultural, and more globally distributed industrial society. By the end of the twentieth century, the West had lost much of its superior political status and its ability to occupy and colonise other people's territories, and it was well advanced towards losing both its domination of trade and finance, and its monopoly on industrial production and technological innovation.

But how can it be said that the West has had its day when it is Western ideas (state, market, science, nationalism, maybe democracy) that are going forward with such force, and when the West has just won the Cold War and still occupies the top ranks of world economic, political, military and cultural power? Clearly the narrow understanding of the West implied in the declinist argument does not come to grips with its real strength and essence. The West is more than just the set of powers rooted in Western Europe that successfully transplanted itself to the Americas and Australia.

It is true that we have now come to the end of the era when this narrow West directly dominated the world through occupation. But 'the West' is a more subtle force, more concerned with ideas than mere physical domination. In this sense, the West can be said to have begun with its Judeo-Christian roots which intermingled with aspects of classical Greek and Roman culture. The Enlightenment clearly has direct links to these intellectual traditions. But as the ideas grew and were given power, they changed. Indeed one of the keys to understanding the power of the West is to understand how it can absorb the best of the ideas it encounters. Thus Western power that began in Europe was deeply enriched by the experience of creating the modern states of the Americas. It was the revolution in Britain's thirteen colonies in North America that gave us the vibrancy of individual rights and enhanced the openness of Western ideals. It has been more than two centuries since Europeans physically controlled the Americas, but few can doubt that people on both sides of the Atlantic are part of what we call the West.

If the West is conceived as a set of ideas and the social consequences of their application, then it would seem to be in robust condition despite (or in some views because of) its retreat from empire. In this sense we are talking more of the continuing power of Westernisation, rather than of the power of the core Western states as such. Historians rightly distinguish between a core culture and its converts: thus Greek and Hellenised, Roman and Romanised, Chinese and Sinified. Ideas often long outlive the state powers that produced them. Greek and Roman ideas about law, religion, citizenship, philosophy and art flourished for over a thousand years after their military and political power had crumbled. In the same way, we need to distinguish between the West, as one of perhaps only six distinct great centres of civilisation in human history, and a much wider sphere that is in various degrees and depths Westernised.

The old Western core is now at the end of a unique period of direct global dominance. Just like the Greeks and the Romans, it leaves behind a vast penumbra of peoples and cultures influenced by its ideas – the sphere of Westernisation. And unlike any previous cultural sphere, this one is global in extent. Unlike the Greeks and the Romans, the West still remains a powerful player into the post-Western era, but it is only *primus inter pares*. Other ancient cores of civilisation, most notably those centred in East Asia, are increasingly able and willing not only to defend themselves, and project power into their own regions, but to assert the legitimacy of their own cultural values, and the power of their economies and traditions. But these other cultures are now heavily penetrated by Western ideas, and since many of those ideas are crucial to the generation of wealth and power, it is a safe bet that they will continue to be influential, and to give the old Western core some advantages in world politics. So just as the nearly two-millennium period of Hellenistic civilisation (from Alexander's conquests to the fall of Byzantium) can be distinguished from the five hundred years of classical Greek civilisation that preceded it, so too can the 500-year period of 'classical' Western civilisation be distinguished from the more multi-centred and multicultural period of 'Westernistic' civilisation that we are now entering.

Armed with this wider understanding of the West, the end of the twentieth century is far less obviously the end of the Western era. Much of Africa and the Middle East are notionally independent but cannot pose serious challenges to the existing Western powers. South Asia may be a different case in the longer-term. But for the time being it is only East Asia that has succeeded in making the miraculous leap that the Atlantic states made from poor peasant countries into modern, highly developed economies and societies. The rise of East Asia is indeed an event of epoch-making importance, but one that may well be far less threatening to the West than many people appreciate. In one sense we are just seeing a reprise of East Asian power, not a wholly new event. According to some estimates, China was still the world's largest economy as late as 1850. And there is nothing distinctly East Asian that unites all the countries on the rim of the Western Pacific – no cultural bloc to fuel a 'clash of civilisations'. To take only the most obvious example, Japan and China have fundamentally different social structures, not to mention the variations with and within Southeast Asia. All the signs suggest that as East Asians grow rich, they eventually follow a path of modernisation not unlike that followed in Europe and North America. What appears to be culturally distinct is often little more than superficial, or accounted for by stage of development. The rise of East Asia has only been made possible because its people have accepted most of the basic features of Western intellectual, political and economic organisation.

The continuing success of East Asia seems to depend on it retaining the fundamental features taught by the Atlantic world.

Every successful economy in East Asia has accepted the logic of a market economy. Every society that has done so has also moved down the road to a variation of political liberalism and primary stress on the rights of individuals. The trend is lumpy but no state goes backward in any of these key respects of Westernisation and still remains an economic success (Singapore is perhaps the exception that proves the rule).

This is not to say that the West will not be changed by the experience of a rising East Asia. Remember how a rising United States enriched rather than destroyed the societies that gave it the principles for its success. In the last years of the millennium it is likely that the peoples of the Western core will rise to the challenge posed by the new East Asia.

If there is a threat to the West, it comes more internally, from doubts about its ability to handle the social consequences of applying its own ideas, than from external challengers. To the extent that the old West will learn something from the rise of Asia, the new Westernised powers may be the trigger for its renewal. The old West may well have to re-learn from Asia some of its ideas about how to sustain a community rather than just a collection of individuals. The West may already have begun to learn that it must cut the role of the state and encourage individuals and their families to re-take greater responsibility for their own welfare. People in the West may also have to rediscover the work ethic once called The Protestant Ethic or Victorian Values.

But learning from Asia will be the easy part. Much more challenging will be the need for the West to find the inspiration to bring economy, society and politics back into a sustainable balance. How will the West forge new social stability, at a time when women are empowered, family structures are evolving into new forms, and identity is far more complex?

As much as the East Asians stimulate the Western core to re-learn old lessons and find new answers to new problems, the East Asians will find that they are changing much faster towards the model of the old West. East Asia will face the same kind of demographic and social pressures that the more developed countries are about to tackle. It could be that in twenty years time, when the Atlantic world has reformed its social and welfare system, and East Asians just begin to contemplate much steeper demographic challenges, that the notion of a Pacific Century will seem every bit as silly as it did when the idea was talked about in the last half of the nineteenth century.

The rise of East Asia demonstrates the extent to which we have made a single human space. Within a few short centuries one centre of civilisation pulled together all of the break-throughs necessary to complete the project of making this space. As argued in chapter 2, by doing so it pre-empted an alternative line in which steady parallel expansions from several centres of civilisation might eventually have formed a world system. With the withdrawal of the West from direct imperial control, and the world-wide diffusion of its sources of power, elements of that older, multi-centred and multicultural pattern begin to re-emerge. But they do so in a context of the shared culture of the Westernistic era. This Westernistic world will be the one that soon faces both the end of unrestrained expansion in human numbers and mobility, and the need to answer the question of how the human community as a whole is going to relate to the planet that it has so recently filled up and inte-grated. This biggest of all the eras confronts us with the biggest questions about the future, and provides us with a powerful reason to look forward now, before we jump.

PART III

MEMORIES FROM THE FUTURE

ON PROGRESS

14

Before we can anticipate where we might be going, we need to pause to reflect on a key part of the very notion of 'going'. Do human beings make progress, or do we merely mistake change and difference for progress? Looking at the story of human development from several million hunter-gatherers to several billion people, most living in industrialising or post-industrial societies, some might consider this a stupid question. Even allowing for all of its setbacks and horrors, what else could this story represent but progress? How could such huge advances in knowledge, scale and sophistication of social organisation, and material welfare be anything else?

Yet there is such a widespread mood of millennial pessimism prevalent in much of the developed world, that the question needs to be addressed. Does the human story thus far represent progress? Put another way, do the things we think of as progress outweigh the developments that we might think of as degenerate or retrograde? If they do, how is progress measured and of what does it consist? Is it guaranteed or fragile? Have we merely been lucky, and is our luck about to run out? Is the dark side of human development about to overwhelm the progressive side? Many of the pundits now trying to peer ahead into the next century are taking a gloomy view of the human future. Some see economic crisis. Others predict ecological catastrophe. Yet others fear social atomisation, cultural decay, and the spread of lawless and violent behaviour. A few still worry about the return of large-scale war. It has become fashionable amongst many in the chattering classes to believe that progress is perverse, that the future (or at least their future) will be worse than the present.

How can this fashion be explained? One obvious answer is captured by Francis Fukuyama's jibe that: 'a naive optimist whose expectations are belied appears foolish, while a pessimist proven wrong maintains an aura of profundity and seriousness'. For professional pundits, pessimism is a safe strategy. And an inclination to the negative may be reinforced by theories that build in expectations of conflict. Realists, who base a world view on the dominance of the dark side of human nature, expect

---

More on Progress

Tomorrow is an old deceiver, and his cheat never grows stale.

Samuel Johnson, letter, 24 May 1773, to Hester Thrale (published in *The Letters of Samuel Johnson*, vol. 1, no. 311, ed. by R. W. Chapman, 1952).

Nothing recedes like progress.

e.e. cummings, *Jottings*, in *Wake*, no. 10 (1951; repr. in *A Miscellany*, ed. by George J. Firmage, 1958).

Progress is not an illusion, it happens, but it is slow and invariably disappointing.

George Orwell, *Inside the Whale and Other Essays*, 'Charles Dickens' (1940).

. . . ask an impertinent question, and you are on the way to a pertinent answer.
Jacob Bronowski, *The Ascent of Man*, ch. 4 (1973).

It's the same each time with progress. First they ignore you, then they say you're mad, then dangerous, then there's a pause and then you can't find anyone who disagrees with you.

Tony Benn, quoted in *Observer* (London, 6 Oct. 1991).

violence and struggles for power to be a permanent feature of human history, past, present and future. In their view, bad times will always return. Marxists may see utopia at the end, but before we get there a long process of class conflict and misery has first of all to be endured. Those of a more mildly negative disposition see not great catastrophes, but a decline into illiteracy, alienation, parochial perspectives, cultural sterility, and surrender to short-term gratifications.

There are others who find the discussion of progress to be cosmically insignificant because life on our planet is in fact subject to much larger forces. Some think that the fatal blow will be delivered by nature, in the form of comet or meteorite strikes, or the return of ice ages. Others look to self-destructive tendencies in humankind. Although the possibility of nuclear suicide has fallen out of fashion, new scenarios are available in pollution-induced climate change, and 'super-bug' plagues. Those in the grip of apocalyptic religions embrace the belief that this is how it will end, often dressing it up as divine retribution for sin.

Such extreme fatalism is thankfully quite rare. More disturbing forms of congenital pessimism come from those who believe, for example, that we are locked into business cycles. Many academics and hard-headed money-makers think that booms are followed by busts, or on the larger scale of 'long cycles', that spectacular periods of technological innovation and growth are followed by spectacular periods of stagnation and slump. Some of these theories build expectations of major wars into their cyclical processes. Since we have just lived through a great boom time, such thinking underlies much professional pessimism about the next decades. It doesn't necessarily mean that believers in this sort of theory take a gloomy view of the whole of the human prospect, though some doubtless do. But it does mean that they will predict bad times ahead, sometimes relatively short and shallow, but sometimes long, deep and destructive.

As a rule, those who question progress carry one or more of: a dim view of human nature, a lively sense of impending catastrophe, a cyclical theory of political economy, or a cynical evaluation of their plausibility as pundits. Their stock-in-trade is the inability of human institutions to see far enough, adapt well enough, or mobilise fast enough to meet the crises that loom. Those who embrace progress often have a transcendent view of human nature. They have faith in the ability of humans to learn and adapt, and to invent solutions faster than they create problems. Both may agree with H.G. Wells' idea that civilisation is a race between education and catastrophe, but optimists think humankind will win the race, pessimists that we will lose it. Catastrophe, failure and decline are easy to understand, but what exactly is meant by progress?

Macaulay on Progress

Time advances: facts accumulate; doubts arise. Faint glimpses of truth begin to appear, and shine more and more unto the perfect day. The highest intellects, like the tops of mountains, are the first to catch and to reflect the dawn. They are bright, while the level below is still in darkness. But soon the light, which at first illuminated only the loftiest eminences, descends on the plain, and penetrates to the deepest valley. First come hints, then fragments of systems, then defective systems, then complete and harmonious systems. The sound opinion, held for a time by one bold speculator, becomes the opinion of a small minority, of a strong minority, of a majority of mankind. Thus, the great progress goes on.

Thomas Babington Macaulay, 'History of the Revolution in England', in *Edinburgh Review* (July 1835; repr. in *Lord Macaulay's Essays*, 1889).

Progress derives from the Latin for walking forward. Although it can be used in a negative sense (he made progress towards the gallows), its general meaning is of movement towards some higher level of development, complexity, completion or perfection. Perhaps its first entry into human awareness dates from the emergence of Judaism, with its belief that human beings can measurably change their lives for the good as they work towards a world fit for the coming of the messiah. Until then, and for long after, most of the major religions and cultures of the ancient and classical world held cyclical views of human existence, and had no linear concept of history. Human life was as one with the repetitive wheel of the agricultural seasons that governed their lives. For the Chinese or the Hindus, life was cyclical. History was not expected to progress anywhere, and if individuals might progress through some form of karmic stages, this was mostly an individual path to heaven, or some other form of detachment from the world, and not necessarily for the improvement of society. Although Judaism acknowledged a large dose of evil and tragedy in life, its central belief was that all this could be overcome by human behaviour. Christianity and Islam also saw themselves as progressive revelations. As they spread out to influence much of the rest of the planet, the ideas gained wider currency, eventually colonising nearly all parts of the globe.

Modern Europe picked up Christianity (as well as law) as part of its legacy from classical Rome. Once Europe was in the grip of both the scientific and industrial revolutions and the ideology of liberalism, it became the absolute embodiment of progress. A whole series of innovative thinkers in the natural and social sciences pumped wave after wave of new and powerful ideas into Western society. From Copernicus, Bacon and Gallileo to da Vinci, Newton and Einstein, and from Hobbes, Kant and Smith, to Mill, Marx, and Keynes, an endless stream of intellectuals, engineers, artists, and scientists set out an ever-expanding vista of how the material and social worlds could be reshaped to improve the human condition. These thinkers energised and empowered Western society, embedded in it a permanent sense of progress, and forever changed humankind's sense of its place in the order of things.

The European Enlightenment – an eighteenth-century philo-sophical movement that embodied the idea of progress – had at its core the belief in the value of reason, scepticism, and regard for the individual. Scepticism was a key feature because the great menace to progress was not so much ignorance as the illusion of knowledge. Hence the virtue of negative discoverers (e.g. Copernicus' discovery that the sun does not circle the earth and the subsequent understanding that our solar system is not the only one). At the peak of the West's power the ideas of the Enlightenment were projected around the globe. Other cultures and civilisations were ruthlessly confronted with the superiority of Western weapons, medicine, transportation, capital and po-litical organisation, beginning a world-wide process of adapta-tion or extinction that continues today.

Another input into the European Enlightenment came from the classical Greek invention of science – the notion that objective truth can and should be tested, and that what was learned was cumulative. Remarkably, the first recorded use of the word 'scientist' was not until 1840. Chinese civilisation also understood aspects of the scientific method, and several of its discoveries, including gunpowder and the compass, were important inputs into the European development. But the Chinese never developed science into a philosophical system. Science, as it was practised by the heirs of Hellenism, was also slow to accumulate knowledge. Galileo Galilei in the sixteenth century was perhaps the first to make serious progress with the scientific method of objectively observing and measuring what he saw. The spread of the scientific method also required myriad other intellectual and material changes, including an understanding of the rights of the individual, the virtues of openness, and the joys of criticism. As the social anthropologist Ernest Gellner pointed out, the specific, and still not fully understood mix of factors that produced the Enlightenment, the rise of capitalism and the conquest of the planet from Europe, seems to have been a unique and far from inevitable process. But once humans stepped through the door of history that led to industrial society, there was no going back, just as there had been no going back after the shifts from hunter-gatherers to agrarian society, and from village life to cities. If knowledge could be systematically accumulated, and if the technological fruits of that knowledge were continuously fed into society, then a powerful and seemingly open-ended engine of progressive change was in place. This progress would be strong in material and knowledge terms, and these would feed into the creation of larger, more elaborate and more sophisticated societies. But whether progress in these domains would enhance or degrade the moral and spiritual condition of humankind was, and remains, more open to question.

The idea, and indeed vivid evidence, of progress was clearly a Western inspiration. Its heyday was the nineteenth century, but that incarnation was articulated and shaped by the ideas of Francis Bacon and John Locke. In the seventeenth century Bacon wrote of the individual's relationship to progress in time and laid the basis for modern individualism. Locke gave us some elements of the modern sense of secular progress – not only by developing the empirical path to scientific knowledge, but also by unfolding the notion that the happiness of the property-owning, rights-bearing individual and the larger political community is only possible when the individual is freed from living

Richard Dawkins, delivering the Richard Dimbleby Lecture on BBC TV on 12 November 1996.

Aristotle was an encyclopaedic polymath, an all time intellect. Yet you know more than he did about the world . . . Such is the privilege of living after Newton, Darwin, Einstein, Planck, Watson, Crick and their colleagues . . . The point is . . . that science is cumulative and we live today . . . Here is a small sample of the things you could tell Aristotle . . . The earth is not the centre of the universe. It orbits the sun – which is just another star . . . Living species are not isolated types with unchanging essences . . . For the first half of geological time our ancestors were bacteria . . . Aristotle was a distant cousin to a squid . . . The brain is not for cooling the blood . . . It is a three-dimensional maze of a million million nerve cells.

. . . The process of accumulation does not stop with us. Two thousand years hence, ordinary people who have read a couple of books will be in a position to give a tutorial to today's Aristotle . . . There is much that we still do not know. But surely our belief that the earth is round and not flat, and that it orbits the sun will never be superseded. That alone is enough to confound those, endowed with a little philosophical learning, who deny the very possibility of objective truth.

. . . Meanwhile, there is so much that we do not yet know, we should proclaim those things that we do, so as to focus attention on problems that we should be working on.

within traditional constraints. Rousseau's picturing of the 'noble savage', freed from the artificiality of civilised life, presages much of our modern flirtation with the notion that there is no progress, only sustainability of some idyllic original state of nature. But history passed Rousseau by. The empiricism of Locke and J.S. Mill, and the individualistic liberal republican political philosophy of Locke, Mill, Paine and others triumphed, as did the market-based liberalism of Adam Smith. The French, American and industrial revolutions were built on different mixtures of these ideas.

Another thread in the conception of progress grew out of Darwin's notion of evolution. Victorians saw evolution as the quintessence of progress, embodying the sense that progress is an automatic, built-in aspect of the unfolding of nature. Just by getting on with the business of survival in a changing and competitive environment, life reaches new forms of complexity, intelligence and sophistication. Progress seemed to be an inherent part of nature (or as some would see it, of God's plan). But out of Darwin grew eugenics, Nazism and the unparalleled horrors of the Holocaust. If that too was progress, then something was terribly wrong. It seems obvious that as in the evolution of the species, not all change is good or successful. Change does not happen smoothly or constantly, and often the process of change involves periods of chaos, conflict and destruction. But out of the competition of genes and/or ideas comes – eventually – improvement.

Mark Twain on Evolution

Evolution is the law of policies: Darwin said it, Socrates endorsed it, Cuvier proved it and established it for all time in his paper on 'The Survival of the Fittest.' These are illustrious names, this is a mighty doctrine: nothing can ever remove it from its firm base, nothing dissolve it, but evolution.

Mark Twain, 'Three Thousand Years Among the Microbes', ch. 8, in _Which Was the Dream?_ (ed. by John S. Tuckey, 1967).

A similar pattern was evident in the way in which Marxist notions worked their way through the story of progress. Marxism was a reaction to the evident failings of a capitalist system in the first part of the nineteenth century. As it grew in strength and influence, the liberal capitalists were forced to adapt, developing a wider franchise for the working class and a welfare system and social legislation. Taxes increased and the state assumed a far larger role in the life of the individual. But the more direct heirs of Marxism created communist party states and the horrors of Stalin, Mao and Pol Pot. Although some so-called communist parties are still in power, their ideology is effectively dead. An amended and improved capitalism and liberalism survived because it changed enough, but did not change so much that it lost the features of openness and pluralism that gave it strength in the first place.

In the late twentieth century, after fascism and communism had been defeated, the believers in progress had a brief moment of triumphalism. But that moment did not last long before it was swamped by the pessimism that swept into fashion as the millennium approached. Yet the current pessimism cannot hide the very tangible progress that led from the amoeba to human-kind. (Though as Bertrand Russell pointed out, 'whether the amoeba would agree with this opinion [about progress] is not known'.)

The modern layman's sense that although there is much progress, there is also much more worry, stems from an inherent aspect of progress – the notion of chronic change. As the pace of change increases, so does the sense of insecurity and the diffi-culty in standing back to see where we stand today. Thus the key to a common sense understanding of progress is to take a perspective longer than a mere generation or two, and to acknowledge that progress is not smooth, constant or apparent in all aspects of life. For those living in the most developed parts of the world, common sense is compelling. Ask almost anyone in the developed world if they would want to live their grand-parents' lives, and most would say they would prefer to live as they are. The degree to which people reach this judgement owes a great deal to the extent to which their material life has improved. Although there has also been important material progress in many poor parts of the world, it is far less obvious and certainly less real than in the developed world. Neverthe-less, it is also worth reflecting that one major Physical Quality of Life Index study has shown that 100 years ago the United States had roughly the PQLI score of modern sub-Saharan Africa.

In most parts of the world, and certainly in the developed world, most people have an intuitive sense that they have never had it so good. Their grandparents did less interesting work, had less leisure, died younger and were far less well educated. The layman's sense of progress is perhaps best understood in the simple categories (to borrow from the United States' Declaration of Independence) of life, liberty and the pursuit of happiness. There can be no doubt that humans live longer than ever before. They could, and probably will, live even longer in the future. The ability to prolong life only came when we understood the scientific basis of life, disease and good health. Progress in these realms is less than 200 years old. It is manifest in the wonders of organ transplants, but most lives are prolonged by what we know about diet, hygiene, and about microbes and how to prevent them killing. Genetic engineering is still in its infancy and so we still have a great deal to learn about the basics of life.

> ### Hume and Mill on Happiness
>
> The great end of all human industry is the attainment of happiness. For this were arts invented, sciences cultivated, laws ordained, and societies modelled, by the most profound wisdom of patriots and legislators. Even the lonely savage, who lies exposed to the inclemency of the elements and the fury of wild beasts, forgets not, for a moment, this grand object of his being.
>
> **David Hume**, _Essays Moral, Political, and Literary_, pt. 1, 'The Stoic' (1742; repr. in _The Philosophical Works of David Hume_, vol. 3, 1826).
>
> Ask yourself whether you are happy, and you cease to be so.
>
> **John Stuart Mill**, _Autobiography_, ch. 5 (1873).

Medical progress is complex and its social impact equally so. The machineries of evolution mean that many advances against disease are only temporary. The use of antibiotics, for example, stimulates the development of superbugs immune to the existing pharmaceutical armoury. And as each new step is taken in the science of life, there exists potential for misuse. Preventing and curing disease is one thing, prolonging the meaningless existence of the terminally ill or brain dead is quite another. One of the reasons that people often feel worse in the course of progress is that by prolonging life, there are more people alive to suffer more chronic medical problems in old age. These risks are part of the process of progress. But in the past such risks have been overcome in the process of open inquiry and debate that lies at the heart of the mechanisms of progress. There is no guarantee that this process will continue, but there is certainly no denying that there has been enormous progress so far in understanding the basic science of human life.

The critics of such scientific triumphalism quickly note that science is double-edged. Technology, in the words of Edward Tenner, 'bites back' in that some improvements (e.g. safety devices) conjure up problems (complacency). Technology has also allowed us to develop far more effective ways of killing millions of people. That tens of millions of people have died in wars in the twentieth century surely casts doubt on the notion of progress. We can kill with chemical, biological and nuclear weapons as well as a huge range of exotic conventional ones. We have cluster bombs, smart bombs, shrapnel that is invisible to X-rays, and humble landmines that kill and maim in unprecedented numbers. Despite the formation of rules and laws of warfare, some people on this planet still manage to break all of them. Torture is widespread, although less so in the richest and most democratic states, and concentration camps and attempts at genocide are still with us despite the horrors of Stalin and Hitler. In several parts of the planet, tens of thousands regularly die of starvation, are disabled by preventable diseases, or are mentally crippled by malnutrition. So how much real progress have we made?

No one can doubt that our superior ability to kill people arises from the technologies and social organisation of progress. Many steps forward carry with them major risks. Advances in transport, communication, chemistry and learning methods benefit criminals and dictators as much as law-abiding citizens and democrats. But at the same time the number of people on this planet has never been greater, nor education and prosperity more widespread. Neither is it clear that we kill a greater percentage of our population than we did in the past. The bottom line is that there are more living people, more able to realise their full human potential, than ever before. Progress is not uniform, and it is always accompanied by setbacks and new problems, but by the common-sense criteria of quantity and quality of life and knowledge, the good outweighs the bad.

It can of course be argued that we have been too successful in creating and sustaining life. We are now at the stage where we think that the creation of ever more and ever longer lives on this planet is not necessarily a good thing. People in richer countries contemplate the costs of sometimes painful and empty old age, and worry that overpopulation and high standards of living jeopardise the environment. Birth control, in some form, is seen by most as a virtue. Euthanasia is much more controversial, but many people in the rich world are demanding some choice over the conditions under which their lives can be prolonged. We have yet to fully understand what it will do to human notions of life and its link to progress when we decide that we do not want more people. Until our own generation, we mostly assumed that progress meant more and longer life. Perhaps we are about to rethink that part of progress, putting more emphasis on quality of life and less on quantity.

The other two features of progress – liberty and happiness – are too closely connected to be easily separated. The key problem, to hark back to Bertrand Russell's quip, is whether we understand what makes for happiness, and whether we have made progress in increasing its quality and quantity. For many people, nothing recedes like progress, in part because of the notion encapsulated in that sixteenth-century epigram – 'If youth knew; if age could'. It was Longfellow who noted, 'each subsiding century reveals some new mystery; we build where monsters used to hide themselves'. But new monsters keep appearing. Is there any evidence that humans have made moral progress?

Classical Greeks had the Sisyphean image of morality – progress was sought but never sustained. In our modern world we have rules and institutions to limit immoral behaviour, but it is far less clear that the natural morality of humans has improved. We may only be better at managing our own immorality (although that in itself is no small achievement). As our societies became larger, we had to become more sophisticated in how we handled social relations. Some suggest that the standard of public and private morality has sharply declined in comparison to village life, but social historians are revealing just how vicious and immoral village life usually was. Making slavery not just illegal, but also immoral has to count as one striking example of moral progress, and can be seen as foundational to the wider campaign now underway to establish legal criteria for universal human rights.

In a related way, we can also speak of having made progress in devising better forms of government. Hunter-gatherers were held in thrall by superstition. Agrarian society had ruthless ruling warrior and priestly classes. Most peasants had an unthinking belief in religion. When agrarian society eventually formed states, found literacy, and became specialised enough to develop the notion of reason, the stage for revolution was set. The process was protracted and far from inevitable, but the point is that it did develop. Industrial society eventually empowered individuals and abandoned superstition for science. Far more humans could then choose a social order and increasingly their place within it. Few can doubt that eventually this third stage of development produced much more opportunity, and in so doing greatly extended the range of liberty. And yet liberty and happiness are not the same thing. The rise of the individual necessarily meant that society would become more fragmented, and individuals more set adrift in a sea of identities.

Nor is it immediately obvious that a more material meaning of happiness demonstrates progress. In our longer lives we clearly have more to do. We spend more time on formal education, on coping with the demands of bureaucracy, on moving from place to place, and on thinking. Total annual working hours are longer than in the agricultural age, although the working day and working year is shorter than in the early age of the industrial revolution. Sweat-shops have largely given way to more civilised working conditions in the developed world. There is said to be more stress in average lives, but this is hard to quantify. An ability to articulate a concern with stress seems to be an especially modern problem born out of an increasing sense that the individual should be much more aware of their own state of mind and interests. Society in the developed world is clearly far more complex than ever before. Individuals have more choice, and in that sense more liberty. But choice means carrying more personal responsibility for dealing with the consequences of unwise or unlucky decisions. In some important senses the most developed societies have become more atomised and individuals within them more anomic. Family structures are shattered earlier and more often. The developed world has invented state-provided welfare, but the agricultural age had family-based networks. As the nature of society changes, mechanisms are found to cope, but coping is not the same as progress. In modern, wealthy countries, the search for a new form of family values is testimony to the sense of dissatisfaction with current arrangements and the need to find a better way to organise society.

Deciding whether humankind has made progress in these complex aspects of happiness is probably an impossible task. Not surprisingly the main part of the debate about whether humans make progress deals in these far less tangible aspects. The difficulty in reaching judgements about human happiness has a great deal to do with the fact that we made much progress in moving towards a basis where these questions are to be judged by individuals, not mystics, clerics or tyrants. We only ask these questions about happiness because we have the freedom to do so. Phrases like 'ignorance is bliss' or 'what you don't know can't hurt you' suggest that we used to live in a world where we were not expected to think about progress in terms of human happiness.

But here we are in the late twentieth century and we are asking these questions. By and large it is a sign of progress that we can and still want to do so. But just as with other aspects of progress, it is far from clear that there is only one road to greater human happiness, let alone whether any of the possible roads are smooth. The debates about happiness do not take place in the poorest parts of the world, for there the basic material elements of happiness still depend on whether wealth and peace can be brought up to much higher levels. The core of the debate about what makes for happiness takes place in the rapidly developing world, and especially in places where wealth and prosperity seem far more assured.

In the richest part of the world there is what Robert Hughes calls a 'culture of complaint' and what Francis Fukuyama calls an 'entitlement culture of victims'. These critics from the conservative wing of the spectrum argue that people complain too much about what is wrong with their lives. They pay insufficient attention to the gains that have been made and the reasons why. By grouching and demanding entitlements, they misunderstand the competitive instincts that must lie at the heart of human progress. What the critics of the critics misunderstand is that the very process of dialectical criticism is what makes for competition and innovation. A degree of a culture of complaint is creative and is what was so deeply embedded in the Enlightenment's notion of scepticism

The Western world is also berated by the *nouveaux riches*, especially in East Asia, for having abandoned the Victorian values (what they call Asian values) of thrift, hard work and family unity. These critics are claiming that they have discovered a new route to progress – one that is based on distinctive cultural values. This is a vexed question. To what extent is progress dependent on culture, and what is culture anyway? Cultural arguments are often the refuge of sloppy thinkers who find it hard to explain seemingly distinctive features of society. If Singaporeans save more money than Spaniards, is that because they have a cultural predilection to do so? Or do Singaporeans save because their government forces them to do so, or because such saving is a normal practice at their stage of development? Victorians used to talk of Protestant ethics and modern critics of developed countries call for a return to these supposed Victorian values.

But what seems more likely is that the East Asians are on a path of progress already well trodden by inhabitants of the Atlantic world. To be sure, the Canadian, Norwegian or French version of modernisation is somewhat different, and culture may help explain some of those differences. But there is nothing unique or miraculous about the values that East Asians have when they are in the high boost phase of their economic growth. They too will soon discover that they have to debate family values versus individualism, environmental values versus materialism, and the degree of complaint to be tolerated in multi-cultural societies when their economies mature. The challenges of demographic bulges will hit the East Asians a generation or so later than they did in the Atlantic world, and they will be more intense, just as their economic modernisation was more intense. But it is unlikely that they have discovered some new path to economic progress, let alone to human happiness.

In most of the developed world, it may well be that the joys of criticism have gone too far. But the creation of greater wealth does seem to depend on encouraging the right of individuals to define their lives, thereby restricting the rights of societies and their institutions to set limits. This is a process of give and take that can only be discussed in an environment where individuals get to define how they wish to make progress. The search for new senses of community or new forms of a 'stakeholder' society are only the most recent efforts to resolve what is a natural and indeed inevitable tension between individuals and their societies. But civil society is not static. Victorian or supposed Asian values cannot be retained or regained when everything around them is changing. When the contraceptive pill has been invented, it is foolish to argue that women must stay at home to rear children. And if women can work like men, then their rights must be equal.

If such notions are accepted – and they increasingly are – then modern wealthy societies must move on from the ethics of their parents who took it for granted that women stayed at home and only men worked and competed in a wider world. The liberation of the talents of half of humanity must be seen as an enormous opportunity for humankind, even though it will, as always, bring with it unexpected and sometimes undesirable change. It may well be true that some women might prefer not to have been 'liberated', but it is patronising for the liberated, whether men or women, to say so. It has been apparent for some time that there is a need to find new ways to build family structures and there is already plenty of evidence, certainly in the most developed countries, that the decline in 'family values' (e.g. as seen in divorce rates) has stopped. In many respects, the anxiety about social decay in the wealthy West reflects the immediate memory of the unusual period of the supposedly 'golden age' of the 1950s and early 1960s. In reality, the health of society looks far more robust when compared to the period before the 1940s. In the developed world, a higher percentage of people are married than was the case a century ago. Communities may no longer be built around Rotary clubs and more people may be 'bowling alone', but there are also sharp increases in new forms of community building, including more popular communal sports (football), and more fathers are taking an active role in their children's schooling.

Under such circumstances, it is obvious that our understanding of happiness and the ways in which we judge the quality of life or the 'feel-good factors', must also change. One of the important reasons why we are at a turning point at this millennium is because the potential for such vast social change is only now being unleashed. Of course, as George Bernard Shaw noted, 'the reasonable man adapts himself to the world; the unreasonable one persists in trying to adapt the world to himself. Therefore, all progress depends on the unreasonable man.' That is why debate about progress in creating happiness in free societies is inevitable and necessary. Judging the quality of life must remain a subjective process. But the basic building blocks of society have changed before and they are bound to change in the future.

Our layman's common-sense verdict will invariably be that life in the late twentieth century is better than a century earlier. At least in the developed world, there is no child labour, women have more rights, individuals have far more freedom from disease, and adults have more leisure. Individuals have far more freedom to choose their own lifestyle. Of course, that very ability to choose brings new tensions and challenges: Longfellow's monsters again. Few would choose not to have that freedom to choose, but the choice is not without costs, some of them substantial. It reminds us of that common-sense notion of 'two steps forward and one step back'. But just because there is 'one step back', few would choose not to take two steps forward.

In choosing to step forward, most people recognise the imperfection of the process. Part of the explanation for why people choose to move forward is their desire for a bigger house, more gadgets or a better life for their children. Some are motivated by altruism and compassion. But an important part of the explanation is also found in the search for status and power. The mix of these and other reasons is hard to fathom. But the fact that the mixture produces more happiness for most people is hard to deny. Of course it is not utopia – for that would suggest that progress has an end, or at least a foreseeable end. Neither is it dystopia, although those who endured German, Soviet, or Maoist concentration camps, or the killing fields of Cambodia, or Rwanda, could be forgiven for thinking so.

In between utopia and dystopia lies a range of options. The current wave of pessimism has been described as heterotopia – a place where things are different but the existence of difference makes no difference. It is a belief that the 'grand narratives' of history, and the grandest of them all, the belief in progress, is over. It is an assumption that we are into an age of sustainability, and that progress is not possible. But this peculiar version of 'the end of history' is only one of a range of possible futures. Its trendiness no doubt has much to do with the fact that we have recently ended a major phase of the struggle for the future of progress, and as yet we do not know where we go from here. These attitudes are somewhat reminiscent of a nineteenth-century economist David Ricardo's gloomy notion that scarce land and diminishing returns would inevitably undermine the future, or early twentieth-century economist John Maynard Keynes' notion that wealth creation would taper off and capitalism would be replaced by community and egalitarianism. But as the modern-day economist Paul Romer has argued so persuasively, technological change accounts for 80% of growth and there are no signs that the growth of ideas that lies behind technological change has become more scarce.

What we have tried to argue so far is not only that there is somewhere to go – this is not the end of history – but that there is evidence that the somewhere can be better than where we have been. In the long view, there is compelling evidence for sustained progress in both material and social terms as the underlying reality of the human condition. Not everyone will agree about what constitutes progress, but few would opt for stagnation or decay, and there are some common cores on which the commitment to progress is widespread. Would it not be better if we could kill, torture, alienate and marginalise fewer people? Surely there is a virtue in more satisfying work, more (and more effective) education, and more comforting or stimulating leisure. We want more justice. We probably want more control over, but less destruction to our environment. We want faster and easier travel. We want more knowledge about the basics of life, and about life beyond our planet. We might be able to have much of this, but we will probably only have it in a more complex world. That complexity and the process of change will bring challenges and no doubt set-backs. Perhaps the greatest challenge will be in evolving new forms of society. Our ever-increasing multiple identities will make for ever more complex civil societies. Judging whether we are happy, when we are so many more types of people, will obviously be harder, but perhaps more satisfying.

But before we begin the detailed anticipation of where we are heading, it is worth reflecting that even if we understand that there is something called progress, it is mostly achieved without any central control or conscious steering. This is not to say that there is a drunkard's walk to catastrophe, for the system we have seems to have self-correcting mechanisms based on criticism and debate. It is the essence of a system based on individual choice, scientific study, and market forces that it produces conflicting and ever changing assessments and options. The essential role of scepticism and criticism in this system means errors can be spotted and solutions found. Errors can be major and long-lasting, but so far there is no compelling evidence that errors cannot be retrieved. Our current fashion for pessimism is, in fact, part of our strength. Pessimists and their warnings, as well as optimists and their hopes, are a kind of steering mechanism.

In this sense, the modern, pluralist idea of progress is almost synonymous with Westernisation. Although the whole of human history can be seen in retrospect as a form of progress, the West has embodied the concept as a basic part of its self-definition. So fundamental is this synthesis that the permanent willingness to question and reconsider the criteria by which progress is evaluated has become part of the Western idea of progress itself. Progress is neither a single quality nor a fixed programme. It is a continuously debated and adjusted set of values covering all aspects of the human condition. This set of values shapes and is shaped by the open-ended self-transformation of industrial society. Their combination, and the expectation of further progress, is the unique hallmark of Western civilisation, and the reason for its fascination with the future.

It is to that fascination that we now turn. Part of the process of progress in the Western tradition is to question the present's view of itself. One way of doing that is to treat the present as history.

Civilisation and the West

People sometimes tell me that they prefer barbarism to civilisation. I doubt if they have given it a long enough trial. Like the people of Alexandria, they are bored by civilisation; but all the evidence suggests that the boredom of barbarism is infinitely greater.

Kenneth Clark, Lord, *Civilisation*, ch. 1 (1970).

Increased means and increased leisure are the two civilizers of man.

Benjamin Disraeli, speech, 3 April 1872, Manchester, England.

Civilization is a stream with banks. The stream is sometimes filled with blood from people killing, stealing, shouting and doing the things historians usually record, while on the banks, unnoticed, people build homes, make love, raise children, sing songs, write poetry and even whittle statues. The story of civilization is the story of what happened on the banks. Historians are pessimists because they ignore the banks for the river.

Will Durant, *Life* (New York, 18 Oct. 1963).

Civilization is drugs, alcohol, engines of war, prostitution, machines and machine slaves, low wages, bad food, bad taste, prisons, reformatories, lunatic asylums, divorce, perversion, brutal sports, suicides, infanticide, cinema, quackery, demagogy, strike lockouts, revolutions, putsches, colonization, electric chairs, guillotines, sabotage, floods, famine, disease, gangsters, money barons, horse racing, fashion shows, poodle dogs, chow dogs, Siamese cats, condoms, pessaries, syphilis, gonorrhea, insanity, neuroses, etc., etc.

Henry Miller, *The Cosmological Eye,* 'An Open Letter to Surrealists Everywhere' (1939).

Mahatama Gandhi, on being asked for his view on Western civilisation attrib.

'I think it would be a good idea.'

THE VIEW FROM 2050

15

'Anticipating the future' is a carefully chosen phrase. Our business in these next three chapters is not to predict the future, but to find a way of having the future tell us what is important about the present. Only by knowing what is important now, can we begin to anticipate the future that will grow out of our own time.

What will historians of the future think is important about our time? What will the texts used to teach students about the late twentieth century say? Will they look upon us as living through times of great transformation that shaped their own world, or see us as part of some humdrum historical era of interest only to specialists? If we are at a turning of eras, how big a change will future historians see as occurring in our time? Will it rank high, comparable with how we see great moments in history such as the rise of Europe and the world transformation that began circa AD 1500 or the dawn of civilisation starting in the fourth millennium BC? Or will it look more like the First World War or the Russian Revolution, very important in its own time, but clearly part of a larger process rather than a key turning point in itself?

The answers to these questions will of course change according to how far into the future we move our perspective. As a rule, distance in time changes how things are interpreted. The further back big events are, the easier it is to see how they fit into larger patterns, and the closer they are the more difficult it is to judge their significance. Distance in time can also affect what is remembered and what is not, though here the effect is more uneven. In general, more remote events are more easily forgotten and so have less influence on the present. But particular cases can remain strong despite being long past. Old history is active in present-day politics in Northern Ireland, in ex-Yugoslavia, in Israel/Palestine, and between Vietnam and China to name just a few. The Second World War still looks like a huge event to us, because we live not far downstream from its turbulence. But from a longer distance even such huge events fade in significance. The First World War is already beginning to feel remote, and the Napoleonic Wars hardly figure at all in how most people think about the present day. Only specialists now know about the nearly millennium-long war between the Roman/Byzantine empires on the one side, and the Parthian/Sassanian empires on the other. And of course historians continually rewrite history in the light of their own present. One view of the historian's job is that it is to make the past intelligible in terms of the preoccupations of the present. What seems important about the past is shaped by what seems important in the present. Interpretations of history are as much a way of understanding the present as they are of understanding the past.

Camus on the Future

Real generosity towards the future lies in giving all to the present.

Albert Camus, *The Rebel*, pt. 5, 'Beyond Nihilism' (1951; tr. 1953).

Our problem is that the more remote from us our future historians are, the less we know about their particular conditions. We have to assume that there will be historians in our future, and to that extent we are already biased against the whole swathe of gloom-laden scenarios that involve the extinction of humankind. Excluding such catastrophes, fifty years ahead we can make some good guesses about what circumstances our historians will be in. Five hundred years ahead is much less certain, with much more room for unanticipatable developments. Five thousand years ahead, we basically don't know anything for sure. We have to assume that there is a civilisation still existing on this planet which sees some connection between itself and the story told in Part I of this book, and therefore has an interest in our history. We do not have to assume that the inhabitants of that civilisation are human in the same sense as we are.

The relative risk

Astronomers believe that an asteroid large enough to kill up to half the world's population strikes once every few hundred thousand years. It's a low-probability event but with potentially devastating consequences, and therefore the odds of dying by cosmic impact are relatively high.

Cause of death	Probability
Car accident	1 in 100
Murder	1 in 300
Fire	1 in 800
Firearms accident	1 in 2,500
Electrocution	1 in 5,000
Asteroid impact	**1 in 20,000**
Flood	1 in 30,000
Tornado	1 in 60,000
Poisonous bite or sting	1 in 100,000
Fireworks accident	1 in 1 million
Food poisoning	1 in 3 million

Source: Chapman and Morrison.

One firm thing about the future is the sense of scale that distance gives any observer of the total pattern of history. We can get some of the feel of a future historian's perspective on our time by reflecting on how we see times that are a similar distance in our own past. With this parallel in mind, we have built these chapters around three jumps ahead of fifty (AD 2050), five hundred (AD 2500) and five thousand years (AD 7000). Doing so mirrors our own perspectives on the beginning of the Cold War, the beginning of European expansion, and the beginning of civilisation.

Some readers will object that this comparison of past and future is false. A future historian's view of our time will not be the same as our view of our own past. For one thing, record keeping is likely to be better between now and our three points in the future than it has been between now and 3000 BC (though one cannot rule out major disruptions and losses along the way).

For another, the analytical tools of a more sophisticated future (assuming that it is more sophisticated) will almost certainly be better than ours (think of what we can do now with genetic analysis of ancient bones and tissues, versus what archaeologists could do just a few decades ago). For another, our future historians will be looking back to a civilisation well established and with a long history, rather than, as we do, to the beginning of civilisation itself. And for another, history may be accelerating, meaning that future generations will be further separated from us by the magnitude of their accomplishments than we are from our ancestors. If the human future moves faster than its past, then these distances will not mean the same thing in both directions. At the same distance in time, we will seem further removed and more primitive to our heirs than our ancestors seem to us. All of these things will make a difference (and many others besides if one imagines what future civilisation(s) will be like). They must be taken into account. But unless our heirs have solved the puzzles of time travel, these points do not override the fundamental fact that distance in time, just as distance in space, shapes the view you get in a number of big and simple ways. A few turning points will perhaps stand as epochal for as long as anyone still thinks about human history. In this league one would find the agricultural revolution, the founding of urban civilisation, and humankind's first ventures into space. But all else will be subject to the logic of relative distance in time, and that fact gives us a way to connect our own time to a set of increasingly remote and unknowable futures.

In our first look back, we move fifty years into the future. Fifty years is the distance that we now stand from the end of the Second World War and the beginning of the Cold War. It is only two generations away, and so sits solidly within living memory. It will be within the realm of expected knowledge for most educated people too young to remember it directly (like the authors of this book). At fifty years' distance connections from past to present are still numerous, obvious and strong. Many direct effects of main events half a century before will still be visible. We can, for example, still see big effects of the Second World War, and the beginning of the Cold War, in the division of Korea, the constrained positions of Japan and Germany as great powers, the problem of Israel, the conflict between India and Pakistan, the construction of the UN and most other intergovernmental organisations, and many other elements in today's world.

But things will also have moved on. In the course of half a century quite large events can play themselves out. In the fifty years separating the mid-1990s from the mid-1940s, at least two world-reshaping events came and went: the Cold War, whose two-power rivalry threatened humankind with nuclear Armageddon; and decolonisation, which transformed a world of empires into a world of states. Half a century can also see a lot of changes. Since 1945, among other things, television, antibiotics, nuclear technologies, satellites and computers have come from nowhere to occupy major positions in society; passenger ships have given way to mass air transport; and at least in the rich world, there have been wholesale changes of attitude towards the environment, and towards gender relations. A view from half-a-century's distance, in other words, will almost certainly contain a mixture of strong continuities and quite big changes. It will see a world whose outlines still feel familiar in many ways, yet which is different enough to feel like another age.

Some of the people reading this book now will still be alive in 2050. It is not inconceivable that among them will be the authors of the words you are reading as well as the fictional historian through whose eyes we look back at our present. We can project with reasonable assurance some of the characteristics of the world in which that historian will sit. Its political and cultural framework will be quite similar to our own. Most of the familiar states and nations and major languages will probably still be there, as will many of the international and transnational organisations (or their recognisable successors). Large parts of Asia will have carried through their process of modernisation, though whether this will have been achieved without wars in the region is less certain. The world will still be heavily divided by patterns of uneven development and inequality. The restraints on war amongst the leading world powers will probably be stronger and somewhat more widespread, but so too will the problem of failed states and the proliferation of privatised violence. The development of the global economy and global communications will have continued, and be much deeper rooted, and more widespread. The world population will be something like double what we now have, but it will be peaking, with only a few areas still showing sharp growth. A great redistribution of population will have taken place, with the old West having shrunk to a smallish percentage of the world's people, and containing a relatively even mix of age groups; and the rest of the world containing the bulk of humanity, and with a preponderance of younger age groups.

What will the historians of 2050 say about us? Here follows a chapter from one of their textbooks: *INTRODUCING MODERN HUMAN HISTORY: The Making of World Society from 1500–2050.*

Chapter 11 – Legacies of the Late Twentieth Century

The late twentieth century was in many ways a major turning point in the making of world society. Anyone looking for legacies from the past is bound to come up with a mixed picture. Just as those who lived after what was called 'The Second World War' saw good things (the defeat of fascism) and bad things (the nuclear terror and the vicious world-wide rivalry between communism and capitalism), so we also see a mixed picture. What we see as good or bad reflects not just who we are, but also the forces that won the battles of history to shape who we are.

Although the historical place of the late twentieth century seems clear to us it was not at all clear to the people living through it at the time. Throughout the first decade of the twenty-first century the transformation was viewed with a mixture of confusion, alarm and complacency. Confusion arose from the suddenness with which the communist world imploded. Four decades of what was called 'The Cold War' had created a strong sense of stability about the world's economic and political order. The one big, simple, durable issue of the Cold War gave way to myriad smaller, and often nastier, issues whose importance was difficult to judge. For a time, there was in some quarters even nostalgia for the great simplification of nuclear confrontation that had held a knife to humankind's throat for several decades.

Confusion also had deeper causes. People were aware of the erosion of the state and the growing power of the market, but they did not know whether this was a good or a bad thing, and had little idea of what to do about it. Many people were disorientated by the pace of technological change, finding themselves confronted by machines they could not operate and did not understand. Many also, at least for a time, found themselves unable to gain, or keep, access to the economy and society through employment, and pundits spoke of 'a dark gash across society'. The dizzying pace of change reinforced a generation gap, widening the social universes of the old, the middle-aged and the young.

Alarm was caused by fears of social crisis and breakdown, both local and global, and by fears for traditional patterns of identity ranging from family to nation. In the West, the nuclear family was under pressure from the mass re-entry of women into the labour force, and the sustained exposure of children to powerful media influences. After the end of the Cold War there were violent episodes of state failure in Cambodia, Somalia, Yugoslavia, and several places in sub-Saharan Africa. Even where the state survived, many people experienced growing levels of criminal violence, and in some places powerful mafias became a major force. A wave of cheap small arms washed across the planet threatening social stability in many countries. It was a time when ultra-nationalism was enjoying a revival in some parts of the world, especially the ex-communist countries. This, along with a surge of religious fundamentalism in several other areas, kindled the flames of political violence. Together, these extremisms fed both terrorism and a rash of vicious civil wars.

Kaplan on the Coming Anarchy

We are entering a bifurcated world. Part of the globe is inhabited by Hegel's and Fukuyama's Last Man, healthy, well fed, and pampered by technology. The other, larger, part is inhabited by Hobbe's First Man, condemned to a life that is 'poor, nasty, brutish and short' . . . Although both parts will be threatened by environmental stress, the Last Man will be able to master it: the First Man will not.

From Robert Kaplan, 'The Coming Anarchy' in *The Atlantic Monthly*, p. 60.

Perhaps the most far-reaching threat came from what some described as 'the atomising forces of the market' which seemed to erode social structures from family through local community. Those same forces also seemed to be mounting an assault on the planetary environment. Fears of global breakdown were fed by weakening American leadership, and a newly unleashed financial system that seemed unable to stop itself from generating repeated currency crises and credit collapses, and periodic failures of major institutions. Many feared for their own identities, for the stability of their societies, and even for the sustainability of the whole human adventure.

Complacency stemmed from a more optimistic school of thought which assumed that the West's victory in the Cold War meant the dawn of a new age of triumphant global liberalism. With its last challenger defeated, no obstacle seemed to stand in the way of an unrestrained spread of Western ideas. The world seemed to be so safe for the liberal values of markets, individualism and democracy that some thoughtful analysts at the time seriously argued that humankind had reached the 'end of history'. By this they meant that solutions had been found to age-old questions about how to organise the political economy of human societies so that they would be both peaceful and prosperous, without at the same time being weak. This being the case, there were no great tensions left to drive the dialectics of history. Evidence for this was found in the economic liberalisation of even the Chinese economy, and the emergence of nascent liberal democracies in Japan, Korea, Taiwan and South Africa.

This cacophony of conflicting interpretations deprived the inhabitants of the late twentieth century of any coherent view of their own time and place, and indeed, of any coherent view of history. On balance, negative views of the future dominated debates and perceptions. The *fin de siècle* fashion was for environmental disasters, waves of unwanted migration, ethnic conflict and social collapses on a large scale, incurable new plagues, and economic crises. Psycho-historians have subsequently attributed much of this to a millennial miasma that ran strongly through Western society for more than a decade.

Quite the most curious aspect of the miasma was the gloom about inter-civilisational conflict. It was almost as if the major societies of the day could not bear to live without the idea that they were existentially threatened from outside. A relatively mild form of this was the debate about 'Asian values' that raged on through much of the 1990s. This debate can perhaps best be seen as a kind of eastern retaliation against the excesses of Western triumphalism and complacency. The new Asia did not want to see itself merely as a Western clone, and reacted sharply to the suggestion that its own culture had little or nothing other than some exotic food, arts and games, to contribute to world civilisation. In this it simply mirrored Western triumphalism in its own image.

A harsher version was the debate about a so called 'clash of civilisations'. The basic idea was of a declining, post-colonial West being increasingly challenged by rising civilisations in East Asia and the Islamic world. Its vision was of a neo-classical world of distinct and separate civilisations somehow equipped with all of the modern means of communication and warfare. It ignored the cross-cultural fusions that undermined one of its assumptions, and blithely overlooked the more potent fact that most of the civilisations were too strongly divided within themselves to operate as a combined unit in a power rivalry with others. But this idea nonetheless had influence. It fed into trade disputes, first between the United States and Japan, and then between the United States and China, and more generally between the old West and the new Asia. For a time, it seemed to threaten, and even to encourage, a radically different and more conflictual future.

Huntington on Clashes of Civilisations

Human History is the history of civilizations . . . Civilizations are the ultimate human tribes, and the clash of civilizations is tribal conflict on a global scale . . . Peoples and countries with similar cultures are coming together. Peoples and countries with different cultures are coming apart . . . Power is shifting from the long-predominant West to non-Western civilizations . . . At the micro level, the most violent fault lines are between Islam and its Orthodox, Hindu, African, and Western Christian neighbours. At the macro level, the dominant division is between 'the West and the rest' . . . The dynamism of Islam is the ongoing source of many relatively small fault line wars; the rise of China is the potential source of a big intercivilizational war . . . In the clash of civilizations, Europe and America will hang together or hang separately . . . Multiculturalism at home threatens the United States and the West; universalism abroad threatens the West and the world . . .

From Samuel Huntington, *The Clash of Civilizations and the Remaking of World Order*, pp. 40, 207, 125, 29, 183, 209, 321, 318.

The clash of civilisations idea was, in the end, a curiously defeatist view of the West's own historical project. It ignored the fact that, for better or for worse, the West's imperial and post-imperial phases had successfully constructed a world economy and aspects of a world culture. The economic development was, as is historically normal, well in advance of its cultural and political companions. As the twenty-first century entered its stride, it became clear that for the economically developed and developing worlds, there was a lattice into which a new civilisation could grow. What the inhabitants of the late twentieth century might have found most pleasantly surprising was the extent to which this new lattice was held together by ties of interest and culture at both a global and very local level. The late twentieth century had laid the basis for complex identities that drew on components from global as well as local culture. A few popular writers on communication at the time wrote about the simultaneous virtues of 'broadcasting' – the globalising forces, and of 'narrowcasting' – the ability to satisfy the interests of smaller groups with tighter and more robust ties of community. This version of 'glocalisation' was more correct than they knew.

MONDO CULTURE

One of the most important achievements of the late twentieth century was laying the foundations for a stable, pluralist sense of identity that began to embrace most of humankind. Though scarcely visible at the time, it is a very clear development in retrospect. It was only when humans had filled the space of the globe that they began to learn how to live with each other in greater harmony. The early phases of living in a more crowded world had resulted in horrific exploitation, conflict, and in places, deaths on a genocidal scale. The first attempts to deal with a world where different groups of people intermingled were dominated by imperialism, racism, virulent nationalism, and myriad forms of social and political inequality. But by the end of the twentieth century, and first apparent in the most economically developed parts of the world, there began to emerge a more layered, less exclusive, and more tolerant sense of identity. People moved away from the overriding sense of national identity that had dominated, and in many ways disrupted, much of the nineteenth and twentieth centuries. While not abandoning it entirely, they added to it both a rediscovered localism and many non-geographical threads of linkage to communities of shared interest varying from professional to sexual, and from political to hobbyist. Many people also began to discover, or rediscover, a vaguer sense of belonging to much larger communities, of being European, Western, Muslim, or just of being a member of the human race. There was room in this scheme to take pleasure in multiculturalism rather than seeing it as a threat. One could be a female; Londoner; British; European; software author; lover of Beethoven's music; Westerner; and member of the human community all at the same time.

As people expanded and diversified their own sense of identity, it became easier for them to take a welcoming, or at least tolerant, attitude to those belonging to other human communities. The idea that human rights are a universal value began tentatively to take hold, albeit accompanied by large amounts of opposition, backsliding and hypocrisy. In coming to this understanding, the developed world, and first its Atlantic components, began to moderate, if not yet abandon, its own long tradition of racism and cultural superiority. It was the first major civilisation to do so, and challenged the world's many other xenophobic cultures to follow suit.

The process of shifting from exclusivist, and often racist, cultural attitudes towards more open, multicultural ones was slow and very uneven. Even today it is far from complete, and many pockets of ethnic hatred still blot the political landscape. But there is no doubt that an important change took firm root in the late twentieth century and has continued to unfold ever since.

This transformation of identities paved the way for what eventually became known as 'Mondo culture'. Mondo culture was about the move away from a world of tightly bounded and geopolitically separated nations and states, and towards a more complicated multicultural world in which cultures penetrated each other, and up to a point blended and fused. In part it was about the creation of a cosmopolitan world culture, but that was not its main feature. In almost no sense was there a significant move to replace a world fragmented into many identities with a world homogenised into one. Mondo was primarily about humans learning to live with each other more closely while retaining their myriad identities. It was a shift from walling different identities off from each other into distinct territorial compounds, to having them live much more intermingled. Supporting this more intimate cultural pluralism required the spread of elements of common culture. Without them the cultural mix would be too explosive to sustain. Mondo was thus a blend of globalising and localising forces, each dependent on the other. The story of how it emerged is worth telling in some detail.

The roots of Mondo culture can be traced back several decades before the classical Western period actually ended, but the process did not really begin to gel until the last few years of the century. Two earlier developments combined to lay its foundations. First was the release of Asian and African peoples from Western control during the 1940s, 50s and 60s, and the release of European and Asian ones from Russian-Soviet control during the 1990s. Second was the American-led globalisation of trade, production and finance that got seriously underway during the 1960s. Some more technically-minded historians refer to this development as 'Westernistic civilisation', but when awareness of it surfaced strongly after 2010 it found the popular label 'Mondo culture'. Westernistic is a more accurate description, for it was Western culture that provided most of the common threads with which much of the world was woven together. But the driving force behind the new age was a sense of liberation from the Atlantic-dominated era. Asians in particular felt free to assert their own cultures, and the West felt free to abandon its imperial past, its ideological rivalries and internecine wars, and, as a consequence, also to abandon its responsibility for keeping world order. Mondo culture expressed this mixture of unity and diversity in a term acceptable to nearly all.

As early as the second half of the twentieth century, there were powerful forces of intercultural linkage that laid the basis for our currently complex sense of identity. In the first stage, most ruling elites and professionals in virtually all of the colonised world quickly acquired Western education, style, and in many respects behaviour, while at the same time retaining many of their own distinct cultural practices. What was more remarkable was that this mixture of cultural synthesis and fragmentation deepened after decolonisation, and not just as an extension of relations between ex-master and ex-ruled.

A crucial second stage in this process took place when migrants from the ex-colonial world moved into the home territories of the Western metro-politan states after decolonisation. The United States found itself absorbing waves of immigrants from South America and to a much smaller extent from Asia. Many of the countries making up the European Union found themselves having to function with substantial minority populations of Arabs, South Asians, West Indians, Africans and/or Turks. Where the Europeans had rolled back and largely replaced the native populations, as in the Americas, Australia and parts of Southern Africa, the transplanted Western societies were slowly but steadily re-penetrated both by the indigenous native cultures they had overrun, and (in the Americas) also by the descendants of the slaves and indentured labourers they had imported in the early phases of their development.

Migrants, natives and the descendants of the slaves and indentured labourers all took on board many aspects of Western culture without at the same time abandoning all of their own. They steadily learned to use the machinery of democracy to establish their rights, often against fierce and racist resistance. Since they had become permanent residents, and in some cases citizens, of the Western core, they acted as bridgeheads from which multiculturalism was projected into the heart of the West itself. Intermarriage between these communities and their Western hosts stea-dily created people who carried the new range of cultural fusions stamped on their faces.

The key to the creation of successful multiculturalism was an under-standing both of the virtues of openness, and also of the fact that the 'multi' in multiculturalism had to be within individuals and not just between easily identifiable and persistently distinct groups. The fundamental openness of classical Western society was vital to its success in taking over the rest of the world. But it also meant that the West could not resist some of the attractive offerings, whether musical, culinary, philosophical, social, or indeed human, available from the cultures it had subordinated (and in some cases nearly exterminated). For a remarkably long time it was thought that the West appeared to be consolidating a global cultural hegemony. In due course, as it became clear that the West was itself being culturally transformed by those whom it had incorporated into its sphere, it became easier to see the reality and virtues of pluralistic identities. Although in the initial stages Western culture continued to set most of the global framework, there was plenty of room for a great mix of cultures to establish their legitimacy and even to compete with some of the basic Western ideas.

In the non-Western world, Western influence diffused steadily into the wider population both from elites and from émigré communities inside the West. As well, of course, it was reinforced by continued commercial, cultural and political contact with the West in both its best and worst forms. By the late 1990s this process was reaching critical mass in China, Korea and much of Southeast Asia. In Japan, Taiwan and Singapore it was more advanced, including most of the population, and had given rise to distinctive and successful forms of political economy in some ways unlike, and some thought better than, their erstwhile Western models. The spectacular economic success in East Asia, where the pursuit of a more open economic strategy made possible real prosperity, and more slowly, political liberalism, quickly exposed them to the same multicultural forces that were remaking the West. East Asian societies, in both their relatively exclusivist variety such as Korea or Japan, and in their more deeply divided variants in Southeast Asia, went through some difficult times in entrenching real pluralism and in learning to accept complex identities. The East Asians, like the inhabitants of the Atlantic world before them, had to learn how to integrate people of different backgrounds. With hindsight it is clear that in having met the challenge of multiculturalism and created complex identities, they became more robust and successful societies. Their eventual success was in no small measure due to the essentially warm welcome they were given by the already more developed states in the Atlantic world. The East Asian societies then went on to become a beacon to others, especially in South America, guiding their subsequent development.

In India, the old civilisation was initially more resistant to Westernisation despite its long and (by the standards of the day) quite benign experience of colonial occupation and exploitation. Its ancient culture retained a powerful appeal to those embedded within its labyrinthine embraces (and some outside them). Its idealisation of spiritual over material values, however much breached in practice, defended it for a long time after decolonisation against the appeal of Western materialism. But Westernisation became much easier to accept once Indian reformers recognised that their culture and ethnic roots were closer to the Atlantic world than to that of East Asia. India also had a head start towards the multiculturalism of

Mondo. Compared to most other post-colonial societies India was successful, despite the obstacles of poverty and illiteracy, in mixing a multiplicity of identities within a stable, large-scale democratic state.

The Islamic world was in a less favourable position. It had the spiritual (and because of oil, the economic) resources to maintain its attraction against the West and was longer able to resist the more open and tolerant patterns of Mondo culture. Its commercial traditions were compatible with the development of an international economy, but two other of its strong traditions worked to its own political and economic disadvantage. First it was unable to find a way of successfully reconciling the idea of the Islamic community as a whole with the need to organise in a system of states. This meant that it was spectacularly vulnerable to political instability, gross materialism and bad government. Second, it was unable to escape from the self-image of being the most successful and expansive world culture. This image dated from the last great period of Islamic expansion before the global triumph of Europe, when the Islamic world spread to incorporate large parts of Africa, South and Southeast Asia, and Southeast Europe. Much of the Islamic world continued to live within this past image, tragically enjoying former glory at the expense of a pressing present need to adapt to changed circumstances. Many Islamic societies hung on to autocratic and theocratic governments long after these had been abandoned elsewhere. Even where these archaic forms were overthrown, they tended to be replaced by dictatorships rather than democracies.

For a time most of the Asian cultures, and generally still today, the Islamic ones, weakened themselves by continuing the worst rather than the best of their own and Western practice in their attitudes and behaviour towards women. In most of Africa, the indigenous cultures were simply too fragmented, too poor, and too politically inept to handle the tricky mix of globalising and localising forces within a stable framework of political order.

Of course this process of cultural mixing was not simply one of Western elements joining with that of once-colonised people. An important accompanying aspect was cultural fusions between non-Western elements. In its imperial phase, the West had unintentionally sown many seeds for this by thoughtlessly shipping substantial numbers of Chinese, Indians and Africans to far-flung locations around the globe. There were also many more local and indigenous blendings such as Arab and African, Tamil and Sinhalese. In many cases the fusions and new ranges of multiple identities were the result of processes of migration that accompanied rather than having been caused by Western policy. The migration of Chinese in East Asia was not the result of anyone's coherent policy, but the unintended effect was to mix different populations together. Where such blendings had occurred, the resulting societies were faced by decolonisation with the job of creating complex identities in order to learn how to live together in a shared state. There were many early failures, as in Fiji, Sudan, Israel/ Palestine and Sri Lanka. Cuba, Brazil and Singapore were in their very different ways forms of early success.

The first concrete signs of Mondo culture, though not recognised as such, appeared in the most culturally mobile of all the arts and entertainments; music, sport, fashion and food. Blues and jazz music in the United States emerged well before the beginning of either external or internal decolonisation, much like reggae appeared in Jamaica and Britain during decolonisation. By the 1960s, the British had learned to love Indian food, the French were eating couscous, and the Americans were eating Chinese noodles. The Olympics had become a properly world-wide event, and football was well on its way to becoming the first true popular world sport.

From these beginnings unfolded an endless blending and inter-penetration of cultures. A few things followed football and the Olympics to become elements of a shared global culture. Some aspects of cinema and pop music achieved this status, and the deaths of rock idols such as John Lennon and Freddy Mercury were mourned as much in Asia as in Europe or the United States. Coca Cola and Pepsi easily switched from being American to being world brands, as did Ford, which pioneered the prophetically-named world car (Mondeo). Clothing manufacturers such as Benetton, Nike, and Reebok, and cosmetic manufacturers such as Body Shop all successfully cultivated cross-cultural world brands. All major cities increasingly had standard Western architectural features, but many also learned from Chinese-born architects and introduced Asian elements.

But as the growth industry of marketing soon discovered in the late twentieth century, there was far less reality than often appreciated in the hype about a global market. While many pundits expected the new communication and transportation technologies to produce homogenised world products, their main effect was to generate globally distributed market segments. It was true that in some cases a local or national image was a liability, but most things became globalised in a more local way. As people and their cultures intermingled, what were once local products with local markets, found themselves with a 'local' audience distributed world-wide. Not surprisingly, some of the first such examples came from East Asia, and especially the Chinese world, where rock idols and TV and movie stars could be worshipped in the Chinese communities of Toronto, San Francisco or Hong Kong. Many previously localised sports such as tennis, golf, motor racing, cricket, baseball and chess acquired global 'local' audiences. Even Sumo could be watched in London and Vancouver, as well as in Tokyo. The new technology also made it easier to spread musical fusions to smaller groups of people scattered around the globe. Western instruments and styles were blended with the local musical resources of Asia, Latin America and Africa to produce a host of other fusion styles. Reggae rhythms spread via 'two-tone' bands into mainstream rock.

Similar trends were evident in activities ranging from eating to architecture. Western-style fast-food outlets went up all over the world, but the West was also counter-colonised by restaurants from Africa, China, Korea, Japan, Thailand, Indonesia and even Afghanistan. At the same time, new syncretic food styles were emerging combining the best (and sometimes the worst) of Asian and Western ingredients and recipes. California (Cal-Ital) led the way, while the French and Chinese looked for ways of enhancing their claims to be the world's greatest cuisine by taking ideas from each other. For the makers of some specifically local products such as whisky, wine, ginseng and some types of cheese, there was much money to be made in being able to target specific markets around the globe.

The ability to reach these audiences was made possible through the burgeoning industry of global communication. CNN pioneered global television news, and was quickly followed by BBC World and Sky. But of equal interest was the fact that these and other supposedly world product ventures such as newspapers or magazines were soon altered for specific markets. Even the likes of CNN had different content in different markets. On close examination, there was far less development of a homogenised global culture, and far more that was sold globally to specific narrow markets. Only exceptionally did global products make commercial sense, and parochial forces likewise prevented any serious move towards a global currency. Only in Europe, and even there after a long struggle, did a significant group of states manage to create a single currency.

By the end of the century the main promoters of Mondo culture were the thousands of companies that responded to the globalisation of international trade, production and finance. Perhaps the most subtly important of these were the software houses such as Microsoft that came to set the standards for the world's burgeoning computer networks. These firms put into place operating packages that quickly shaped both a common experience and a pool of metaphors for hundreds of millions of people across the planet. They reinforced English as the global lingua franca, and generated almost a common language of their own. These companies developed an important element of the framework into which Mondo culture grew, and were the perfect example of the simultaneous globalising and localising that were its hallmark. The networks and some of the software were global, but they connected communities of the like-minded that were scattered all over the planet. Companies with products for smaller segments of the market were quick to use the global reach of the new forms of communication to sell to their scattered target audience.

This liberal business culture proved far more flexible and open than the diplomacy between states that had traditionally dominated the 'international relations' of classical Western civilisation. Business culture did not replace diplomacy. It grew up alongside it, absorbed parts of it, and became a player in the diplomatic game. It steadily shifted the focus of diplomacy from high politics to commerce. Eventually it grew much larger than the diplomatic network in terms of the resources it carried and the consequences of its actions, and increasingly it bypassed political channels altogether. Anyone could join the business culture provided they had the talent or the assets, and this openness meant that as a global network it could grow almost without limit. The rise of a cosmopolitan business culture on a large scale was in many ways the key to the transformation of Western hegemony into the complex identities with which we live today. Mondo culture began to crystallise at the very end of the classical Western period. It would not have happened without the West, but it did not represent a Western victory. Rather, it was a whole new range of cultural syntheses, the emergence of which signalled the shift from classical Western to Westernistic civilisation. The rest of the world was let back into the global game that the West had made.

One of the most interesting legacies of the *fin de siècle* was the so called 'internet', which from small beginnings in the 1980s had by the 1990s mushroomed into one of the trendy transmission belts of the emerging Mondo culture. What started as a slow and primitive system for connecting computer networks around the world was superseded by the far more powerful 'world window' that is now so seamlessly integrated with our everyday lives. During the 1990s, some people predicted that the internet would transform world society, leading it to an inward turn. They thought that much of human society would move into cyberspace, with electronic communication and simulation replacing direct human contact for everything from business and tourism to sex and politics. It is quaint now to read the thoughts of late twentieth-century cyber-gurus who saw the primary virtues of the new forms of communication as necessarily leading to a homogenised global culture.

In the event, the new technologies of communication did not homogenise society, though they did change many aspects of it. They certainly created a widespread subculture of 'nerds', many of whom immersed much of their lives in cyberspace. But for most people the new communications technology was just a much faster, cheaper and more versatile postal system, newspaper and library. The opening up of cyberspace provided enormous opportunity for both the globalising and localising strands of Mondo culture, making it much easier to sustain a strong sense of identity and community divorced from geographical proximity. Since distance mattered less, old diasporas could maintain themselves more easily, and new ones could form whenever an interest or identity strong enough to justify them arose. Alongside the nerds, political and sexual extremists, technophiles, soap opera addicts, environmentalists, pop music fan clubs, academic and scientific associations, and believers in 'alternatives' of all sorts piled into the internet. As they did so, a new non-territorial communitarianism began to establish itself as part of the reaction to the demise of social cohesion that so marked the late twentieth century. The ease with which communication networks could be formed and maintained quite quickly had a political impact, laying the foundations for the development of interest group politics as an element of world politics.

Rather than replacing travel, as some thought it might, the vast improvements in simulation technology simply added a new market to education and tourism, enabling those so inclined to 'visit' everything from the Taj Mahal and the Pyramids to Everest and the Great Barrier Reef, in detail, in privacy, in comfort, and in safety – and with (or without) a guide. The same marriage of simulation and communication was a boon to the world's scientists. It not only linked them into a real global community, but enabled them to plunge every deeper into the micro-universe. Biology, physics and material science all flourished in a world of nearly infinite simulation and computation where the complexities of the ultra-small could be explored in virtual reality. The success of 'world window' eventually made it possible to create the global network of world-class university education (known as the 'silicon league') available to a dispersed and travelling student body.

But the late twentieth-century discussion of the virtues of 'virtual society' was nearly the last example of this kind of technological hubris before more serious efforts were made to nurture wounded societies. The major crises in developed societies, and the salutary example of the rising power of East Asians who trumpeted their concern with 'family values', galvanised the developed world into paying more attention to how they sustained social cohesion. It was recognised that 'virtual society' was an oxymoron. Humans found that virtual reality (another great oxymoron) was ultimately cold and distant. They rediscovered the warmth of a wink or the good vibrations in the firm grip of a handshake. The kinship that comes from 'skinship' – the necessity to build trust through real personal contact, not email – was soon recognised as essential. The internet and its successors added a fabulous new dimension to all of this, but they did not transcend the need for rich human environments and vibrant societies. Although it was once felt that shopping or business meetings could be done on a computer link, it was soon realised that these activities were as much social events as technical transactions. Current sociological research reminds us that those early 'cyber-cafes' were mainly attractive because of the aroma of the coffee and the quality of the friendly chat, rather than because real satisfaction was derived from reading the news on-line from Singapore. The much touted demise of newspapers never happened until it was possible to convey the news electronically on plastic pages that could be read on the couch, carried on a train or read by the swimming pool.

The concern over the demise of social cohesion in the developed world not only encouraged the efforts to help satisfy elements of new, more complex identities by narrowcasting contacts around the globe, but also led to a series of government measures to strengthen the basic threads of the social fabric closer to home. It is odd and dangerously perverse that many people in the late twentieth century felt that the core family as the basis for identity and a firm social fabric did not matter. Just as the anxiety in the developed West was reaching its peak at the turn of the millennium, real efforts were begun to re-define and strengthen the family and wider social fabric. In most developed countries in the late 1990s the divorce rates had stopped rising. As adults married later they had more stable marriages. They had fewer children and so cared more about their future. Children came to know it was the norm for mothers to work. Because parents demanded more flexible working arrangements so as to make child-care easier, a new form of smaller, more intense families was born, as was a whole new industry of support services for them. These included everything from cleaning and technical support, through babysitting and educational and personal interaction sites for kids on the internet, to security and building maintenance. More parents worked from home, and with falling working hours, had more time to spend with their children. The leisure industry created specialised facilities for this new form of family anxious to build bonds in their leisure time. When it became clear that government spending could fall when nuclear families remained together, the tax and public service structure was used to reward these changes in work practices, long-term marriage commitments and a stable environment for children.

This process was undoubtedly made much easier by the fact that in developed countries the populations had ceased growing. In order to get over the demographic bulge whereby a small young population had to support a large older population, the state cut back its provision of basic welfare and people re-learned how to support themselves and their closest relatives. The bonds of family were strengthened, and when the demographic bulge passed, there was a new generation that recognised that society could no longer make the mistake of leaving social cohesion to government. The result is the fundamental lesson that we now take for granted – that the family is the key to identity, social stability and prosperity and that it can and must be re-made as the nature of education, work, leisure and society changes.

But if the reinvention of family – the narrowest of the elements of identity – was all that had happened, we might have merely seen the turning back of the clock rather than making progress towards the more diverse, complex and energetic societies that we know today. What was so remarkable was that while the basic elements of individual identity were rejuvenated, yet more layers were interleaved to create the pluralism of Mondo culture. In the case of these additional layers of identity, the technology of communication played a vital facilitating role. Groups of people – for example lovers of the 'Country and Western' music (born in the USA) – could exchange experiences, at least initially, through computer networks and the mass media. Easier transport made it possible for a greater number of such people to physically get together to share their experiences in much more meaningful ways. When Chai Ling (from Shanghai in the new Chinese federation) took the Country and Western charts by storm in 2025, it was a demonstration of the virtues of fragmented culture, global scale, and complex pluralism.

PROSPERITY, ECONOMISM AND LITE POWERS

Fifty years ago, following the defeat of communism, the impetus seemed to go out of the long-standing struggle to close the gaps of uneven development. Some have argued that the late classical West missed the opportunity to construct a new world order that seemed to open up in the early 1990s. The unfortunate confluence of a rare period of malleability in the world system, and the gutting of political leadership, meant that a substantial possibility of steering the development of international society was lost. Market forces were allowed to run riot in a way that not only threatened social cohesion and democracy in much of the Western and neo-Western core, but also contributed to delaying the prospect for a democratic peace that would extend across all of the major centres of power. Whether there were achievable policies that would have steered the world down a different path is something we can never know for certain, but the international system was allowed to drift into more than two decades of polarisation and crisis.

Part of this drift was the deepening and consolidation of humankind's division into three different worlds of development, all standing in uneasy relationship with each other. There was a world of rich and open societies, a world of closed states, and a world in which the whole political and economic framework was either weak or had collapsed. To some extent these 'worlds' even existed within specific societies, with poor living in a suburb next to the rich. Although the vast majority of the population in the rich and open world managed to find new jobs in the new economy (unemployment never rose above 15%), there continued to be up to 10% of the population that remained alienated, unskilled and disruptive. In the global perspective, the rich and open world contained most of the wealth, knowledge and organisational power. Military power was spread across all the worlds, though the open states retained a significant technological edge. The closed states commanded increasingly significant industrial, and in some cases financial power. In the weak and failed states parts of the decolonisation process unravelled, with quite a number of societies proving themselves incapable of effective, modern self-government in a highly interconnected international system. A rash of failed states was beginning to leave large holes in the fabric of international society.

The defeat of communism and its allegedly egalitarian objectives was probably bound to produce a bout of triumphalism. The most obvious cause was the superior ability of liberal democracies to produce wealth and social and technological innovation. Against this background, and despite the well-known shortcomings of the liberal system, there developed a tendency to draw radical and unquestioning conclusions about its absolute virtue as a system of political economy. The result was a world-wide wave of extreme market liberalism that later came to be called *the cult of economism*.

This cult had built up a head of steam in some of the core countries of the West during the 1980s, and flourished globally almost unopposed for more than a decade in the wake of the collapse of communism. While the sources of the policy – the belief that prosperity comes from freedom of the individual and markets – was well grounded, the ideas were dangerous when unbounded by a deeper concern with maintaining the basics of a social fabric. The driving idea of economism was to make market values the highest priority of society. One of its early leaders, Margaret Thatcher of the former United Kingdom, said in an unguarded moment that 'there is no such thing as society'. The more extreme advocates of economism argued that all other social projects were to be ruthlessly subordinated to the criteria of economic efficiency on the grounds that this would maximise wealth creation, and therefore both breed more freedom and make available more resources for other social projects. Its greatest successes were in East Asia, where it unleashed modernisation, and in the financial sector where something close to complete liberalisation had been achieved by the end of the century. It was not the first time such a cult had run its course across the face of world history. Something similar had evolved during the nineteenth century, and its instabilities had played a major role in causing the catastrophes of the first and second world wars that brought it down.

The late Western cult of economism had learned some lessons from the earlier disaster. But it could not avoid the fundamental instability inherent in its basic idea that the social and political life of humankind can and should be subordinated to the dictates of the market. In the transitional decades from the late twentieth to the early twenty-first century, the lesson steadily became apparent that placing any one facet of social organisation rigidly above the others was a serious mistake. Just as Soviet communism's attempt to subordinate society and economy to politics could never produce a sustainable and efficient political economy, so also the same fate awaited economism's attempt to subordinate society and politics to the economy. By 2010 substantial elements of the business class had come around to the view that if profits were to be maintained, the 'political' needed to be put back into political economy, and the 'eco' back into economics. New understandings of political economy gained ground, seeing it as a world of continuing evolutions and revolutions, where learning is possible, but where there is a continuous remaking of basic conditions because of technological, economic, environmental and social changes. The market remained central to economic organisation, but increasingly lost its right to dominate political and social issues, and to threaten the structure of family life. This understanding gave rise to the new political consensus that eventually came to dominate the centre of the spectrum under the label '*the social market*'. New forms of measuring, accounting and taxation were developed that both gave a global view of the world political economy, and incorporated a wider range of social and environmental variables into the calculation of product, profit and loss. The fatal flaw of economism – that subordination of the social and the political to the strictly economic is incapable of supporting the framework of order and stability that its own functioning requires – was increasingly widely recognised and accepted.

The history of economism was another example of how the powerful ideas of the West worked best when they were accompanied by criticism and an openness to further reform. The essential Western concepts of individualism and the necessity of free markets, although taken to an extreme in economism, remained central to economic success. The likes of Mrs Thatcher, for all their extremism, were enormously successful in transforming the agenda in the rich world so that the core of their reforms remained an essential part of the centre of the political spectrum by the end of the 1990s. Economism was a short-sighted application of these ideas and after a run of nearly a quarter of a century under mounting criticism it was, during the first decade of the new millennium, defeated by the social market. The economistic revolution certainly generated substantial benefits, most obviously in Asia. In the West, it can be given credit for pushing forward the dialectics of post-industrial social development. But these benefits were purchased at the cost of heavy damage to the social, political and environmental fabric of the planet before it had run its course. Although it was the pampered societies of the old West that suffered most from economism, all three worlds were badly affected, both internally and in their international relations.

Despite the cult's promises of economic regeneration, nearly all of the old centres of capitalism slid into low growth, de-industrialisation, political drift, and social anxiety and depression. All of this was made worse by the fact that economism coincided with the challenge of getting over the massive adjustment to deep changes in the age structure of society in the advanced industrial countries. The demographic hump began in the late twentieth century, and only ended around 2020 when the large bulge of people born in the 1950s and 1960s began to die out. When combined with lower birth rates in subsequent generations this hump created a serious imbalance in the proportions of older and younger generations. It is still a matter of great debate amongst economic historians just how much of the problems of the late twentieth and early twenty-first century were due to bad policies, and how much to the scale of the demographic challenge. In our own age, East Asians are only just emerging from the worst of their own demographic challenge, suggesting that even with clear warning about the problem, the challenge remained enormous.

What was once referred to as the Anglo-Saxon economies were the first to embrace economism but they were also the first to deal with its excesses and to undertake the difficult reforms of the welfare state that eventually led to the social market. The emergence of 'ethical investment funds' in the 1990s was an early sign of the ability of capitalism to heal itself through market forces, even though they did not begin to pay big dividends until economism was no longer the ruling doctrine. In the late twentieth century growth rates in the most open states averaged 2–3%, although they, and especially the continental Europeans, faced serious challenges in reforming their welfare states for many years. In these years of massive economic restructuring and major changes to the nature of education and work, it was not surprising that rates of unemployment seemed stubbornly high. In such a fluid economy, some unemployment was 'necessary' in order to keep inflationary pressure under control.

By the first years of the twenty-first century it had become conventional wisdom in the open states that the role of the state in providing welfare and social support had to be substantially replaced by the role of the market. Many features of the post-1945 welfare state were either dismantled, shrunk, or privatised. In the places where economism was most strongly entrenched this was done with a ruthlessness and lack of attention to market alternatives that threatened social cohesion. The stripping out of the welfare state sometimes seemed to be more about transferring resources to the pockets of the already rich, rather than facilitating a transfer of responsibility from the state to the citizens. But once the rising economic, social and moral costs of economism began to bite, more balanced approaches to this transformation emerged. The state came to define its role primarily as a support-net for the weakest 10–15% of the population and as the guarantor of effective mechanisms (education) for individuals to improve their position. The state legislated for private savings for welfare but competition among pension and health providers ensured more efficient provision of services. As we have already noted, the newly re-defined family was a crucial part of this transformation.

One symbol of the social disorientation that accompanied the changes at the time was the rash of terrorist cults that infected most of the post-modern world. Exploiting the resources and vulnerabilities of advanced urban societies, even single individuals could (and did) inflict widespread da-mage and death. Some of them were bizarre and nihilistic, having no apparent aim other than the entertainment of their members. Others were more socially focused, pursuing environmental and political causes without much concern for the cost to innocent bystanders. These terrorists reflected both the breakdown of social restraints and the weakening of state control. They were paralleled by a new kind of cyber-vandalism on global computer networks. Again, some of this was childish and nihilistic, making a sport of launching ever more sophisticated viruses into cyber-space with little care for the huge damage done to innocent bystanders. But some of it was purposeful, counterattacking against state and corporate attempts to control or close off parts of the network. The use of chemical and biological agents at the height of the transnational terrorist campaign was the final straw that led to a concerted international effort to manage the threat.

Crime also flourished. As it did, the provision of security became increasingly privatised, and detached from the state. The rise of globally organised crime cut across all three worlds. Mafias were the dark side of economism's obsession with openness and freedom for capital, and to some extent the dark side of the global business culture itself. The weakening, and in some cases elimination, of the state increased their room for operation. The softening of state boundaries to facilitate trade, finance and competition made criminal transactions easier. As the state was hollowed out, it had less capacity to control globally organised crime. Integration of national police forces and interior ministries proved slow and difficult even within the zones of highest integration, such as the European Union, and almost impossible elsewhere. As laws and norms were changed to allow for the unrestricted operation of capital, some seemingly criminal activities became legal. A large grey area developed connecting legal businesses with illegal ones, and this spilled over into government with rising concerns about political sleaze.

The mafias occupied dangerous niches in the trades in arms and nuclear materials, but made no essential difference to the commercially backed spread of these technologies. They played a significant, though again not determining, role in the smuggling of migrants and the revival of something close to a slave trade. But the big problem with the global mafias was drugs, which was by far their most lucrative and most destructive business. By the late 1990s, drugs had become one of the world's major businesses, and its huge profits gave the mafias sufficient resources to penetrate the political and economic life of many states and virtually to control a few poorer and weaker ones. Its ever more exotic products became integrated into the numberless subcultures into which open societies had allowed themselves to be fragmented.

Crime in general, and the drugs trade in particular, eventually proved to be one of the Achilles' heels of economism. They exposed the flaws in the argument that the market was the best solution to all social problems by showing in acute form the costs of hollowing out the state and down-grading society and family. By doing so they underpinned the reaction against the excesses of economism that got underway early in the twenty-first century.

Domestic decay had international consequences. The cult of economism was one of the key factors weakening the major centres of power politically at the time when they were most needed to manage the emergence of a more multicultural and multi-centred world system. Capital became truly international, largely detaching itself from the state, and even constructing its own system of self-regulating institutions, like the Bank for International Settlements and the International Organisation of Securities Commissions, to protect itself against the instabilities of its own operation. But capital had no political vision except to get society and politics out of its way, and no goals other than the accumulation of wealth. This divorce between economic power and political responsibility meant that the hollowed-out states that remained had neither the resources nor the will to take up many of the traditional responsibilities of international management. Even the integration project of the European Union, once thought to be largely in the interest of capital, was in some ways deformed by the loss of political vision and leadership. It suffered heavy blows from financial interests, and although not destroyed, developed more feebly and more slowly, making it harder to take advantage of the political opportunities thrown up by the ending of the Cold War.

Several other factors helped to emasculate the powers. One was the demographic effects of one-child families, and the consequent reluctance to suffer military casualties for peripheral causes. Another was declining trust in the wisdom and honesty of government bureaucrats and politicians. The more complex and fragmented international politics after the Cold War also encouraged the attitude that regions should look after themselves. The absence of any galvanising ideological crusade or intense power rivalry meant that there was little external stimulus to overcome the domestic reluctance to take on the responsibilities of international management.

The resultant 'lite powers', as the US, the EU and Japan came to be called, were introverted and anxious to avoid any entanglements that would cost them money or blood. While this helped keep the peace among the open states, it also made them more reluctant to foster a sense of global political management. There were even calls for what in effect was neo-colonialism to deal with the rash of failed states, but the lite powers were not interested in bearing anything but burdens that were clearly in their economic self-interest. At the end of the Cold War they failed to undertake any serious reform of the United Nations, and particularly the Security Council, to reflect the new order of power. Instead, they left the organisation crippled by a structure that reflected the outcome of the Second World War, by that time old history. The United States and some of its allies systematically and intentionally overburdened and under-funded the United Nations and most of its agencies so that international institutions became discredited, marginalised and unable to play a significant stabilising or moderating role.

The lite powers neglected world policy more than they had bad policies. They made some gestures in the form of arms control regimes on nuclear, chemical, biological and missile technology. But although sales of finished weapons dropped from Cold War levels, the search for profits and market share was such that many militarily significant technologies could be, and were traded, sometimes openly, often covertly. The lite powers were, though, generally careful to keep the leading edge in military technology to themselves. They rested behind their belief that their superior technology allowed them to control battlefields in real time, at long distances and with low casualties. Their ability to have real-time vision of hundreds of miles of a battle zone ensured that they did not feel the need to arm proxies or place many troops outside allied states. Uncertainty about China, the much diminished Russia, and the bubbling cauldron of the Middle East, kept the Atlantic alliance in being and expanded its zone into central and eastern Europe.

In contrast to the weak international political management, an important part of international affairs continued to be the remarkable survival of a largely open global economic system. In the international economic realm, the malign effects of economism were held in check, albeit only barely, by some of its very own motives. For example, the strong belief in the virtue of open markets helped ensure that the World Trade Organisation survived as an important international institution. The value of economic openness ensured tacit and formal co-operation with the WTO. Perhaps even more significant was the rise of *geoeconomic diplomacy* as a result of the increasing interplay of business and political global relations. An early, but initially ill-understood, case for geoeconomic diplomacy was the crisis in Bosnia created by the break-up of Yugoslavia. After a hesitant and largely disastrous opening intervention, the Europeans and Americans started to shape the evolution of the new mini-state system that succeeded the wars of separation. They did so by wielding the levers of diplomatic recognition, economic aid, and access to the world economy to reward or punish domestic policies in the new states and sub-states. Wielded over time, and in relation to consistent goals such as peace, tolerance, openness, and democracy, these levers could be used to raise the costs of excessive nationalism or dictatorship to a level unsustainable in the middle- and long-term. After being refined in the larger challenge posed by a rising China, geoeconomic diplomacy eventually became the new form of global international society that emerged during the 2040s.

The economic crises that were endured in the past fifty years would be understandable to those living in the late twentieth century, for they too talked about the tensions between regionalism and globalism in economic affairs. Regionalism might well have ruled the day, and for a time it looked as if a world of three economic regions (the Americas, Europe, East Asia) might emerge. But in the event none of the regions proved able to consolidate itself as a world actor, though each of them remained an important focus for economic, political, social and strategic activity.

The limits on European unity were already clear in the late twentieth century. There was a parallel between the evolution of a more complex understanding of personal identity, and the evolution of a more complex sense on the part of Europeans of their own social and political identity. It is useful to recall the awkward phrase used in those days – 'subsidiarity' – to describe a situation where policy decisions that were best taken at a local level were left to the local level. Much the same was done for individuals in liberal democracies, and hence the new stress on the family and complex personal identities. This Europe of many spires, with its formal unity on many issues, but its _de facto_ multiple identities and sub-polities, laid the basis for closer relations across the Atlantic.

The dreams of a unity of the Americas never developed as far as the European form. This was both a matter of timing and a far less evenly balanced set of power relations in the Americas. But it was also super-seded by the trend towards closer relations with the Europeans. Europe, like the Americas, had begun by integrating northern and southern components. The large-scale migration of Hispanics into the United States was clearly an important dimension that underlay the policy process. With the added Hispanic factor, it was not surprising that Europeans and Americans again looked at their shared cultural roots across the Atlantic. The relative absence of such connections in the much-hyped trans-Pacific connections helps explain why the Americas never developed the same pattern of warm relations across the Pacific. The rise of the China challenge, and virulent Chinese nationalism in the early twenty-first century, had a great deal to do with the way the trans-Pacific dialogue was limited and channelled.

The centrality of open markets also helped drive the open states to take a relatively firm line against China as it emerged as the world's second largest economy. Because there was so much premature and exaggerated discussion of China growing into an economy larger than that of the United States, the open states managed to insist that China be more changed by the global trading system than able to change it to suit Beijing. The struggle with and within China in the first decades of the twenty-first century was the defining issue in international affairs. It now appears remarkable just how slow the policy makers in the late twentieth century were to see that Russia was a faded power and China was to become the main focus of great power rivalry. But in the end the liberal instincts of what some referred to as the Euramerican world were vital in making the China challenge appear very high on the agenda and making possible the firm measures necessary to tie China into the international system.

In part because China too was constrained by the forces unleashed by economism, and in part because it benefited from open markets, the people of East Asia look back on the cult of economism with far more recognition of its positive features than do many in the old West. The rapidly growing states of East Asia benefited from the huge inflows of investment, and the opening up of trade. Many states in East Asia, and a few elsewhere, climbed out of poverty and laid the foundations of industrial society. The extreme rapidity of their development inevitably had many adverse effects. As in the open states, it polarised and destabilised society, assaulted the environment, and weakened the state, though on the whole these negative effects compared favourably with the harshness of the West's own industrialisation in the nineteenth and early twentieth centuries.

But in parallel with the West's earlier experience, industrialisation in Asia also triggered the growth of xenophobic nationalism. In some places, most notoriously for a while in China, but also in the Middle East, it sustained and empowered ruthless authoritarian governments who exploited the nationalist phase to the full. This nationalism was fed on long-standing historical and territorial disputes and enmities. It gained strength from the dizzying changes in the balance of power within regions that came as rapid economic growth financed expanding military and political reach, suddenly elevating lucky states to new heights of power, and new ability to threaten their neighbours.

In the case of China, this process reached an extreme pitch. At first, the lure of the China market brought in huge amounts of trade and investment from near and far, with little regard for the regional or global power consequences. But as China became a rogue force in the global political economy the Western powers became tougher in demanding that it open its markets and play by international rules. At first China's neighbours in East Asia shied away from confronting it. But as China began taking markets in the developed world from some of its East Asian neighbours, and resorting to direct forms of military bullying in the region, they too joined, mostly tacitly, in learning to constrain Chinese behaviour. The East Asians learned many useful lessons from the Western experience, and began to evolve their own form of geoeconomic diplomacy. Their problem was that they had to use it to reform a great power, albeit with help both from the West and from within China.

Japan, which had suffered the most from Chinese bullying and was forced to accept unfair trade demands from Beijing, eventually chose to work more closely with the Atlantic powers in constraining China. The brief Taiwan Independence Crisis was the defining moment for Japan. After having offered logistical support to American forces, and then been threatened with nuclear attack from China, Japan joined the Atlantic world's ballistic missile defence programme and began working with other Asian countries to help shape a firmer geoeconomic line against a rising China. It is from this time that Japan became a full partner in the Atlantic world's cyberwar programme. The resulting tension in East Asia might have turned out more bloodily, but in the event the weaknesses inside China, and the community of purpose outside it, made even the giant of Asia susceptible to external pressure.

The rise of China and the various attempts to meet that challenge also go a long way to explaining why Asians never achieved their own unity. Japan was the first Asian power to realise the scale of the Chinese challenge, and it soon chose to work more closely with the United States in keeping the global market economy open, and China under control. India was another key power to both join the global market economy in an open and positive way, and to play a role in the balance of power. The states of Southeast Asia persisted with their more placatory policy towards China for the longest period, but when a wobbly Indonesia sought to build unity at home by talking up the China threat, there was little doubt that there would be severe constraints on China's ability to dominate Asia. China's foray into Central Asia in search of energy and new influence was seen, even at the time, as an admission that it was failing in its primary mission to cast the far more important Pacific rim states of Asia into a subordinate position. Of course these efforts to manage China also meant that Asian unity was never possible and it was therefore easier to keep the global economy open and prosperous. Now that a more open and liberal China (or at least most of it) seems to have chosen to join the international system as a status quo force, there is far more optimism about the prospects for the global economy.

Although the global disengagement of the lite powers was a problem in the early stages of the contest with China, the scale of the challenge posed by China was always likely to ensure that it would be the focus of a great power struggle in the early twenty-first century. What did come as a surprise to many was just how easily the lite powers found it to stay out of the wars in the Middle East and yet not suffer as a result. New technology of oil exploration, breakthroughs in solar and other so called 'alternative' forms of energy, and better management of energy use in the developed world, all ensured that the oil in the Middle East lasted longer, and was less crucial to the stability of the world economy, than many had thought possible. Rising oil demand from East Asia did drive up prices, but this made more oil exploitable elsewhere, and brought other energy sources into the market, thus substantially diminishing the intensity of great power interest in the Middle East.

In the Middle East, oil sustained a variety of anachronistic regimes, from absolutist monarchies, through totalitarian dictatorships to theocracies. It also sustained purchases of arms and military technologies, but increasingly the weapons were bought from the new economic powers of Asia in exchange for oil to power their economies. Even though the Atlantic powers knew the risks in such activity – having done much the same themselves in the late twentieth century – there was little they could do to persuade the oil-rich, but tense and fragile states in the Middle East from wasting their money on arms, or to persuade the East Asians to curb their arms sales. Russia, whose economy otherwise was still finding it hard to sell goods into the markets of the developed countries, was also anxious to sell weapons in the Middle East.

After years of unrest, the outbreak of full scale civil war in Saudi Arabia and most of the Gulf emirates in 2012 both destroyed the West's system of protectorates in the Gulf, and unravelled the fragile post-colonial political fabric of the whole region. Within a few years these events triggered the second Iran–Iraq war, which, with all of its rival interventions, quickly expanded into the seventeen-year-long Great Middle Eastern War. This crisis lasted from the revolutions and civil wars in Saudi Arabia and the Gulf, to the treaty of Sao Paulo finally signed in 2031. Unlike the Cold War, the world crisis of the Middle Eastern War was not about a direct confrontation between great powers. Instead, it centred on a complex regional clash that was in one sense between Iran and the Arabs, and in another between the Sunni and Shi'a sects of Islam. This clash was in the tradition of deeply rooted patterns of ethnic, territorial and political conflict in Mesopotamia going back to ancient times. It was facilitated by the freer range given to regions after the Cold War, and the oil factor ensured that the rest of the world took sides, albeit remaining aloof from the fighting.

The war enveloped much of the region from Turkey to Egypt and resulted in a massive redrawing of political boundaries. China supported Iran as part of its policy to consolidate an anti-Western axis. So also did Russia, which had drifted into anti-Western forms of nationalism. On the other side, the European Union, the United States, India, Egypt and Israel, all with long-standing grievances against Iranian support for radical Islamist movements, supported what eventually became New Assyria. Each side in the war was given such extensive political and military support by its backers that a stalemate of some sort was the only possible outcome. This global polarisation reinforced the alienation that had grown up between China, Russia and the West during the twenty years following the Cold War.

The war itself was a long, slow process with short periods of intense conflict interspersed with lengthy and unstable cease-fires. Terrorism was widely used by both sides. The war had elements of nuclear deterrence, with Iran flaunting its own weapons, and Israel, with American backing, providing extended deterrence for the Arabs. Conventional war between the local parties raged under this nuclear umbrella, but nuclear deterrence was one of the factors that kept the outside powers from intervening more directly. There was never much danger of war being triggered amongst the great powers. Nuclear deterrence, economic interdependence, and domestic liteness constrained them. Once the West's allies in the Gulf had been eliminated, they did not put their own forces directly into the fray. But there was a clear balance of power centred on the struggle to control a crucial, albeit diminishing global resource.

Although causing much ruin in the region, and cementing inter-Islamic rivalry for decades to come, this war was on balance an Arab victory. The Arabs eventually restored and held their north-east boundary against Iranian power. By replacing their post-colonial fragmentation with a single state stretching from the Levant to the Gulf, and incorporating much of the northern Arabian peninsula, they also succeeded in recovering some of their traditional world power status. But the Iranians did not lose. They extended their sphere to include most of the erstwhile emirates in the eastern end of the Gulf, and parts of Baluchistan and Afghanistan. They also extended influence into the Caucasus and Central Asia, and re-established some of their traditional claim to world power status. For the rest of the world, the division of the Gulf's oil between two rival regional hegemons was an acceptable guarantee against monopoly. The division of Islam into two rival cultures was also more than acceptable to most of the outside world.

The wars in the Middle East, as fearsome as they were, never really looked like drawing in the great powers in a direct way. While it is true that the Atlantic powers remained highly suspicious of the new superpower – China – it was also true that Beijing knew the limits of its own power at such a distance. For China, and Euramerica, the main contest remained in Asia. Like the Cold War in the second half of the twentieth century, the struggle with China never really broke out into major direct conflict. The Taiwan crisis apart, the struggle was mainly in the minds and the markets of the countries of the richest parts of the world. Unlike the Cold War, China was such a large economic power that it had the ability to give more pause to the hard-liners in Euramerica. But China was also constrained because as it became tied into the global economy, it gradually turned into a lite power. There were very difficult times in the first third of our century, but the Chinese role in the Middle Eastern conflicts was really their last gasp at taking on the interests of Euramerica. China was ultimately a weak state because of internal divisions and the power of market forces and political liberalism to turn it into a lite power.

Map 6 – Geopolitical changes by 2030

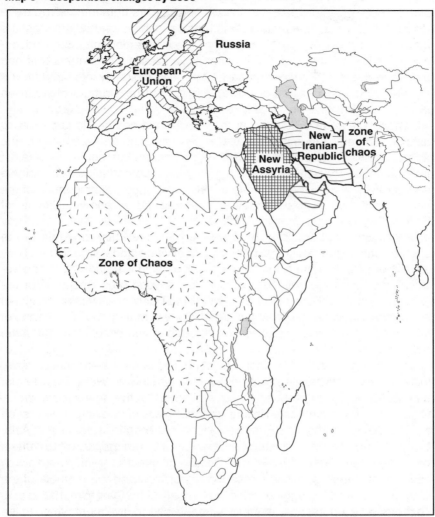

The ability of the Euramerican world to manage the transition of China into being a more status quo power must rank as one of the great achievements of power politics. Critics of the geoeconomic diplomacy school said it could not be done. In part they were correct, for the contradiction between the lure of China's markets and the fear of its power was extremely difficult to resolve. With hindsight it is remarkable that the newly developed transnational geoeconomic diplomacy could eventually cope with a challenge the size of China.

The twin, and often related events in the Middle East and East Asia go a long way to explaining why the United Nations, although not completely killed off, never played a major role in managing international society. The death of so many states in Africa, which led to a draining of United Nations membership, was only a minor reason for its continued irrelevance. What pundits in the late twentieth century never expected – a new concert of powers – was the essential regulator of important aspects of international affairs. Chance provided a useful symbolic event in 2029, when a 1 km-diameter meteorite on a collision course with earth was intercepted and deflected by joint American, European, Russian, Chinese and Japanese action. This victory over a threat from nature, which was made possible by earlier multinational collaborations in space science, led to the founding of the International Space Watch Organisation (ISWO), and helped to accelerate a shift towards more co-operative international attitudes that was already underway for other reasons.

The treaty of Sao Paulo in 2031 was also the occasion for beginning a long-delayed major reconstruction of global institutions around the new concert of powers. The UN had been in decline ever since the financial crisis forced upon it by the United States in the mid-1990s. Some of the lite powers, most notably Japan, continued to support it, but as friction between China and Russia, and the West, grew, the Security Council became increasingly paralysed. When the Middle East crisis broke, the remnants of the organisation were pushed to the margins with only a handful of the specialised agencies continuing to function. But the improved atmosphere of the 2030s, the narrowing political gap between the old West and the new Asia, and the growing awareness of serious collective problems laid the basis for a rebuilding of international institutions. Like the League of Nations before it, the UN was formally dissolved into a successor, the World Management Organisation (WMO), which was structured to reflect the actors, agendas and powers of the day.

Elsewhere there was much less fundamental change over these decades. States either struggled to make the best of the global market, as in most of South America, or tried to limit and control its penetration, as in Russia, or simply tried to avoid toppling into the expanding zones of chaos, as in parts of Asia and Africa. India was the only major power outside of East Asia to make major progress in transforming itself into a richer place. Indian reforms were never as spectacular as those in China, and the success of the Indian economy never provoked the same worry as China's did. India had the benefit of being a rough-and-tumble democracy with a more or less effective system of law. It also had the benefit of living in a region with neighbours that were far poorer and therefore of little strategic interest. India was thus free to prosper in the global market economy. It was welcomed as a bargaining chip by companies anxious to force the Chinese to behave properly towards foreign investors, and by other powers who wanted to build a balance against China.

With all the concern in the old West about the vices of economism, it was often forgotten that these decades marked an era of enormous economic prosperity for the majority of the people on the planet. The growth in China and India alone was cause enough for loud cheering. Despite low growth and the ravages of economism, the people of the Atlantic world did not suffer any generalised economic shrinkage such as accompanied the great depression of the 1930s. And despite losing their privilege as the exclusive club of the rich, they remained firmly in the top ranks of wealth and power, soundly refuting the argument that new economic powers could only arise at the expense of the old ones. The pattern of growth in much of East Asia was nearly the opposite to that in the Atlantic world, with rapid growth rates in the early twenty-first century giving way to slower growth in the face of rising welfare costs and demographic distortions. In aggregate, the past fifty years have been the era of the fastest economic growth ever seen.

Nevertheless, lest our own generation fall prey to its own version of economism, it must be remembered that most of the areas covered by weak and failed states have been disastrously bypassed both economically and politically. The weak state structures and fragile societies left behind by decolonisation in parts of Africa and Asia needed, and still do need strong support from the international community in order to survive in the modern world. Many of them were not in any meaningful sense capable of self-government up to international standards. They needed outside aid and expert advice on a day-to-day basis, and it was far from clear that many of them would be capable of fully joining international society for many decades even with that assistance. The economistic revolution ripped away much of this support, exposing this world to forces that it was not equipped to handle. The United Nations, which provided them with affordable diplomatic capabilities, was reduced to a gutted shell. With the onset of wars and power rivalries, and the reassertion of vetoes, most of the organisation faded into irrelevance. From as early as the 1980s, aid programmes were slashed, and replaced with commercial loans, which quickly and repeatedly built themselves into crippling debt crises. Multi-national companies were allowed free reign, and international mafias established their presence. Under the impact of these conditions, and in several cases aided by the crippling effects of disease and civil war, quite a few of these states disintegrated. Unless they were somehow crucial to the wider world economy, or embarrassingly close to a zone of wealthy and open states (as was the case in Haiti and what was once known as 'Yugoslavia'), most of them were simply allowed to collapse.

From the 1990s onward, three effectively stateless zones of anarchy began to grow. One started in Liberia, spread slowly through other parts of West Africa, and by 2010, when Nigeria imploded, embraced most of the region. A second started in east-central Africa with Rwanda and Burundi, and eventually spread to much of Zaire and Uganda, and large parts of several neighbouring states. By 2018, these two zones had effectively merged. The third zone started in Afghanistan, spread into parts of central Asia, and after the civil war of 2013 in Pakistan grew to incorporate most of the north-west frontier, Kashmir and parts of Baluchistan. Some other regions that might have gone the same way – Central America and the Caribbean, Myanmar or Cambodia – were saved by regional interventions. Within the zones of chaos, violence and disorder were endemic, and political life consisted of a shifting pattern of local warlords, tribal alliances, and mercenary forces of various kinds. Some companies established their own fortified en- claves, as did several mafias, but in general the zones were outside the sphere of diplomacy and law. Geoeconomic diplomacy had few useful ideas about what to do in areas where the formal political structures had collapsed into anarchy.

These continuing zones of chaos are a warning that not all problems have obvious solutions. The events of the past fifty years are also a warning about the risks of hubris that might lead to economistic-type errors. One of the main lessons of this period is that governments now have a sharper sense of what they can and cannot do better than other levels of our more complex society. But in the end, we have to be grateful that during those turbulent decades there was more good news than bad, and above all that so much of Asia managed the difficult transition from poor peasant countries to modern and more-or-less stable pluralist systems.

THE DOGS THAT DID NOT BARK

If we recall that in the last decades of the twentieth century there was much apocalyptic talk of the twin crises of a population explosion and environ- mental damage, it is evident now that both challenges have been more or less successfully contained. In the case of population control, the outcome is very clear. The sense of panic was rooted in the uncertainty about how and when the exponential growth in overall human numbers would stop. A strong secondary issue was what the final outcome would look like in terms of the overall global racial balance. Many in the old West, and not just racists, were acutely aware that while their own period of massive expansion had subsided into stasis decades ago, the numbers of Arabs, Asians and Africans were continuing to explode.

It was only in the early decades of the twenty-first century that people in the developed world stopped worrying about these issues. By then it was apparent that the same forces that had slowed and stopped their own demographic explosion were at work in rapidly developing East Asia. Confidence developed that total human numbers would peak around mid-century, and that in most regions the peak would be sustainable. Confidence increased as the Indian economy joined the Chinese one in producing the necessary mix of forces to stabilise population size. This change in attitude was helped along by a growing consensus about what made for good population control: government policy that fostered sustainable economic growth, political choice, and education for women. These objectives became part of the geoeconomic programme. Worries about the cultural and power effects of racial redistribution also mostly faded, not least because the spread of Mondo's multiculturalism steadily subverted the assumptions on which they were based. Although illegal migrants were a continuing problem in many places, control mechanisms proved adequate, and the success of development in Asia meant that most people were content to stay within their own regions.

Parts of the Middle East and Africa were much less successful in controlling population. They did not achieve any of the key criteria: economic modernisation, political pluralism or education of women. The stress of overpopulation in these areas contributed to the expansion of the zones of chaos, and in some places helped bring on desertification and other environmental crises. All of this created a serious and sustained migration problem of which Europe was the main target.

But overall, the global population 'crisis' never materialised. Once the general outcome became predictable, as it did around 2015, the sense of crisis passed. What remained was the still serious problem of a very large global population. In some regions, most obviously the old West, the peak population size was perfectly sustainable. In others, most notably Asia, the peak was mostly manageable, but too high to be desirable in the longer run. In a few countries, most notably Egypt, Bangladesh, Algeria and Indonesia, and also in parts of China and India, overpopulation created serious local crises. More generally, the overabundance of humans fed a growing sense of planetary claustrophobia. This, in turn, shifted attitudes on a whole range of issues from birth control and euthanasia to individual rights and ecology. Thus while population faded as a global problem, the very high human numbers contributed both to significant changes in society, and to ongoing pressure on the stability of the planetary environment.

The issue of the planetary environment was always more difficult and more long-term than population. Whereas population dynamics had been fundamentally understood almost since Malthus, and had simple and direct outcomes, environmental dynamics were much less well understood, and frequently had complex and indirect outcomes. The operation of the planetary ecosystem had innumerable components, many of whose inter-actions and interdependencies remained obscure. Given the primitive climate models and short data sets available fifty years ago, there was no effective way to assess the effects of pollution or to understand the operation of natural cycles. There were grounds for thinking that human activity was beginning to make a significant impact on the ecosphere, and grounds for worrying that the climate could undergo cataclysmic change. But there was no way of knowing for sure how big or how immediate the problem was, or even in which direction change might go. Fed by short-term fluctuations in weather patterns, fashionable panics over supposed cooling or warming trends alternated with alarming frequency.

That makes it all the more remarkable that even in the last years of the twentieth century it was possible for governments to agree some significant environmental policies. Most important was that which would eventually repair the damage to the ozone layer by stopping production and use of the main ozone-destroying chemicals. Some other useful constraints on pollution were also put into effect. Perhaps most remarkably, the plague of unsafe nuclear fission reactors that had taken off during the 1970s was substantially brought under control by the end of the century. A notably odd coalition of greens and economistic radicals eventually killed this unhappy progeny of Cold War military nuclear development in much of the West, though the process took several decades longer in Russia and Asia. Although a long-term legacy of nuclear dumps and decommissioned reactors still remains a burden for us today, this victory helped to open the way for development of solar power. The late classical West thus began to rediscover on a planetary scale the wisdom of many primitive peoples about the necessity of keeping human activity and nature in some kind of sustainable relationship. The old West certainly did not succeed in putting the 'eco' back into economics, but it did initiate a transformation of attitudes towards the environment. It also began the long process, still far from completion in our own time, of accumulating systematic knowledge about the air, water and living systems of the planet, and the complex interactions amongst them.

But despite these signal achievements the underlying problem of human pressure on the ecosphere remained. As the new millennium dawned, it was clear that a potentially difficult period lay ahead. The ecosphere already seemed noticeably, though not fatally, altered by the impact of five billion people only a quarter of whom had achieved industrialisation. What would the impact be when twice that number, more than half of them in industrial societies, had to be sustained, as was going to be the case in the coming decades? Two dangers loomed. The clearest was that the rising tide of human numbers would take a terrible toll of other species before it peaked. Hunting, fishing, logging, land development and pollution would drive thousands of species to extinction, with large mammals being the principal victims. Much less clear, but at the end of the day far more significant for the fate of humankind itself, was how the inevitable increase in pollution from so many more people, and so much more industrialisation, would affect the planetary climate and the human habitat. These two questions were linked to the extent that the living fabric of the planet was itself one of the keys to maintaining the chemical, and therefore climatic, stability of the atmosphere.

The worry about mass extinctions turned out to be fully justified. But the fact that an invaluable and thorough catalogue of genetic information and samples for many species was saved, ensured that the outcome was not wholly catastrophic. Rapidly developing genetic engineering ensured that whole new life forms were eventually created, and some lost ones restored.

The future of the planetary climate is still unclear, though the most pessimistic predictions were wrong. It remains the subject of scientific debate whether global warming or global cooling will define a future environmental crisis. Two hundred years on from the industrial revolution we are still unsure about the extent to which our various pollutions of the atmosphere pose a long-term climatic risk. Sadly, it was impossible to stop the countries in East and South Asia from repeating many of the polluting mistakes of the old West. They paid the same domestic price for this behaviour as did the first-round industrialisers, and they eventually learned the same lessons. The planet paid some price in a modicum of global warming, some substantial local changes in climate, and a half-metre rise in sea levels. A few places, mostly in the poor world, suffered badly from flooding and climate change, especially the overpopulated deltas of the Nile and the Ganges. But the old and new industrial worlds were mostly able to defend themselves with sea walls and other measures. Losses of agricultural land in Bangladesh, Egypt, Southern Africa and the United States were made up in the global scale by defrostings in Canada and Russia. More problematic was the change in the geographical distribution of several diseases that took advantage of rising temperatures to increase their range. Large parts of Europe and North America found themselves exposed to malaria, dengue fever and other tropical diseases to which their societies were not accustomed. Thanks to intense publicity and a rapid diversion of resources, casualities were statis- tically tiny, although anxiety was high.

Now that the main bulk of primitive industrialisation is over, the immediate threat of massive global warming seems to have passed. China and India have moved beyond dependence on grossly polluting forms of energy and production, and the advanced economies have the technology to increase wealth without proportional increases in pollution. The human population has peaked in size, and there are no great surges of new primitive industrialisation on the horizon. Uncertainties in our knowledge about the workings of the planetary climate means that we cannot be complacent, but there are rising grounds for optimism that we are past the worst threat.

The ability to meet these challenges seemed wildly optimistic to those who stood on the cusp of the third millennium. That we managed to do so owed something to good fortune and something to good policies (however belated). But it owed even more to the Westernistic ability to remain constructively sceptical, admit mistakes, and adapt to change.

THE VIEW FROM 2500

16

In our second look back, we move 500 years into the future. Five hundred years is the distance that we now stand from the great voyages of discovery and the beginnings of Europe's ascent from feudal obscurity to world domination. It is twenty generations distant, and very few people other than nobility and genealogy enthusiasts will have any sense of personal connection to it through their ancestors. Most educated people will have had some introduction to it in school, but unless they have the misfortune to be locked into a community obsessed with its history, few will remember more than a handful of names and stories – Da Gama, Columbus, Magellan – and a vague sense that some important things happened then in a world of kings, explorers, religious fanaticism and frequent wars. At 500 years' distance connections from past to present are weak, but still present. Those with sufficient knowledge will still be able to see direct connections between then and now. Several of the main civilisations from 1500 still exist (Europe, Islam, India, China), as do all of the main religions, and quite a few states (e.g. France, Japan, Iran, Egypt, Spain, Poland, Russia). The effects of European navigation around Africa and across the Atlantic and Pacific are still visible in numerous ways, from the populations of the Americas and South Africa, through the transplanted crops and animals, to the shipping routes of world trade.

251

But beyond these few familiar landmarks, things will have moved on very considerably. In the course of half a millennium the whole setting of the world stage changes dramatically. In the 500 years separating the end of the twentieth century from the beginning of the sixteenth, the human population multiplied itself by a factor of twelve from 500 million to six billion, and the political and cultural maps of the world have been transformed. At least two major civilisations have disappeared (Inca, Aztec) along with numerous states and empires (Ottoman, Holy Roman, Venetian, Mameluke, Song, British, etc.). Dozens of new states now occupy the map where there were none before, including the most powerful state on the planet, the USA, and intercontinental ethnic and cultural mixing has taken place on a huge scale. Technological and scientific knowledge has gone through several revolutions: mechanical, metallurgical, chemical, electronic, nuclear and biological. Over a 500-year gap, the knowledge and technological environment is almost unrecognisably different, so much so that a citizen of 1500 transplanted to our time would be by turns amazed, confused, disorientated, horrified and terrified by the everyday experiences of late twentieth-century life. A view from half-a-millennium's distance, in other words, will see rather few and faint continuities and large numbers of very big changes. It will see a world whose outlines are only barely familiar; a different age, albeit one still recognisable as a direct part of our own history. We can still appreciate the literature of this time, feel its humanity connected to our own, and share spiritual and linguistic identities with it.

An historian writing in 2500 about the world 500 years back would reflect this greater distance and detachment. Here follows an extract from chapter 6 of *AN INTRODUCTION TO EARLY MODERN HISTORY: The Classical West and Westernistic Civilisation, 1500–2300.*

6.3. Computing, Biotechnology and Information Systems – The Transformation from Western to Westernistic, and the Search for a New World Order 1989–2038

This period was an extraordinary time in the human story. It marked both the culmination of Western power that began with the European maritime explorations, and the shift of a Western-dominated world into the beginnings of the first truly global civilisation. Tremendous social and technological forces were in play, many for the first time, and the learning curves were often steep and dangerous. The wave of transforming technological developments that had first become apparent around 1850 continued relentlessly. As each new technology burst forth it required and facilitated massive adjustments in the whole organisation and self-perception of humankind. This process in some ways repeated, though more intensely, the human experiences of the agricultural revolution and the first rise of urban civilisation. In all three cases human social relations were transformed by technological developments. But the industrial transformation was far more rapid and more widespread than the other two. In no sense was it under control, and it generated spectacular successes as well as spectacular disasters.

The economic, social and political life of the species were in a state of continuous adaptation and upheaval. The rate of political, economic and social innovation was forced to keep pace with the new technologies even though no one knew what the consequences of each new development would be. It is clear that this half century marks a key turning point in world history. During these turbulent decades, humankind shifted from its historic norm of being basically fragmented culturally, politically and economically, to being basically integrated economically, and having the first rudiments of global culture and governance. Although elements of the long fragmentation are still with us today, it was at this point in history that the balance changed forever in favour of integrative forces. This transformation took place in the shadow of the peaking of human population, and some theorists see a causal connection between the two. The extraordinarily rapid and extreme increase in human numbers and density of occupation of the planet that accompanied the industrial revolution were also part of its cause. At the same time, however, this whole process pushed the carrying capacity of the planet to a potential crisis point, generating the first concerted efforts to engineer both the planetary environment and the political and economic organisation of nations.

Despite its chaotic circumstances, this period produced some remarkable technological and social developments. In terms of technology, five things stand out as particularly relevant to our own time:

- the development of machine intelligence
- the resumption of human physical evolution
- the first level integration of human and machine worlds
- the capability to manipulate the planetary environment, and
- the first stages of the venture into space.

The development of machine intelligence was apparent only to a few visionaries during this period. Nevertheless it was the essential moves made at this time that opened the way to the synthesised human–machine culture that we now enjoy. Simple computing had developed apace all through the latter half of the twentieth century. But not until the late 1990s did the linearly designed and serially programmed first-generation machines inspired by von Neumann begin to give way to the parallel designs and evolutionary programming of the second

---

Kelly on Humans and Machines

The greatest social consequence of neo-biological civilisation will be the grudging acceptance by humans that humans are the random ancestors of machines, and that as machines we can be engineered ourselves . . . Machines are a dirty word now. This is because we have withheld from them the full elixir of life. But we are poised to remake them into something that one day may be taken as a compliment . . . When the Technos is enlivened by the Bios we get artifacts that can adapt, learn and evolve. When our technology adapts, learns and evolves then we will have a neo-biological civilisation . . . Neo-biological culture welds engineered technology and unrestrained nature until the two become indistinguishable.

From Kevin Kelly, *Out of Control*, pp. 71, 606.

generation, and the quantum physics of the third. Although the best of the first-generation machines gave notice of what was to come by beating the top human players at chess, the von Neumann machines were inherently limited. They could not easily learn, and they became increasingly the victims of flaws in their massively complicated serial programs. Only with the second-generation machines and the taking of an evolutionary approach to programming, did the first glimmerings of machine intelligence begin to appear.

The resumption of human physical evolution occurred in parallel with this development. It had long been understood that the onset of civilisation had largely taken humankind out of the Darwinian treadmill of natural selection. Human beings seemed to have no challengers at the top of the evolutionary scale. In the 1900s it was already understood that evolution had shifted into the social sphere. People might not change much, but their cultures, and their social, political and economic organisations could and did. Human development moved into the collective, where different modes of organisation competed for survival, and the fittest became the foundation for the next cycle of evolution. By this process, human societies grew ever larger, more knowledgeable, more intricately structured, and more capable. But at the end of the second millennium it was begun to be understood that the basics of the modern human being did not have to remain fixed.

Technological advances made in the late twentieth and early twenty-first centuries made possible a resumption of human evolution, albeit not on Darwinian principles, but on engineering ones. It was then that the key work was done to understand the handful of genes that separated humans from apes. It became possible to manipulate and mutate these genes as well as create new ones. The human genome project opened the way not only to myriad new medical opportunities in the treatment of diseases and disabilities, but also to the redesign of the human organism itself. Given the acute and widespread vulnerability of unmodified human bodies to damage and disease, the pressure to pursue this line of knowledge was very great apart from its intrinsic scientific interest. Early efforts focused on making people live longer by finding ways to slow down the ageing process. It was only much later that genetic breakthroughs made possible the creation of designer bodies, and the ability to gestate young outside the womb. This early work was derided as the 'eyes in the back of the head' school, but eventually began to change fundamental features of how humans lived their lives. By the fourth decade of the twenty-first century pressure was also growing from those who wanted to colonise space, for without radical changes to the earth-based human form permanent residence off-planet would be much more difficult and expensive.

But society at large was not ready for attempts to improve the organism in other than curative ways. Notions of human equality were too recently established after the age of imperialism, and the racist ideologies that accompanied it, to allow any consensus on taking up the opportunity of eugenics. Thus although the pioneering work was done at this time, it was not seriously exploited (indeed, it was seriously repressed) until nearly two centuries later. The struggle against scientists peddling 'designer genes' was protracted and inevitable given the commercial power unlocked by discoveries in this field. The renegade 'rejuvenation clinics' established on Caribbean islands in the 2080s attracted a mixture of brilliant scientists and perverted minds, but their operations were eventually made illegal, and closed down by a concerted international action. There were also major anxieties about how to prevent military applications of genetic technique. Only when the population crisis of the twenty-first century was clearly over, and humankind settled into a more sustainable balance with the planet, did the climate ripen for the intensive development of the human species itself.

Rapidly deepening knowledge about the architecture of both human and machine intelligence was accompanied by dramatic improvements in ability to interface between the two. Out of the primitive 'gophers' and 'search engines' of the early internet evolved first a variety of network personal assistants (PA), and later our own personal companions. These increasingly sophisticated utilities started out as solutions to information overload. They took on the burden of monitoring the internet, and of flagging and retrieving items of interest to their users. Network PAs could be configured to the personality and interests of their user. They responded to specific requests, but could also explore creatively on behalf of users whose profile they knew in detail. By the end of this period these PAs were sophisticated enough to begin acquiring personas of their own. They could hold quite sophisticated conversations with their users, play games with them, and offer advice on everything from stock prices to medical symptoms. In the rich world children acquired their own PA at an early age, the two in a sense growing up together.

Simulators of all kinds began to marry human perceptions with machine ability to generate images. The same types of linkage also opened the way to numerous telekinetic devices, both practical and entertaining, that fused humans and machines into a single behavioural unit whose two parts could be separated by substantial distances. There were some experiments in long-range sex, but more popular were things like drone flying, where individuals could link into the 'eyes' and controls of sophisticated model aircraft. This development had revolutionary implications for both entertainment and education, as well as for surgery, mining, deep-sea exploration and a host of other dangerous or difficult activities.

Deeper and in the long run more significant work was also going on. Although scarcely noticed at the time, experiments in the late 1990s successfully passed information from a computer chip to a nerve cell without killing the cell. Like the understanding of the human genome, this development also offered both appealing solutions to medical problems and highly controversial possibilities for creating cyborgs as a superior form of human. The idea of being able directly, and perhaps permanently, to link one's mind into a computer network was profoundly attractive to some and deeply abhorrent to others. But this path too was for a long time closed off by fears of its potential to assault the still newly achieved and fragile value of human equality.

The fourth technological breakthrough was the beginnings of planetary environmental management. Again, this was largely unrecognised at the time, consciousness being focused on the ways in which the earth's climate and ecosystems were coming under pressure from the seemingly cancerous growth of humankind and its industrial activities. And this was indeed the age of massive pollution and destruction of species. In the turbulent century when human population peaked it was perhaps not surprising that much more attention was paid to the human impact on the planet than to the longer-term threats to civilisation from earth's natural climate cycles. We can only look back in astonishment at the chemical barrage our ancestors inflicted upon the planet, sometimes as a by-product of their wasting of precious fossil fuel resources. Their nuclear dumps remain with us still, and there is no need to retell the story of how several of these remain major hazard zones and polluters of groundwater. But all of this uncontrolled pollution of the atmosphere, land and sea was in one sense a gigantic (and very risky) experiment. Observation of pollution effects on the planetary climate and ecosystem was the beginning of learning about how to control the natural cycles and systems of the planet. This learning effect accelerated once pollution control measures began to be attempted. The two late twentieth-century landmarks here are the moves to stop the disintegration of the ozone layer, and the experiments in seeding the oceans with iron to increase the growth of phytoplankton (thus both generating a food resource and taking CO_2 out of the atmosphere).

Although it took several decades to consolidate, the shift from the idea that the planetary environment was either a static or a random variable in human affairs, to the idea that it was a central collective management problem of the species can clearly be seen to have begun at this time. With the advantage of hindsight, one of the most striking features of this turning point is the relative confusion and helplessness of both policy makers and scientists caused by inadequate data. Intensive and systematic statistical monitoring of both human and planetary systems had made great strides in the late twentieth century. But most of the data was only a few centuries long, and not yet capable of capturing the larger cycles. The relative feebleness of computing power, which was then only a few decades old, greatly limited what could be done with modelling the complex interplay of oceans, atmosphere and biosphere. Although some progress had been made in collecting longer-term climate data from ice cores and fossils, understanding of climate dynamics was at best patchy. The combination of fear of climate change and weak knowledge of causes and effects meant that there was much dispute and many false alarms. Short-term fluctuations were mistaken for long-term ones, and scientists were unable to distinguish between natural cycles and human impacts. Nevertheless, despite all its confusions, this time laid the foundations for the great geo-engineering project that our Planetary Management Corporation is now preparing to extend the Holocene interglacial. From the knowledge that began to be accumulated in response to human pollution of the planet in the late twentieth century, we have now built the theories and capabilities to fend off the ice age that nature would otherwise deliver seven hundred years hence.

The fifth development, the first ventures into space, was actually more significant in social than in technological terms. The technology was for the most part exceedingly crude, representing a triumph of old ideas pushed to their limits rather than a breakthrough into a new future. But in social and political terms space played quite an important role in helping to find solutions to the world order problem as humankind made the turbulent shift from a basically fragmented to a basically integrated mode of being. Space became the mirror that enabled humankind to see itself as a whole for the first time.

At the very beginning of the space age this social effect was not much in evidence. The first photographs of earth from space helped to inspire environmental consciousness, and the landing of a man on the moon had an intense, but short-lived symbolic importance. But otherwise the first explorations of the moon and the planets were simply an annex to the military rivalry (the 'Cold War') between two so-called 'superpowers', the United States of America (despite the name, at that time comprising only the central band of North America) and the Soviet Union (a short-lived manifestation of the Russian Empire). Indeed, when that rivalry ended in 1989, it seemed for a time as if the whole commitment to space exploration and development would be greatly diminished and delayed, if not quite given up altogether. Manned exploration of the moon was abandoned, and budgets for space science dropped steadily. Without the impetus of political rivalry it seemed impossible to sustain the necessary resource commitments and vision, a problem made much worse by the assault of economism on government projects of every sort.

But towards the very end of the twentieth century a new and quite different attitude towards space began to form. Its origins can perhaps be dated to a series of discoveries and realisations in the mid-1990s. First was that meteorite impacts played a big role in the periodic catastrophes that have affected the evolution of life on earth. Second was the discovery that the space near earth was not empty, but surprisingly full of rocks and iceballs, some of them worryingly large and close. Third was the confirmation, after a protracted dispute which itself helped to stimulate further exploration, that evidence had been found for a primitive form of life on Mars. And fourth was the discovery that planets were commonplace rather than exceptional, and that many stars in our part of the galaxy were accompanied by planets. More generally, the astronomical discoveries of the late twentieth century, and the images of the planets returned by early space probes, had transformed people's sense of their place in the larger scheme of things. As the planet filled up, it lost the sense of openness and new geographical frontiers that had been a feature of all of human history. But as earth reached closure, new technologies brought the solar system and the near stellar environment into much clearer view, and up to a point within reach. Humankind was offered the opportunity to relocate its sense of self from a single planetary space to a much larger neighbourhood.

At first, these discoveries just played into a strong subculture of interest in space that was pervasive in the developed world. Part of this subculture was driven by the classical Western spirit of adventure, exploration and colonisation, and by 2010 this was strong enough to have begun financing its own moon colonisation project. There was also a more commercially motivated drive to cash in on orbital tourism. The bulk, however, was more negative, even paranoid, in attitude. There was a widespread belief that hostile aliens were already present on earth, and that governments were keeping this fact secret.

This belief was ruthlessly exploited and reinforced by the entertainment industry, which found that hostile extra-terrestrials sold better than friendly ones. It provided fertile ground for political manipulation.

The demonstrable threat from meteorites spurred calls for the development of a spacewatch and defence capability to protect the planet. In addition, the idea that life was a normal product of organic chemistry, and that the abundance of planets suggested that the forces of life would not be short of venues, diminished sharply the possibility that earth was the sole supporter of higher life-forms. It was no longer possible to think of space as an empty place which might be scientifically or eventually economically interesting, but which was not threatening and which there was no particular urgency about coming to terms with.

Although initially treated rather dismissively by the pundits of the day, these discoveries marked a turning point. Not surprisingly, the space agencies and high-technology industries that had been hard hit by the winding down of great power military rivalry were the first to spot the opportunity of exploiting the changed attitude towards space. If space could be presented as threatening, then priority could be restored to the budgets that favoured their activities. The lobby in favour of a spacewatch organisation thus found powerful industrial backers.

Politicians and managers of the world economy were slower on the uptake, but by the first decade of the twenty-first century many began to see space as a potential threat. The result was a decision to keep in being high-tech weapons research without having to justify it against another country. Defending the planet against meteorites would require capabilities with many other possible applications. It was agreed to create a joint project linking together all of the major powers and advanced societies. After the ending of the American–Russian rivalry, declining budgets had required multinational co-operation for much of space science, which meant that a rudimentary framework for a globalist approach to space was already in place. The project was presented not only as a powerful symbol of the democratic and capitalist peace, but also as a practical and economically efficient demonstration of the benefits of international co-operation.

One of the most important, albeit vague forces behind the new attitudes to space was the possibility of changing the political psychology of humankind by reorienting its security concerns from an inward to an outward-looking perspective. Such a policy had long been pursued by state managers in their attempts to make governing easier within their own territories. But in a world ever more densely occupied and economically integrated this policy was no longer either appropriate or possible. The idea of threats from space offered the opportunity to play the same strategy on a planetary scale. Doing so did not require cultivating paranoid expectations of imminent invasions by hostile aliens. In the first stages nature itself could be adequately cast as the antagonist. This policy received massive support with the successful multinational intercept of an incoming meteorite in 2029, an event which led to the founding of the International Spacewatch Organisation. In the background however, lay the idea that life was almost certainly a pervasive feature of the galaxy. This understanding made it both more interesting and more prudent to develop humankind's capability to explore and operate in space. Although slow to develop, and obstructed by the international turbulence in the first three decades of the twenty-first century, the move back into space on a collective basis began almost in the first year of the new millennium. Its progress from that point has been a benchmark of the transition from a fragmented to an integrated human civilisation on earth.

These technological developments played strongly into a variety of no less significant transformations in the social sphere. In the five decades (1989–2038) under consideration here, a series of policy experiments took place (most of them with decidedly mixed outcomes) to find suitable and sustainable forms for the community of humankind. These experiments involved a whole series of bold reconsiderations of the relationship among politics, economics and society, and various attempts to apply these to human affairs. Underlying them was the enormous pressure of human numbers, then undergoing the final cycle of doubling to over 12 billion souls.

For the first time the human species was consciously and unconsciously seeking forms of social organisation that included important elements of global scale not only in the economy, but also for identity and governance. At stake were several powerful ideas that had underpinned the rise of the West, most notably sovereignty [the idea that all powers of government should be concentrated into distinct and separate territorial packages called 'states'], and nationalism [the idea that each group of people sharing a culture and language should have their own state]. Also under pressure were ideas about power, which had up to then mostly focused on the state, and ideas about religion, which were under pressure from many different directions. Although these ideas were closely associated with the success of the West, by the late twentieth century they were becoming visibly obsolete. As the balance of human affairs shifted relentlessly from fragmented to integrated forms, these culminating ideas from the past looked less viable as organising principles for the future.

This period of great change set the basic scheme of human organisation for the next two centuries. The question was how to organise the political economy of human society on various levels including on a global scale, so that its component parts would be peaceful and prosperous both within and between themselves. The twentieth-century's wars of industrial ideology had eliminated the autocratic and totalitarian options from the running, and the experiments were mostly driven by belief in markets, in pluralism, and in complex patterns of individual identity, loyalty and responsibility. By the second decade of the twenty-first century a consensus was developing in the rich world that the answer had to be found in a balance among the social, political and economic spheres. No one sphere could be allowed to dominate the other two without putting both peace and prosperity at risk, especially not at a time when the human population was reaching its peak in both size and level of polluting activity. This idea came in many versions, but was generally labelled the *social market*. At the beginning of this period, some people (most notably in China) spoke of *market socialism*, but such an attempt to square a circle was recognised as an oxymoron, and did not last long. China, like the rest of East Asia, eventually accepted the Western notion of a social market – a genuine synthesis between market logic, social policy and pluralist governance.

This synthesis, developed first in the richer and more open societies, was found in a complex mixture of layers within and between which the needs of society and prosperity were carefully managed and regularly adjusted as a result of continuous open debate. Markets, political authority and social identity all had to operate simultaneously on several layers: local, state, regional and global. Letting any one layer dominate produced the same instabilities as letting any one sphere determine the others. Keeping them all in play dampened down many of the destructive forces, and sustained desired degrees of diversity, without placing too massive a burden on the efficiency of the markets.

To achieve this complicated balance of forces many things had to change. The rigid concept of state sovereignty had to be loosened and opened up so that each element of governance could be performed on the level most appropriate to it. What was then called the European Union led the way in this experiment in the political domain, although its ungainly term for the process – 'subsidiarity' – like so many other EU terms, never caught on. The World Trade Organisation applied similar principles in the economic sphere – and was more successful with its image of the global economy as a 'city of many spires'. In parallel with the hollowing-out of the state and the construction of new layers of governance, nationalism, and in some places religion, had to be softened, and removed as the central focus of political legitimacy. This could only be done if control over culture was left at the appropriate level. It had also to be accompanied by increased political significance for other layers of personal identity, thus giving individuals and groups a stake in the various levels of governance in which they were embedded. While politics at the state level, both domestic and international, grew less significant, local, regional, transnational and global politics all grew in importance, many acquiring new institutions as they did so.

To handle all of this, monitoring, management and accounting tools had to be made hugely more sophisticated, accessible and flexible, a process that would have been impossible without the widespread availability of vast amounts of cheap computing power. Mondo culture played a crucial role, helping to stabilise both the hollowed-out multicultural state and the interdependent global political economy. These changes meant that the whole understanding of power had once again to be reinvented. The traditional understanding of power as being essentially linked to the military capability of the state had not surprisingly held firm right through the three world wars of the twentieth century. But it was coming unstuck even before the end of the 'Cold War'. As the global economy began to replace war as 'high politics', and as burgeoning information, organisation and communication networks cut through state borders, the old meanings of power became less useful. Since wars were no longer fought between the major states, the measure of their ability to do so declined in importance, although never completely disappearing. The propensity to use brute force seemed greater when confronting less developed people. What mattered far more in the emerging global political economy was power in the form of information, ideas and capital. The combination of information, ideas about what to do with it, and capital resources to implement it became the key to success in both political and economic life, increasingly replacing brute forms of coercion. But while fear of war and domestic repression declined in the rich world, fears of the new forms of power arose to take their place, and political life shifted towards these new security issues and debates.

All of these developments took place in the context of the early stages of the turnaround from an essentially divided to an essentially integrated organisation of humankind. Not surprisingly in this increasingly cosmopolitan universe, the traditional notion of 'the foreign' began to be eroded. As foreign became more familiar, it started to lose much of both its essential meaning and its social and political significance. Symbolic of this was that these decades were a time of massive and uncontrolled mixing of human cultures and languages. As human numbers approached their peak, cultural diversity expanded in an unprecedented fashion, although it was paradoxical that the mechanism for this diversity was the spread of powerful means for global communication. While early thinkers had feared that the result of global communication forces might be a Mondo homogeneity, in fact the result was the precise opposite. While more than two-thirds of the 5,000 living languages existing in 1990 were extinct by 2050, thousands of new dialects that resulted from the cultural mixing took their place.

But the logic of uneven development was still operating strongly during this period. Unlike our own time, where unevenness has become mostly a matter of choices about different *styles* of development, in the early twenty-first century it was still very much a matter of different *degrees* of development. Already by the 1980s it was becoming clear that the world was dividing into three zones. In the inner zone were found the core of rich, open states. These possessed both the resources and the sophisticated civil societies necessary to undertake the transformation towards the social market. In the middle zone were the late industrialisers. These were half open and half closed, but they had sufficient economic, political and social resources so that they could be first associated with, and then absorbed into the core. This was a process that lasted many decades. The core states used the sticks and carrots of geoeconomic diplomacy to steadily reshape the societies of the middle zone into their own image. As they did so, the core became larger and more influential, and by the end of this period was beginning to take shape as a new and more integrated form of international society. Some even thought of its complex interweaving of political, cultural and economic life as a new form of international system. In either view, the founding of the World Management Organisation in 2034 was a benchmark occasion.

But the outer zone was much more problematic. The unbalanced market preoccupations of the economistic period had allowed a substantial swathe of the planet to sink into political chaos. Many of the weak post-colonial states collapsed altogether, and even those that struggled through lacked the political, economic and social resources to follow the revolutionary transformation going on in the core. In this zone, violence remained endemic both within and between states; or where states failed, among the warlords, tribes and mafias that succeeded them. The whole social and political structure was either so weak, or so disintegrated, that it was beyond the remedial techniques of geoeconomic diplomacy.

These poor areas were marginal to the global economy, and their problems were overshadowed by the huge developments in Asia and the long war in the Middle East. The failure of several attempts during the 1990s to find a workable formula for humanitarian intervention led to a growing compassion fatigue and doubt that anything could be done. In thinking about this episode it is important to remember how strong the values of sovereignty and nonintervention still were, especially for these parts of the world where imperial rule had so recently ended.

While these attitudes increasingly froze governmental action, they did not stop a rising tide of individuals and groups within the civil societies of the core. Some of these were descendants of an earlier generation of migrants whose parents or grandparents had come from these areas. Some represented humanitarian interests keen to promote the principles and the practices of global human rights. Some were engaged in organised crime, eager to find bases of operation outside the reach of the law. Others set themselves up as providers of commercial military and political services, and hired themselves out to the local powers. There was even a small but significant migration from the core into the outer zone. This was mostly composed of people who found the security and civilisation of the inner zone too cloying or dull. They sought adventure and liberation, and sometimes just a chance to live within an older set of values. These various forces often worked at cross purposes, but they did get around the political paralysis of nonintervention, and they did keep the outer zone in contact with the core. They also played a substantial role in the long and often painful process of development that the peoples and societies of the outer zone had still to go through. War remained a major part of the political and social learning process in this zone for nearly two more centuries. It took that long for the development of locally rooted civil societies and political institutions strong enough both to control violence, and to handle the more open forms of political and economic relations necessary to begin integration with the core.

THE VIEW FROM 7000

17

In our third and last look back, we move 5,000 years into the future. Five thousand years is the distance that we now stand from the dawn of civilisation in Sumeria and Egypt. It is the dividing line between history and prehistory, more than 200 generations distant. Across such a gap, nobody will have any sense of personal connection to it through their ancestors. Most educated people will have had some introduction to it in school, but few will remember more than a handful of names and stories – perhaps Hammurabi and his code of laws, and the Pharaohs and their pyramids. Probably the most common sense of connection across the distance will be in the form of religious legends and old testaments. At 5,000 years' distance connections from past to present are almost non-existent. None of the civilisations, states, peoples or main languages of that time can be found today, and their literature and art do not figure much in our culture. We marvel at the remaining works of that time partly because of their scarcity, partly because of their dramatic contrast in sophistication with the relative nothingness of prehistory, and partly because of the extreme crudity of the technologies with which they accomplished seemingly huge feats like the pyramids and the irrigation systems. Since the dawn of civilisation almost everything has changed. Virtually all of the states, peoples, languages, religions and cultures are new. Technological and scientific knowledge is simply in a

267

different universe, with perhaps a few tenuous connections in areas such as animal and plant breeding, pottery, and bronze casting. A view from five millennia's distance in other words will see virtually no continuities and a panorama of massive transformations in almost all aspects of human life.

When we look back five millennia we are looking at the lives and works of humans who are the same species as ourselves. It would be remarkable if the same were true when our ancestors five millennia hence look back at us. We can already see in our own technologies the emergent capability for humankind to remake itself. In the not too distant future it will be possible for our heirs both to remake their genetic codes and to fuse their biology with mechanical and electronic machines. It will also be possible to make intelligent machines. The application of these capabilities will almost certainly be resisted, perhaps for a long time. They threaten not only the sense of human identity, but also the hard won principle that all humans, regardless of race, class or (dis)ability should be seen as equals. But it is hard to imagine that humankind will forever resist the temptation to play god, either with its own evolution, or with machine intelligence. And the long view suggests that there is nothing sacred about any particular human form. Modern humans (homo sapiens sapiens) only emerged some 100,000 years ago, and before that there is a sequence of increasingly primitive hominid types stretching back at least two million years to australopithecus.

> ### Trotsky on Humanity
>
> The historic ascent of humanity, taken as a whole, may be summarized as a succession of victories of consciousness over blind forces – in nature, in society, in man himself.
>
> **Leon Trotsky**, *The History of the Russian Revolution*, vol. 3, 'Conclusions' (1933).

The physical evolution of humankind is thus not new. What may well be new is that the next stages of evolution might be consciously directed by humans themselves. By the year 7000, it is highly probable that the people looking back at us will do so with an anthropological perspective. They may be an evolved form of hominid or a fusion of human and machine. Conceivably they could just be machine intelligences. Whatever they are, they will see us as physically and mentally primitive. They will marvel at the fragility and vulnerability of our bodies and at the limitations on our minds. They will also see us as socially and technologically primitive. Just as we look at the Sumerians through the lenses of the numerous revolutions in ways of living that separate us, so the people of AD 7000 will be separated from us by a host of technological, social and political transformations most of which we cannot conceive. Their analysts of ancient events will take a similarly long view. Here follows an extract from AN INTRODUCTION TO THE SECOND ERA OF THE ANCIENTS: The First World 'Civilisation' 1500–2500.

Wells on Biology

Biologically the species is the accumulation of the experiments of all its successful individuals since the beginning.

H.G. Wells, *A Modern Utopia*, ch. 3, sct. 4 (1905; repr. in *The Works of H. G. Wells*, vol. 9, 1925).

Introduction

Modes of evolution divide the human story quite neatly into three epochs: pre-civilisation, when physical evolution dominates; ancient, when social evolution dominates; and own epoch, when physical and social evolution unfold together. During the incredibly long and slow-moving epoch of pre-civilisation, the main theme is the accelerating physical evolution of the hominid line towards the peak of natural selection in homo sapiens sapiens. only towards the very end of this time, around 8000 BC, when the first population crisis forced the shift from hunter-gathering to agriculture, did social evolution begin to take over as the central theme in human development.

The epoch of the ancients runs for nearly six millennia, during which time social evolution takes over the story, and the physical evolution of humankind moves into the background. It is conventional to divide this epoch into two eras: *high agrarian*, and *industrial*. The high agrarian era stretched from 3250 BC to AD 1500, and comprised the initial struggle for civilisation, particularly the development of cities and high cultures. Its main feature was localism. Technical and physical restraints on transportation and communication meant that cities, empires and civilisations developed largely in isolation from each other. In consequence, the human story, though progressive, was fragmented — almost a world of separate worlds.

The industrial era, which is the subject of this work, comprised a single turbulent millennium. The sources of this turbulence were two. First was the rapid connecting together and integration of the scattered human worlds of the classical era. In its early stages this process was often forceful and generally resisted. Some civilisations experienced the connection as a short circuit and died. Others survived to participate in a global fusion, but the development of a collective sense of humanity was centuries slower in the making than the physical welding together of peoples into a single human space. For many generations the process of connection and integration fuelled fierce conflicts.

The second source of turbulence was the shift from agrarian to industrial political economy. The industrial revolution provided the means and motives to overcome the localism of the classical era. But it also subjected humankind, and indeed the planet, to twenty generations of unprecedentedly high levels of change and stress. Around the middle of the era, the ancients encountered the two so called 'first hurdle' crises of existence that are common in form to the history of all known planet-based sentient species: the option of self-destruction; and the limits of environmental sustainability. As is normal for life on class-M planets, these crises came not only close together, but also before the process of globalisation had created a level of social and political coherence sufficient to handle them safely. In other words, the ancients had to face the first hurdle crises while still half locked into the fragmented and conflictual framework of their classical era. There was a real risk at this point that the human story would either terminate or suffer a massive setback.

The option of species suicide emerged abruptly during the second half of the twentieth century with the first primitive unleashing of nuclear energy. In some ways this development was a natural accompaniment of industrialisation, but most historians agree that its onset was hastened by the peculiarly high levels of socio-political fragmentation, war, and militarisation of technology that were a feature of the twentieth century. Either way, the nuclear revolution marked the key shift for humankind from the ever-present, but then not much worried about, danger that random forces of nature would extinguish a life-form or a planet, to the much higher, and much worried about, probability that the species would perform this disservice for itself. Nuclear weapons were quickly followed by varieties of chemical, biological and then genetic possibilities capable of terminating all higher life on the planet. compared to some other planetary systems, humankind was lucky in having the Jovian shield to limit nature's bombardment of the inner planets. It was unlucky to acquire the means of self-extinction so early in the process of building a global civilisation, but survived nonetheless. The main period of danger lasted less than fifty years, and the much studied story of this peculiar and intense moment in the history of the ancients is told in chapter 7.

The second existential crisis — the limits of environmental sustainability — followed almost immediately after the first, and was much more drawn out. It is conventionally seen as spanning the last doubling of the human population that took place between 1995 and 2057, bringing the total number of humankind to nearly 13 billion. But the crisis was not over until nearly the end of the twenty-first century, and it took nearly two centuries to fully recover from this peak. The sheer weight of human numbers, and the extraordinary lack of concern about their quality of life and development, is perhaps the most difficult aspect of this time for us to grasp. The great explosion in the volume of humankind was accompanied and fed by the rapid spread of primitive industrialisation, which was extraordinarily productive and innovative by the standards of what came before. But this mode of production remained rooted in the assumptions of the high agrarian era, when the human population was much smaller, and its technological capacity was too limited to make much impact on the planet. It thus not only consumed the capital of the planet at a prodigious rate, but also spewed myriad pollutants in huge quantities into the seas, air and land-water systems.

The combination of accelerating human numbers, and the rapid spread of industrialism to most of them, created a real danger of overloading the planetary ecosystem. great damage was indeed done. The atmospheric shielding of the planet was seriously degraded. some parts of the land were rendered uninhabitable [though astonishingly, people often continued to live in them]. substantial swathes of several generations were exposed to debilitating pollutants and drug-resistant diseases. A great extinction of species took place that dangerously narrowed the bio-resource base, and in combination with atmospheric pollutants, is now thought to have come close to triggering a major climate change. yet by a combination of luck and foresight, this crisis also was narrowly survived. one interpretation sees this survival as a curious side-effect of the highly uneven pattern of development that shaped the industrial era. because one part of humankind 'called "the west"' had embarked on industrialisation well before the rest, it became aware of the environmental sustainability problem at an early stage. by moderating its own pollution, monitoring the planetary systems, developing less wasteful technologies, and pressuring the late industrialisers to avoid at least some of the worst practices, it made just enough difference to avoid a world-wide catastrophe.

also worth mentioning as a historical landmark for the species were the first human ventures into space which took place at the point where the nuclear and the environmental crises overlapped. this was a great symbolic moment for humankind, although serious moves into space had to await two further technological revolutions. the venture was accomplished with amazingly crude and dangerous technologies, and is a testament to the courage and vision of those who undertook it. some analysts identify this event as the symbolic termination of the high agrarian fragmentation of humankind, and the opening move of a global civilisation.

there are many fascinating subjects for study in the industrial era of ancient civilisation but perhaps the most interesting is the rapid and massive fluctuations in population size. within this relatively brief span of a thousand years, the human population first expanded twenty-four-fold from over 500 million to nearly 13 billion, and then shrank back to around 8 billion. as can be easily imagined, this process had an immense impact on the development of the ancients' civilisation. in some respects, it resembled the birth of civilisation itself, five millennia earlier, when unprecedented human numbers concentrated in a few locations, gave rise to the first city-states and high cultures. the second great concentration occurred between 1800 and 2100, and was likewise accompanied by a huge flowering of art, technology, and social and political innovation. the period of shrinkage that followed is almost equally interesting. in much of asia, particularly south asia, populations had grown too large to be either sustainable or desirable in the long run. but reducing them was peculiarly difficult. in earlier times, when plagues sometimes cut human populations by a third or more over short periods, the population loss was distributed across all age groups. but in this shrinkage, only the young age groups shrank, making for massive distortions in the structure of these societies for a period of many decades. The dynamics and social impacts of industrial era population changes will be explored in more detail in chapter 5.

In many ways the industrial era of the ancients can be seen as a transitional time between the epoch of the ancients, and our own epoch, in whose fourth era we currently move. It not only laid the foundations for civilisation on a global scale, but also made many of the technical innovations that paved the way for the resumption of human physical evolution that distinguishes the third epoch from it. It was at that time that the first steps were taken in genetic engineering and machine intelligence that have been so crucial in making our modern world possible. Here also we find the origins of geo-engineering and the idea of planetary management. These later culminated in the terraforming of Mars begun in 2400, and the successful staving off of the second-hurdle crisis during the fourth millennium, when a return of the ice age threatened to undo the climatic stability on which human civilisation depended.

But perhaps the main accomplishment of the industrial era was simply to survive the two great crises that were its fate both to create and to confront. Failure would have been easy, and some argue that it was not avoided by much. But in the end, the last generations of the ancients proved up to the task, handing on to us not only an intact planet and an unbroken historical line, but also the makings of a new humanity.

FURTHER READING

This guide is intended to be indicative rather than exhaustive. Given the interconnections of the various parts of the book, this reading list should also be used with interconnections in mind. In the late 1990s it would be foolish to suggest that a list of books begins to be sufficiently comprehensive for a modern reading list. We have benefited a great deal from material available in electronic form, both on the Internet and on compact disks. If you have not yet had the pleasure of browsing the Encyclopaedia Britannica on CD and on the World Wide Web, then those might be the most stimulating places to start.

General

Anderson, Perry. **Passages from Antiquity to Feudalism**. London: Verso, 1974.

Barraclough, Geoffrey (ed). **The Times Atlas of World History**. London: Times Books, 1978.

Bloom, Harold. **Omens of Millennium**. London: Fourth Estate, 1996.

Boorstin, Daniel. **Cleopatra's Nose**. N.Y.: Vintage, 1995.

Boorstin, Daniel. **The Creators**. N.Y.: Vintage, 1992.

Boorstin, Daniel. **The Discoverers**. N.Y.: Vintage, 1983.

Braudel, Fernand. **A History of Civilizations**. N.Y.: Penguin, 1987, 1994 (trans. Richard Mayne).

Briggs, Asa and Daniel Snowman (eds). **Fin de Siècle: How**

Centuries End 1400–2000. New Haven: Yale University Press, 1996.

Buzan, Barry and Richard Little. **International Political Science Review**, 'The Idea of "International System": Theory Meets History', 15(3): 231–255, 1994.

Cohen, Bernard. **Revolution in Science**. Cambridge MA: Harvard University Press, 1985.

Crosby, Alfred. **Ecological Imperialism**. Cambridge: Cambridge University Press, 1986.

Dawkins, Richard. **River Out of Eden**. London: Phoenix, 1995.

Fernandez-Armesto, Felipe. **Millennium: A History of Our Last Thousand Years**. London: Bantam Press, 1995.

Fukuyama, Francis. **Trust: The Social Virtues and the Creation of Prosperity**. N.Y.: The Free Press, 1996.

Frank, Andre Gunder. **Review**, 'A Theoretical Introduction to 5000 Years of World System History', 13(2): 155–248, 1990.

Gellner, Ernest. **Plough, Sword and Book: The Structure of Human History**. London: Paladin, 1988.

Gills, Barry K. and Andre Gunder Frank. **Review**, 'World System Cycles, Crises and Hegemonial Shifts, 1700 BC to 1700 AD', 15(4): 621–87, 1992.

Gribbin, Mary and John. **Being Human**. London: Phoenix, 1993.

Gribbin, John. **In the Beginning**. London: Penguin, 1994.

Hodgson, Marshall G.S. **Rethinking World History: Essays on Europe, Islam and World History**. Cambridge: Cambridge University Press, 1993.

Huntington, Samuel. **The Clash of Civilisations**. N.Y.: Simon & Schuster, 1996.

Inkster, Ian. **Science and Technology in History**. London: Macmillan, 1991.

Johnson, Paul. **The Birth of the Modern**. London: Phoenix, 1992.

Kennedy, Paul. **The Rise and Fall of the Great Powers: Economic Change and Military Conflict from 1500–2000**. London: Unwin/Hyman, 1988.

Kenwood, A.G. and A.L. Lougheed. **The Growth of the International Economy**. London: Routledge, 1992.

King, Anthony D. **Culture, Globalization and the World System**. London: Macmillan, 1991.

Leslie, John. **The End of the World**. London: Routledge, 1996.

McNeill, William H. **The Rise of the West: A History of the Human Community**. Chicago: University of Chicago Press,

1963, 1991.

McNeill, William H. **Plagues and Peoples**. London: Penguin, 1976.

McNeill, William H. **The Pursuit of Power: Technology, Armed Force and Society Since AD 1000**. Oxford: Basil Blackwell, 1982.

McNeill, William H. **Review**, 'The Fall of Great Powers: An Historical Commentary', 19(2): 123–43.

Manguel, Alberto. **A History of Reading**. London: Harper Collins, 1997.

Mann, Michael. **The Sources of Social Power**. Cambridge: Cambridge University Press, 1986.

O'Brien, Conor Cruise. **On the Eve of the Millennium**. N.Y.: The Free Press, 1995.

Roberts, J.J. **The Pelican History of the World**. London: Pelican, 1982.

Segal, Gerald. **The World Affairs Companion**. London: Simon & Schustr, 1996.

Stavrianos, L.S. **The World Since 1500**. London: Prentice-Hall, 1982.

Stavrianos, L.S. **Lifelines from our Past**. London: I.B. Tauris, 1990.

Tilly, Charles. **Coercion, Capital and European States AD 990–1990**. Oxford: Basil Blackwell, 1990.

Thomas, Hugh. **An Unfinished History of the World**. London: Hamish Hamilton, 1979.

Thompson, Damian. **The End of Time**. London: Sinclair-Stevenson, 1996.

Toynbee, Arnold. **A Study of History**. Oxford: Oxford University Press and Thames and Hudson Ltd, 1972.

Walker, Martin. **The Cold War: A History**. N.Y.: Henry Holt & Co., 1994.

Watson, Adam. **The Evolution of International Society**. London: Routledge, 1992.

Wight, Martin. **Systems of State**. Leicester: Leicester University Press, 1977.

Wight, Martin. **Diplomatic Investigations**, 'Western Values in International Relations' (Herbert Butterfield and Martin Wight eds). London: Allen & Unwin, 1966.

Woodruff, William. **The Struggle for World Power**. London: Macmillan, 1981.

PART I

Twentieth Century

Barraclough, Geoffrey. **An Introduction to Contemporary History**. Harmondsworth: Penguin, 1967.

Carr, E.H. **The Twenty Years' Crisis, 1919–1939: An Introduction to the Study of International Relations**. London: Macmillan, 1946, 1939.

Kaylor, William R. **The Twentieth Century World: An International History**. Oxford University Press, 1984.

Maynes, Charles William. **Foreign Policy**, 'The New Pessimism', 100, 1995.

Mead, Walter Russell. **World Policy Journal**, 'Trains, Planes and Automobiles: the End of the Postmoden Moment', 12(4): 1995–6.

Hobsbawm, Eric. **Age of Extremes**. London: Abacus, 1995.

Polanyi, Karl. **The Great Transformation**. Boston: Beacon Press, 1996.

Rosenberg, Nathan and Birdzell, L.E. **How the West Grew Rich**. N.Y.: Basic Books, 1986.

Rosencrance, Richard. **The Rise of the Trading State**. N.Y.: Basic Books, 1986.

Rosencrance, Richard. **Foreign Affairs**, 'The Rise of the Virtual State', 75(4): 45–61, 1996.

Ruggie, John. **International Organization**, 'International Regimes, Transactions and Change: embedded liberalism in the postwar economic order', 36(3): 379–415, 1982.

von Laue, Theodore. **The World Revolution of Westernization: the Twentieth Century in Global Perspective**. N.Y.: Oxford University Press, 1987.

Rise of Europe

Anderson, Benedict. **Imagined Communities: Reflections on the Origin and Spread of Nationalism**. London: Verso, 1983.

Anderson, Perry. **Lineages of the Absolutist State**. London: Verso, 1974.

Bartlett, Robert. **The Making of Europe: Conquest, Colonisation and Cultural Change 950–1350**. London: Penguin, 1994.

Bull, Hedley and Adam Watson (eds). **The Expansion of**

International Society. Oxford: Oxford University Press, 1984.

Chirot, Daniel. **American Sociological Review**, 'The Rise of the West', 50: 181–95, 1985.

Davies, Norman. **Europe: A History**. Oxford: Oxford University Press, 1996.

Gellner, Ernst. **Nations and Nationalism**. Oxford: Blackwell, 1983.

Gong, Gerrit W. **The Standard of 'Civilization' in International Society**. Oxford: Clarendon, 1984.

Scammell, G.V. **The World Encompassed**. London: Methuen, 1981.

Tracey, James D. (ed). **The Political Economy of Merchant Empires: State Power and World Trade 1350–1750** and **The Rise of Merchant Empires: Long Distance Trade in the Early Modern World**. Cambridge: Cambridge University Press, 1990.

Wallerstein, Immanuel. **The Modern World-System: Capitalist Agriculture and the Origins of the European World-Economy in the Sixteenth Century**. New York: Academic Press, 1974.

Wallerstein, Immanuel. **The Politics of the World Economy – The States, the Movements and the Civilizations**. Cambridge: Cambridge University Press, 1984.

Wallerstein, Immanuel. **Geopolitics and Geoculture: Essays on the Changing World System**. Cambridge: Cambridge University Press, 1991.

Wright, Ronald. **Stolen Continents: The 'New World' Through Indian Eyes**. N.Y.: Houghton Mifflin, 1992.

Ancient and Classical

Abu-Lughod, Janet L. **Before European Hegemony: The World System AD 1230–1350**. Oxford: Oxford University Press, 1991.

Barfield, Thomas J. **The Perilous Frontiers: Nomadic Empires and China 221 BC to AD 1757**. Oxford: Blackwell, 1992.

Meijer, Fik and Onno van Nijf. **Trade, Transport and Society in the Ancient World**. London: Routledge, 1992.

Begley, Vimala and Richard Daniel De Puma (eds). **Rome and India: The Ancient Sea Trade**. Madison: University of Wisconsin Press, 1992.

Bentley, Jerry H. **Old World Encounters: Cross-Cultural**

Contacts and Exchanges in Pre-Modern Times. Oxford: Oxford University Press, 1993.

Crosby, Alfred. **Ecological Imperialism**. Cambridge: Cambridge University Press, 1986.

Curtin, Philip D. **Cross-Cultural Trade in World History**. Cambridge: Cambridge University Press, 1984.

Diamond, Jared, **Guns, Germs and Steel**. N.Y.: W.W. Norton, 1997.

Drews, Robert. **The End of the Bronze Age: Changes in Warfare and the Catastrophe *ca* 1200** BC. Princeton: Princeton University Press, 1993.

Eisenstadt, S.M. **The Political Systems of Empires**. London: Transaction Publishers, 1992.

Fagan, Brian M. **World Prehistory: A Brief Introduction.** N.Y.: HarperCollins, 1993.

Finley, M.I. **The Ancient Economy**. Berkeley: University of California Press, 1973.

Forbes, R.J. **Studies in Ancient Technology**. Vol. 11, Leiden: E.J. Brill, 1955.

Harris, Marvin. **Cannibals and Kings: The Origins of Culture**. N.Y.: Vintage, 1978.

Leakey, Richard and Roger Lewin. **Origins Reconsidered**. N.Y.: Doubleday, 1992.

Meijer, Fik and Onno van Nijf. **Trade, Transport and Society in the Ancient World**. London: Routledge, 1992.

Neuberger, Albert. **The Technical Arts and Sciences of the Ancients**. London: Methuen, 1930.

Pearson, H.W. **Trade and Market in the Early Empires**. N.Y.: The Free Press, 1957.

Rossabi, Morris. **Voyager from Zanadu: Rabban Sauma and the First Journey from China to the West**. Tokyo: Kodansha International, 1992.

Singer, Charles, E.J. Holmyard, A.R. Hall and Trevor I. Williams. **A History of Technology, Vol. 1: From Early Times to the Fall of Ancient Empires**. Oxford: Clarendon Press, 1954.

Singer, Charles, E.J. Holmyard, A.R. Hall and Trevor 1. Williams. A **History of Technology, Vol. 11: The Mediterranean Civilizations and the Middle Ages c. 700** BC **to c.** AD **1500**. Oxford: Clarendon Press, 1956.

Trigger, Bruce G. **Early Civilizations: Ancient Egypt in Context**. Cairo: American University of Cairo Press, 1993.

Yoffee, Norman and George L. Cowgill (eds). **The Collapse of Ancient States and Civilizations**. Eurospan, 1991.

PART II

Population

Barraclough, S. **An End to Hunger**. London: Zed Books, 1991.

Coclough, C. and Manor, James. **States or Markets**. Oxford: Clarendon Press, 1992.

Dowty, Alan. **Closed Borders**. New Haven: Yale University Press, 1987.

Erlich, Paul and A. Erlich. **The Population Explosion**. N.Y.: Simon & Schuster, 1990.

Hancock, G. **Lords of Poverty**. London: Macmillan, 1989.

Hardin, G. **Living Within Limits**. Oxford: Oxford University Press, 1993.

Huysmans, Jef. 'Migrants as a Security Problem: Dangers of Securitizing Societal Issues', in R. Miles and D. Thanhardt (eds) **Migration and European Integration: The Dynamics of Inclusion and Exclusion**. London: Pinter, 1995.

Loescher, Gill. **Beyond Charity**. N.Y.: Twentieth Century Fund, 1993.

McNeill, William and R. Adams. **Human Migration**. London: Indiana University Press, 1977.

Smith, B. **More Than Altruism**. Princeton: Princeton University Press, 1990.

Woytinsky, W.S. and E.S. Woytinsky. **World Population and Production: Trends and Outlook**. N.Y.: Twentieth Century Fund, 1953.

Environment

Adamson, D. **Defending the World**. N.Y.: St. Martin's Press, 1990.

Bailey, R. **Eco-Scam**. N.Y.: St. Martin's Press, 1993.

Brenton, T. **The Greening of Machiavelli: The Evolution of International Environmental Politics**. London: Royal Institute of International Affairs, 1994.

Brown, L. **State of the World**. N.Y.: W.W. Norton, 1994.

Brown, Neville. **Survival**, 'Climate, Ecology and International Security', 31(6): 519–32, 1989.

Cairncross, F. **Costing the Earth**. London: *Economist* Books, 1991.

Cline, W. **The Economics of Global Warming**. Washington:

Institute for International Economics, 1992.

Crump, A. **Dictionary of Environment and Development**. London: Earthscan, 1991.

Easterbrook, Greg. **A Moment on the Earth: The Coming Age of Environmental Optimism**. Harmondsworth: Penguin, 1995.

Ford Runge, C. et al. **Freer Trade, Protected Environment: Balancing Trade Liberalization and Environmental Interests**. Oxford: Clarendon Press, 1992.

Gore, A. **Earth in the Balance**. Boston: Houghton Mifflin, 1992.

Hurrell, A. and Benedict Kingsbury (eds). **The International Politics of the Environment: Actors, Interests and Institutions**. Oxford: Clarendon Press, 1992.

MacNeill, Jim, Pietr Winsemius and Taizo Yakushiji. **Beyond Interdependence: The Meshing of the World's Economy and the Earth's Ecology**. N.Y.: Oxford University Press, 1991.

Myers, Norman. **Ultimate Security: The Environmental Basis of Political Stability**. N.Y.: W.W. Norton, 1993.

Porter, Gareth and Janet W. Brown. **Global Environmental Politics**. Boulder: Westview Press, 1991.

Identity

Bannerman, P. **Islam in Perspective**. London: Routledge, 1988.

Chay, Jongsuk. **Culture and International Relations**. N.Y.: Praeger, 1990.

Fowkes, B. **The Rise and Fall of Communism in Eastern Europe**. Basingstoke: Macmillan, 1993.

Hassner, Pierre. **The International Spectator**, 'Culture and Identity', 26(1): 136–53, 1991.

Hutchinson, J. and A.D. Smith (eds). **Nationalism**. Oxford: Oxford University Press, 1994.

Ignatieff, M. **Blood and Belonging: Journey into the New Nationalism**. N.Y.: Farrar, Straus and Giraux, 1994.

Kepel, G. **The Revenge of God: The Resurgence of Islam, Christianity and Judaism in the Modern World**. Cambridge: Polity, 1994.

Lawrence, B. **Defenders of God**. N.Y.: Harper and Row, 1989.

Lewis, Bernard. **Islam and the West**. N.Y.: Oxford University Press, 1993.

Lewis, Bernard. **The Middle East**. London: Phoenix, 1996.

Piscatori, J. **Islam in a World of Nation States**. Cambridge:

Cambridge University Press, 1986.

Segal, Ronald. **The Black Diaspora**. London: Faber, 1995.

Smith, Anthony D. **National Identity**. London: Penguin, 1991.

Smith, Anthony D. **Nations and Nationalism in a Global Era**. Cambridge: Polity Press, 1995.

Wæver, Ole, Barry Buzan, Morten Kelstrup and Pierre Lemaitre. **Identity, Migration and the New Security Agenda in Europe**. London: Pinter, 1993.

Wasserstein, Bernard. **Vanishing Diaspora**. London: Penguin, 1997.

Capital

Bhagwati, J. **The World Trading System at Risk**. Princeton: Princeton University Press, 1991.

Gilpin, Robert. **The Political Economy of International Relations**. Princeton: Princeton Universityi Press, 1987.

Haggard, Stephen. **Pathways From the Periphery**. Ithaca: Cornell University Press, 1990.

Haus, L. **Globalizing the GATT**. Washington: Brookings, 1992.

Irwin, Douglas. **Against the Tide**. Princeton: Princeton University Press, 1996.

Jackson, J.H. **Restructuring the GATT System**. London: Pinter, 1990.

Julius, D. **Global Companies and Public Policy**. London: Pinter, 1990.

Kuttner, Robert. **Everything for Sale**. N.Y.: Knopf, 1997.

O'Brien, R. **Global Financial Integration**. London: Pinter, 1992.

Oxley, A. **The Challenges of Free Trade**. N.Y.: St. Martin's Press, 1990.

Paye, Jean Claude. **International Economic Insights**, 'Merciless Competition: Time for New Rules?', 5(1):21–4, 1994.

Radin, Margaret Jane. **Contested Commodities**. Cambridge MA: Harvard University Press, 1997.

Spero, J.E. **The Politics of International Economic Relations**. London: Allen & Unwin, 1985.

Strange, S. **Casino Capitalism**. Oxford: Basil Blackwell, 1986.

Stubbs, Richard and Geoffrey Underhill (eds). **Political Economy and the Changing Global Order**. Toronto: MacLelland and Stewart, 1994.

Volker, P. and Gyothen, T. **Changing Fortunes**. N.Y.: Times

Books, 1992.

Woytinsky, W.S. and E.S. Woytinsky. **World Commerce and Governments: Trends and Outlook**. N.Y.: Twentieth Century Fund, 1955.

Wyatt-Walter, Andrew. **World Power and World Money**. N.Y.: St. Martin's Press, 1991.

Sovereignty

Archer, Clive. **The United Nations**. London: Macmillan, 1994.

Bailey, Sidney. **The United Nations**. London: Macmillan, 1989.

Barkin, J. Samuel and Bruce Cronin. **International Organization**, 'The state and the nation: changing norms and the rule of sovereignty in international relations', 48(1): 1994.

Berridge, Geoffrey. **Return to the UN: UN Diplomacy in Regional Conflicts**. London: Macmillan, 1991.

Buchan, D. **The Strange Superpower**. Brookfield, VT: Dartmouth University Press, 1993.

Camilleri, J. **The Land of Sovereignty?: The Politics of a Shrinking and Fragmented World**. Aldershot: Elgar, 1992.

Ghali, Boutros B. **An Agenda for Peace**. N.Y.: United Nations, 1992.

Hannum, H. **Autonomy, Sovereignty, Self-Determination: The Accommodation of Conflicting Rights**. Philadelphia: University of Pennsylvania Press, 1990.

Hirst, Paul and Grahame Thompson. **Globalization in Question**. London: Polity Press, 1996.

Jackson, R. **Quasi-states: Sovereignty, International Relations and the Third World**. Cambridge: Cambridge University Press, 1990.

Lodge, Juliet (ed). **The European Community and the Challenge of the Future**. London: Pinter, 1993.

Michalski, A. and H. Wallace. **The European Community and the Challenge of Enlargement**.

Murphy, C. **International Organization and Industrial Change: Global Governance Since 1850**. Oxford: Polity Press, 1994.

Righter, Rosemary. **Utopia Lost, the United Nations and World Order**. N.Y.: Twentieth Century Fund.

Walker, R.J.B. **Alternatives**, 'Security, sovereignty and the challenge of world politics', 15(1), 1990.

Weber, Cynthia. **Review of International Studies**, 'Reconsidering statehood: examining the sovereignty/intervention boundary', 18(3), 1992.

Knowledge

Boorstin, D. **The Discovers**. N.Y.: Random House, 1985.

Gay, Peter. **The Enlightenment**. N.Y.: W.W. Norton, 1977.

Hamelink, C.J. **The Politics of World Communication**. London: Sage, 1994.

Jones, S. (ed). **CyberSociety**. London: Sage, 1994.

Kelly, Kevin. **Out of Control: The New Biology of Machines**. London: Fourth Estate, 1994.

Skolnikoff, E.B. **The Elusive Transformation: Science, Technology and the Evolution of International Politics**. N.Y.: Council on Foreign Relations, 1994.

Van Doren, C. **A History of Knowledge**. N.Y.: Ballantine, 1991.

Military Power

Bozeman, A. **Strategic Intelligence and Statecraft**. London: Brassey's, 1993.

Codevilla, A. **Informing Intelligence**. N.Y.: The Free Press, 1991.

Cowen, Karp R. **Security with Nuclear Weapons?** Oxford: Oxford University Press, 1991.

Dunn, Lewis. **Containing Nuclear Proliferation**. London: IISS *Adelphi Papers* No. 263.

Freedman, Lawrence. **The Evolution of Nuclear Strategy**. London: Macmillan, 1989.

Harkavy, R. and Stephanie Neuman. **The Arms Trade: Problems and Prospects**. London: Sage, 1994.

Lacquer, Walter. **The Age of Terrorism**. London: Weidenfeld, 1987.

Segal, Gerald et al. **Nuclear War and Nuclear Peace**. London: Macmillan, 1988.

West, Nigel. **Games of Intelligence: The Classified Conflict of International Espionage**. London: Weidenfeld and Nicolson, 1989.

Wilkinson, P. **Terrorism and the Liberal State**. London: Macmillan, 1986.

PART III

Anderson, Walter Truett. **Evolution Isn't What it Used to Be**. N.Y.: W.H. Freeman, 1996.

Bowler, Peter. **The Invention of Progress**. Oxford: Basil Black-well, 1989.

Buzan, Barry and Gerald Segal. **World Policy Journal**, 'The Rise of "Lite Powers": A Strategy for the Postmodern State', 13(3), 1996.

Cerny, Philip. **Globalization and Structural Differentiation**. Paper presented to the ECPR-SGIR Conference, Paris, September 1995, 62pp.

Crick, Francis. **The Astonishing Hypothesis**. N.Y.: Touchstone, 1995.

De Santis, Hugh. **Beyond Progress**. London: University of Chicago Press, 1996.

Dennett, Daniel. **Darwin's Dangerous Idea**. London: Penguin, 1995.

Dertouzos, Robert. **What Will Be**. N.Y.: HarperCollins, 1997.

Desmond, Adrian and James Moore. **Darwin**. London: Penguin, 1992.

The Economist, 'The Software Revolution', 10 June 1995.

Elliot, Michael. **The Day Before Yesterday**. N.Y.: Simon & Schuster, 1996.

Erlich, Paul and Barbara. **Healing the Planet**. Reading MA: Addison-Wesley, 1991.

Fukuyama, Francis. **The End of History and the Last Man**. London: Penguin, 1992.

Gay, Peter. **The Enlightenment**. London: W.W. Norton, 1977.

Gleditsch, Nils Petter. **Journal of Peace Research**, 'Democracy and Peace', 29(4): 369–76, 1992.

Goldgeier, James M. and Michael McFaul. **International Organization**, 'A Tale of Two Worlds: Core and Perhiphery in the post-Cold War Era', 46(2): 467–91, 1992.

Helleiner, Eric. **Regionalization in the International Political Economy: A Comparative Perspective**. Eastern Asia Policy Papers, No. 3, University of Toronto and York University Joint Centre for Asia-Pacific Studies, 1994.

Helleiner, Eric. **Studies in Political Economy**, 'Great Transformations: A Polanyian Perspective on the Contemporary Global Financial Order', 48: 149–64, 1995.

Herman, Arthur. **The Idea of Decline in Western History**. N.Y.: The Free Press, 1997.

Horsman, Matthew and Andrew Marshall. **After the Nation State: Citizens, Tribalism and the New World Disorder**.

London: Harper Collins, 1995.

Huntington, Samuel P. **The Clash of Civilisations**. N.Y.: Simon & Schuster, 1996.

Johnson, Paul. **Modern Times**. N.Y.: Harper and Row, 1983.

Jones, Steve. **The Language of Genes**. London: Harper Collins, 1994.

Kaplan, Robert. **The Ends of the Earth**, N.Y.: Vintage, 1996.

Kelly, Kevin. **Out of Control**. London: Fourth Estate, 1995.

Kennedy, Paul. **The Rise and Fall of the Great Powers**. N.Y.: 1987.

Kennedy, Paul. **Preparing for the Twenty-First Century**. N.Y.: Random House, 1993.

Lasch, Cristopher. **The True and Only Heaven: Progress and its Critics**. N.Y.: W.W. Norton, 1993.

Lottman, Herbet. **Jules Verne**. N.Y.: St. Martin's Press, 1997.

McNeil, William. **The Rise of the West**. Chicago: The University of Chicago Press, 1963.

McRae, Hamish. **The World in 2020**. London: Harper Collins, 1994.

Miles, Jack. **God: A Biography**. N.Y.: Vintage, 1996.

Naisbitt, John. **Global Paradox**. Avon Books, 1994.

Negroponte, Nicholas. **Being Digital**. London: Hodder and Stoughton, 1995.

Nye, Joseph S. **Foreign Affairs**, 'What New World Order?', 71(2), 1992.

Nye, Joseph S. **The Washington Quarterly**, 'Conflicts After the Cold War', 19(1): 524, 1996.

Pfaff, William. **World Policy Journal**, 'Progress', 1995–6.

Polyani, Karl. **The Great Transformation**. Boston: Beacon Press, 1994.

Ridley, Matt. **The Red Queen**. London: Penguin, 1994.

Ridley, Matt. **The Origins of Virtue**. London: Viking, 1996.

Robertson, Roland. **Globalization: Social Theory and Global Culture**. Sage, 1992.

Rosenau, James N. **Turbulence in World Politics: A Theory of Change and Continuity**. Hemel Hempstead: Harvester Wheatsheaf, 1990.

Rosenau, James N. **International Political Economy: Understanding Global Disorder**, 'Distant Proximities: The Dynamics and Dialectics of Globalization', in Bjorn Hettne (ed), 31–45, Halifax: Fernwood Books, 1995.

Ruggie, John. **International Organization**, 'Territoriality and Beyond: problematizing modernity in international relations',

47: 139–74, 1993.

Segal, Gerald. **Rethinking the Pacific**. Oxford: Clarendon Press, 1990.

Scientific American, 'Key Technologies for the 21st Century', September 1995.

Shapin, Steven. **The Scientific Revolution**. Chicago: University of Chicago Press, 1996.

Simon, J.L. (ed.). **The State of Humanity**. Cambridge MA: Blackwell Publishers Ltd, 1995.

Singer, Max and Aaron Wildavsky. **The Real World Order: Zones of Peace, Zones of Turmoil**. Chatham, N.J.: Chatham House Publishers, 1993.

Sowell, Thomas. **Migrations and Cultures**. N.Y.: Basic Books, 1996.

Schwartz, Peter. **The Art of the Long View**. N.Y.: Doubleday, 1991.

Stopford, John and Susan Strange with John S. Henley. **Rival States, Rival Firms**. Cambridge: Cambridge University Press, 1994.

Strange, Susan. **Hitotsubashi Journal of Law and Politics**, 'Who Governs? Networks of Power in World Society', Special Issue, 5–17, June 1994.

Tarnas, Richard. **The Passion of the Western Mind**. London: Pimlico, 1996.

Tenner, Edward. **Why Things Bite Back**. London: Fourth Estate, 1996.

Toffler, Alvin. **PowerShift**. N.Y.: Bantam Books, 1990.

Van Doren, Charles. **The Idea of Progress**. N.Y.: Praegen, 1967.

Waldrop, Mitchell. **Complexity**. N.Y.: Simon and Schuster, 1992.

Watson, Lyall. **Dark Nature**. London: Hodder and Stoughton. 1995.

Wilson, Edward. **The Insect Societies**. Cambridge MA: Harvard University Press, 1971.

Wilson, Edward. **On Human Nature**. London: Penguin, 1995.

Wright, Robert. **Three Scientists and Their Gods**. N.Y.: Times Books, 1988.

Zacher, Mark. 'The decaying pillars of the Westphalian temple: implications for international order and governance', in James N. Rosenau and Ernst-Otto Czempiet (eds) **Governance Without Government: Order and Change in World Politics**. Cambridge: Cambridge University Press, 1992.

INDEX

Afghanistan 113, 162, 246
Africa 162, 224
ageing xv, 255
agrarian societies 29, 31, 67–69, 203
  villages and towns 68
  the beginning 67–68
  revolution in 68
agriculture *See* agrarian societies
AIDS 111
Alexander the Great 48, 57
Anderson, Benedict 121
animals
  and herding 68
  horses 68
  and trade 59
antibiotics 200
Arabs 241, 242
  defeat of China 58
Asia-Pacific Economic Co-
  operation 153
Association of Southeast Asian
  Nations (ASEAN) 82
astronomy 60
asylum 114–15
Athens 49
Aztecs 60, 252

Babylon 49
Bacon, Francis 197
Balkans 237
Baluchistan 246
Bangladesh 113
barbarians 51–53, 58, 61, 68, 145
  conquest of civilisations 52
Baudrillard, Jean 118
BBC 226
Benn, Tony 193
Bennetton 225
birth control xv
Body Shop 225
Bosnia 116
British Empire 252
Bronowski, Jacob 192
Buddhism 44, 61
Burundi 246
Byzantine Empire 58

calendars xxi–xxii
Cambodia 116
Camus, Albert 212
Canada
  and identity 125
  identity and pluralism 123

289

cancer 111
Carthage 49
Ch'ang-an 49
change
  through chaos 177, 198
  through climate 91
  environmental 65
  and the industrial revolution 31
  through knowledge 142
  through technology 31
China 84, 163, 172–73, 185, 238, 240,
    243
  Arab defeat of 58
  and East Asia 239
  expansion 37
  internal trade 57
  Ming Empire 41
  nationalism 238
  new superpower 242
  and science 196
  technology 44
Chinese Empire 31
Christianity 44, 195
  versus Islam 58
cities 63
  city-states 29, 47, 49, 67, 145
  comparison with other societies 64
  and empires 49
  importance of 47
  migration to 78
civilisations, clash of 218–19
Clark, Kenneth, Lord 209
climate 91–92
CNN 226
coal 30
Coca-Cola 225
Cold War xiv, 7, 8–9, 15, 18, 34, 169–
    70, 180, 215, 236
colonisation 36–37
communications 76, 113, 134, 215, 226
communism 7, 17
  failure of 145, 147
Confucianism 44
Constantinople 49
crime 12

drugs 235
  and mafias 234–35
Crusades 58
Cuba 113
cummings, e.e. 192
Cuzco 49

Darwin, Charles 198
Dawkins, Richard 196–97
Delhi 49
Diderot, Denis 130
disease 249
  AIDS 111
  cancer 111
Disraeli, Benjamin 209
divorce 12, 112
drugs 235
Durant, Will 209

East Asia xiv–xv, 82, 116, 205, 223,
    228, 232, 239, 240, 245
  economy 81
  epoch-making rise 185–87
ecology and environment
  air pollution (UK) 101
  air pollution (USA) 100
  atmosphere 14
  change 65–66
  climatic change 91–92, 249
  green groups 98
  green image as marketing
    gimmick 99
  human impact on 96, 179, 271
  and the 'invisible hand' of market
    forces 102
  manipulation of 254, 257–58
  and market forces 99–100
  nuclear dumps 248
  ozone layer 248
  planetary ecosystem 248
  species diversity 14, 97
  see also Chapter 6, p. 91, _and_
    ecology
economism 231–33
education enrolments, 1900 and

1995 178
e-mail 13
empires
  British 252
  Byzantine 58
  Chinese 31
  Holy Roman 25, 252
  Mameluke 252
  Manchu 52
  Ming 41
  Mogul 41
  Ottoman 34, 37, 41, 252
  Persian 57
  rise and fall of 48–51
  Sassanian 58
  Song 252
  Venetian 252
energy sources 30
  oil 240–41
  solar 240, 248
Enlightenment 195, 196
environment *See* ecology and
    environment
eugenics 198, 256
Europe 237–38
  as destination for migrants 112
  dominance 62
  EU 125, 153, 236, 262
  expansion 35–36, 44
  fifteenth century 25
  French Revolution 33
  Hapsburg dynasty 34
  industrialisation 22
  national states 27
  nineteenth century 28
  population and control 21
  power struggles 33–35
  power, weakening grip on 183
  sea power 36
  and trade 75
  see also Chapter 2, p. 21
European Union 125, 153, 236, 262
  and sovereignty 161
euthanasia 202
evolution

human, engineering of 254, 255,
    268, 273
  Mark Twain on 198
  Victorian view 198

Fagan, Brian 56
families 229
  re-invention of 230
  size of 107, 110
  see also population
fascism 17
  failure of 145
federalism 28
feudalism 25, 29
food 225, 226
  production and population 110–11
  yields, 1950–90 109
Ford 225
Foucault, Michel 4–5
France
  French Revolution 33
  and state spending 149
Fukuyama, Francis 192, 204

G7 (Group of Seven) 161
Galileo 196
Gandhi 210
GDP xiv, 182
  growth of, 1966–2005, 146
  per head, 1900 and 1995, 178
  questionable indicator of
    wealth 150
Gellner, Ernest 196
genetics 179, 200, 273
Germany 141
  division of 7
glasnost and perestroika 78
globalisation 7–8, 13–17
  and capital 235
  communications 13, 215, 226
  diplomacy 15
  economy 9–10, 80, 123, 148–49, 226
  future economy 215
  'glocalisation' 220
  interest rates 149, 161

and the sovereign state 158
stock markets 13–14
transnational organisations 11, 149
    see also Chapter 1, p. 7, *and*
    transnational organisations
Gorbachev, Mikhail 78
Greece 49, 60
greenhouse gases 94
Gregorian calendar xxi
Group of Seven (G7) 161

Hapsburg dynasty 34
Haiti 113, 116
happiness 203–4
Hinduism 44
Hobbes, Thomas 131
Hodgson, Marshall 78
Holocaust 198
Holy Roman Empire 25, 252
horses 51, 60, 68
Hughes, Robert 204
human society 47, 64
    agrarian 29, 67–69, 203
    city-states 29, 67, 145
    feudalism 29
    formation of 66–67
    hunter-gatherers 63–4, 66, 203
    nation-states 123
    and technology 77
    uneven development of 79–81
hunter-gatherers 63–64, 66, 203
Huntington, Samuel 219

IBM 141
ice age 65–66, 92
identity
    ethnicity 121
    gender 118
    language 121
    religion 119
    sub-groups 123–24
    see also Chapter 8, p. 117
Incas 60, 252
India 162, 163, 223–24
    and the global market

economy 240, 244–45
Indus valley 47
industrial revolution 29–31, 59, 78,
    95, 145
    social change 31
International Monetary Fund 161
Internet 134, 135, 141, 227–28, 229, 256
    connected networks, 1988 and
    1996, 178
Iran 163
Iraq 172
irrigation 68
Islam 44, 49, 195, 224
    versus Christianity 58
    divided within 127
    expansion 37
    inter-sect conflict 241
    Sunni–Shi'ia divide 119
Italy
    and identity 125

Japan 185, 239–240
    and pluralism 124–25
Johnson, Samuel 192
Judaism 44, 194

Kaplan, Robert 217
Kashmir 246
Kelly, Kevin 255
Keynes, John Maynard 207
knowledge
    communication of 134
    and the forces of change 142
    freedom of information 133
    as key to power 129, 133
    the knowledge explosion 131
    and language 134
    material sciences 131
    natural sciences 131
    scientific 180
    and social goals 138
    text-book bias 135
    see also Chapter 9, p. 129
Korea 141
Kuwait 163

language
English as lingua franca 16, 134–35, 226
as identity 121
lingua francas 16, 134–35, 226
major tongues, speakers of 122
as repository of knowledge 134
Lao-Tzu 132
League of Nations 11
Lebanon 155–56
leisure
specialised 78
Lennon, John 225
liberal capitalism 17
liberal market economy 147
Liberia 116, 155–56, 246
lingua francas 16, 134–35, 226
Locke, John 197
Longfellow, Henry Wadsworth 202

Macaulay, Thomas Babington 194
mafias 234–35, 245
and drugs 235
Magyars 58
Mameluke Empire 252
Manchu Empire, expansion of 52
Mao Tse-tung 199
Mars, terraformed 273
Marxism 198–99
Marx, Karl 5
mathematics 60
Maya 47, 49
Mercury, Freddy 225
Mesopotamia 68
Mexico 48
Microsoft 141, 226
Middle East 240–41
the Great Middle Eastern War 241
war in 2012, 241
migration 36, 115
to Africa 37
to Australia and New Zealand 37
to Europe 112
official control 113
and population 105–6

to South America 37
to USA 36
within regions 112
Mill, John Stuart 197, 200
millennium xxi
Miller, Henry 210
Ming Empire 41
Mogul Empire
expansion 41
monarchs 28–29
'Mondo culture' 220–21, 225, 263
and food 225
and music 225
Morris, David 180
music 225, 226
Country and Western 230

national state 26–27
nationalism 121–23
nation-states 123
navigation techniques 60
Nazism 198
Nietzsche, Freidrich 5
Nigeria 246
Nike 225
Nineteen Eighty-Four xvii
Nineveh 49
Nobel Prize
chemistry 137
physics 136
North American Free Trade Area 153
nuclear energy 132
nuclear weapons 15, 165, 270
as deterrence 82
fading threat of war 171

oil 240–41
Opium Wars 37
Ortega y Gasset, José 5
Orwell, George xvii, 192
Ottoman Empire 34, 37, 252
expansion 41

Pakistan 113, 162, 163, 246

Patna 49
Pepsi-Cola 225
perestroika and glasnost 78
Persia
  conquests 37
Persian Empire
  expansion 57
Peru 48
Physical Quality of Life Index 180,
  181, 199
plague 95
Pol Pot 199
population 14, 21, 74, 75, 271
  control 246–47
  fifty years on 215
  fluctuations in 272
  and food production 110–11
  impact on other species 249
  increase in 66, 252, 261
  influencing rate of 107
  and migration 105–6
  peak, projections of 107
  and pollution 249
  uneven growth 115
  world, growth in 106
  world projections 108
  see also Chapter 7, p. 105
printing 134
prisons 170

racial superiority 17
Reebok 225
religion 60
  adherents to faiths, mid-1994 120
  and politics 119, 121
  sects 119
  world 119
Ricardo, David 207
Rome 49, 60
Romer, Paul 207
Rousseau, Jean-Jacques 197
Russell, Bertrand 199
Russia
  expansion across Siberia 52
  Middle East weapons sales 241

wealth and power 145
Rwanda 113, 246

Saracens 58
Sassanian Empire 58
Saudi Arabia 241
Schlesinger, Arthur M., Jr. 4
Schwartz, Peter xviii, 92, 117
Shaw, George Bernard 206
Singapore 186
Sky 226
slaves 37
Smith, Adam 198
solar energy 240, 248
Somalia 116, 155–56
Song Empire 252
South Africa 162
sovereignty
  and the EU 161
  and the global market 158
  the sovereign state 155
  and Taiwan 155
  see also Chapter 11, p. 155
Soviet Union 7, 84
  glasnost and perestroika 78
space 258–61
  International Spacewatch
    Organisation 261
space travel 254, 255–56, 272
  social significance 258–59
Spanish conquests 41
Stalin, Joseph 199
Sudan 113, 162

Taiwan 141, 163, 239
technology 253
  China 44
  cyborgs 257
  and killing 201
  machine intelligence 254, 273
  planetary environment,
    manipulation of 254, 257–58
  simulators 256
  societies, effect on 31
  as source of change 31

stagnation of 59–60
uneven development of 77
Tenner, Edward 201
Tenochtitlan 49
terrorism 170, 234
Thatcher, Margaret 231
Third World 10
Tilly, Charles 27
Toynbee, A.J. 4
trade
  and animals 59
  and crops 59
  and disease 59
  global economy 9–10
  long-distance 54, 56–59, 69–70
  luxury goods 69
  and rivers 56
  and transport 75–76
  wider networks 74–75
Transatlantic Free Trade Area 153
transnational organisations 149, 153,
  161, 171, 244
  League of Nations 11
  United Nations 11, 80, 236, 244,
    245
  WTO 262
transport 75–76
Trotsky, Leon 268
Twain, Mark 132, 198

Uganda 246
United Nations 11, 171, 236, 245
  successor to 244
Ur 49
USA 141, 184, 236, 252
  American Revolution 33
  identity and pluralism 123
  multi-ethnicity 28

Venetian Empire 252
'Victorian values' 204–5
Vietnam war 112
Vikings 58

warfare
  Balkans 166, 168, 171
  expenditure and manpower 167
  future restraints 215
  Gulf 166, 168, 171
  Iran–Iraq 168, 241
  as last resort 166
  role of machines 166
  Napoleonic 212
  nuclear weapons 15, 270
  style of 166
  technology 201
  see also World Wars
Wells, H.G. 194, 269
Western ideas xiv–xv
  Judeo-Christian roots 184
  wealth and power, generation
    of 185
Wilde, Oscar 3
women
  education of 107
  emancipation of 12
  role of 111, 206
working hours, 1900 and 1995, 178
World Trade Organisation 153, 161,
  237, 262
World Wars 35
  Europe's strength sapped 183
  First 8, 165, 212
  Second 8, 10, 165, 212
  see also warfare
writing 60

Zaire 246